Portraits of Teacher Preparation

Learning to Teach in a Changing America

Edited by

Patrick M. Jenlink
Karen Embry Jenlink

Published in partnership with the
Association of Teacher Educators

Rowman & Littlefield Education
Lanham, Maryland • Toronto • Oxford
2005

Published in partnership with the
Association of Teacher Educators

Published in the United States of America
by Rowman & Littlefield Education
A Division of Rowman & Littlefield Publishers, Inc.
A wholly owned subsidiary of The Rowman & Littlefield Publishing Group, Inc.
4501 Forbes Boulevard, Suite 200, Lanham, Maryland 20706
www.rowmaneducation.com

PO Box 317
Oxford
OX2 9RU, UK

Copyright © 2005 by Patrick M. Jenlink and Karen Embry Jenlink

All rights reserved. No part of this publication may be reproduced, stored in a retrieval system, or transmitted in any form or by any means, electronic, mechanical, photocopying, recording, or otherwise, without the prior permission of the publisher.

British Library Cataloguing in Publication Information Available

Library of Congress Cataloging-in-Publication Data

Portraits of teacher preparation : learning to teach in a changing America / edited by Patrick M. Jenlink, Karen Embry Jenlink.
　　p. cm.
　Includes bibliographical references and index.
　ISBN 1-57886-269-8 (pbk. : alk. paper)
　1. Teachers—Training of—United States. 2. Teaching—Political aspects—United States. 3. Teaching—Social aspects—United States. 4. Educational change—United States. I. Jenlink, Patrick M. II. Jenlink, Karen Embry.
　LB1715.P63 2005
　370'.71—dc22
　　　　　　　　　　　　　　　　　　　　　　　　　　　　2005005971

∞™ The paper used in this publication meets the minimum requirements of American National Standard for Information Sciences—Permanence of Paper for Printed Library Materials, ANSI/NISO Z39.48-1992.
Manufactured in the United States of America.

To our daughters, Tamira, Amber, and Charla, who have been our constant companions in our journeys of learning to teach. We have constantly reflected on our respective journeys and realize that our learning to teach began as parents to our children, and continued as our daughters became our teachers, sharing their life experiences and allowing us to learn how to be parents. Learning to teach in a changing America has been enriched and made relevant by our daughters, by their questions, by their own learning, by their expressions of love and support, and by their friendship along the way. Our daughters were there with us when we began our journey, with us on the college campus as we prepared to become teachers, with us at home while we were grading and reading and preparing for the next day of classes, and with us in our daily conversations about our work and life as teachers. Thank you for instructing our journey and helping us to learn how to be parents and teachers.

Contents

Foreword   *James W. Fraser, Northeastern University*   ix

Part I   Preparing a Backdrop   1

Overview   5
Patrick M. Jenlink, Stephen F. Austin State University

1 Learning to Teach in a Changing America   13
*Patrick M. Jenlink and Karen Embry Jenlink,
Stephen F. Austin State University*

Part II   Learning to Teach for Social Justice   29

2 Center X: Where Research and Practice Intersect for Urban School Professionals: A Portrait of the Teacher Education Program at the University of California, Los Angeles   33
Brad Olsen, with the help of Sheila Lane, Eloise Lopez Metcalfe, Jody Priselac, Gordon Suzuki, and Rae Jeane Williams, University of California, Los Angeles

3 Collaboration and Inquiry: Learning to Teach at the Lynch
   School of Education 53
   *Kelly Donnell, Andrea J. Stairs, and Nicole Guttenberg,
   Boston College*

4 Reimagining One Urban Teacher Education Program:
   Transformation Through Inquiry, Difference, and
   Field Experience 73
   *Valerie Lava, Laurie Lehman, and Cecilia Traugh,
   Long Island University*

Part III   Learning to Teach in a Democracy 95

5 Keepers of the Flame: The CARE Program for
   Democratic Education 99
   Rosalie M. Romano, Ohio University

6 Cultivating Democratic Learning Communities:
   Three Portraits of Roosevelt University's Department of
   Teacher Education 113
   *Nona Burney, Andy Carter, Elizabeth Meadows, and
   Tom Philion, Roosevelt University*

7 Converging Voices: Teaching and Learning to Teach 133
   Marguerite Sneed and Siri Voskuil, Alverno College

Part IV   Learning to Teach Through
Social Consciousness 151

8 A Portrait in Time and Context: The TE Collaborative 20%
   Internship Program 155
   *Nancy Lourié Markowitz, Patricia Swanson,
   Andrea Whittaker, and Morva McDonald,
   San José State University*

9 Adapting to Meet the Needs of a Growing,
Urban School District 175
*Jeffrey C. Shih, Lori J. Olafson, and Lori A. Navarrete,
University of Nevada, Las Vegas*

10 Teacher Education for Our Schools and Our Community 199
*Beth Berghoff and Jacqueline Blackwell, Indiana
University School of Education at Indianapolis*

Part V Re-Creating Teacher Education: Imagining Possibilities 217

11 Reflective and Aesthetic Inquiry: Seeing the Whole 221
Karen Embry Jenlink, Stephen F. Austin State University

12 Coda: A Portrait of Teacher Education:
Imagining Alternative Possibilities 235
Patrick M. Jenlink, Stephen F. Austin State University

Index 239

About the Editors and Contributors 243

Foreword

James W. Fraser
Northeastern University

Teacher education today is under siege. Everywhere we turn there is another editorial, report, or legislative mandate indicating further dissatisfaction with the nation's schools and colleges of education. Many of us believe that much of this criticism is well earned. We teacher educators have not always held to the highest academic standards. We have not always embedded our preparation of future teachers in the real-world experience of today's schools and today's teachers. And we have not prepared teachers who will have the confidence, the expectations, the commitments, and the skills to ensure that tomorrow's students receive the education that they deserve.

However—and it is a very important however—our critics also have a major fault. Almost without exception, those in government, the foundations, think tanks, and the media who are appropriately critical of "ed schools" have failed to discriminate between the schools and programs that deserve their wrath and those that do not. They have failed to notice when some programs and schools have heard the critique and have changed themselves—sometimes changed themselves quite dramatically. There are today many teacher educators who are as dissatisfied, if not more than dissatisfied, with the old status quo than there are external critics. And these internal critics are bringing about real changes that will, in the long run, do more to improve the actual ways in which tomorrow's teachers are prepared than all of the external voices.

Patrick M. Jenlink and Karen Embry Jenlink's *Portraits of Teacher Preparation: Learning to Teach in a Changing America* appears at just the right time to help transform this debate. Avoiding any self-serving defensiveness, the authors of these chapters—these portraits of teacher preparation programs in the process of transformation—offer clear and powerful evidence that the tide is turning; that in many places the teacher education that has been so harshly criticized does not exist any more; that it has been replaced with something much better. The authors of these chapters are careful not to romanticize the reality in today's universities or the public schools. They are acutely conscious of the sometimes dogmatic rigidity and constricted climate that characterize American education at the beginning of the 21st century. And none of the portraits offered here represent a finished product. The authors are refreshingly honest about what still needs to be done, just as they are clear about what has been done—what they saw in need of change, and what was changed.

If there is a common thread in these chapters—and there is—it is found in their focus on democracy, on issues of equity, justice, community, and in their commitment to transform schools and teachers so that these values receive much greater attention. In all of these case studies, there is a larger purpose to teacher education than simply filling the pool of applicants for the nation's teaching jobs. There is also a great deal of specificity about what it means to prepare teachers who care about equity, justice, and community, including the following characteristics of reformed programs.

- All the programs demonstrate a clear recognition of the need to break down the traditional university-school division; not only has the physical location of many of the education courses moved into the schools, but the university faculty are spending more and more time in the actual school buildings, among the teachers and young people, and the public school teachers are also being invited to the university to serve as colleagues with their university-based partners.
- All the effective efforts take time and many hours of conversation. Effective and democratic transformation cannot simply be mandated though it does require an initiative from some quarter. But before it can be real, university faculty, public school teachers, and education students need to talk to each other, learn from each other, and know when to stand their ground and when to change.

- A substantial change of focus—from preparing teacher education students for schools as they are to preparing them for schools as they ought to be, for schools in which the failure to appreciate and serve all the students is simply unacceptable, and for schools that are deeply engaged with and appreciative of the surrounding community in which the young people live and spend most of their time—is at the heart of these efforts.
- In some cases (I wish it were more) there is also a strong effort to include faculty from across the university, especially faculty from the arts and sciences, who have so much to offer, and sometimes so much to learn from the efforts to prepare effective teachers. Equity includes attention to what to teach and how to teach; as these chapters show, we neglect either half of the equation at our peril. And universities have powerful traditions of their own that can be harnessed to the effort to transform teacher education.

Without exception, the stories reported here are works in progress. Much remains to be done. In some cases, the reforms have taken place at the margins and need to become the norm for all of a given university's teacher education programs. In some cases the next steps are very clear and simply require time, while in others there is a sense of an agenda yet to be developed. But without exception, these are stories of success, of serious efforts to take the needs of tomorrow's students—all of tomorrow's students—seriously and to make the success of those students the primary point of reference for the education of their teachers.

Yet for all their similarities, there is also a wonderful diversity in these chapters.

- The University of Nevada at Las Vegas chapter reports a pilot program in which the traditional theory/practice split is transformed into a single, coherent school-based immersion experience that engages university faculty, veteran teachers, and preservice students as a community of learners while focusing specifically on the urban experiences of Las Vegas, Nevada. A second cohort program for current special education support staff builds on their professional experience in a district-supported accelerated program leading to a baccalaureate degree and licensure.

- At the University of California, Los Angeles, the issue of social justice is moved from the margins, and from the theoretical underpinnings of teacher education, into the very core of the program, bravely engaging prospective teachers in a critique of schooling, including a critique of the university and the education school, even while they also focus on ensuring that "our most, quote-unquote, 'socially active' teachers have to realize that they still have a lot to learn about effective classroom teaching."
- San José State University began with a recognition that the links between university coursework in education and field experiences in the schools were too often weak, while communication between the school districts and the university was tenuous, and decided to do something about it. The program was changed to ensure placement of university students in a school classroom over the course of two full years through a part-time internship in Year I and a full-time internship in Year II linked to coordinated coursework and an effective effort to break down the traditional separation of school and university faculty.
- Roosevelt University focused on a number of approaches that took its long-standing, universitywide commitment to democracy seriously. In one case, the faculty revised their work with cooperating teachers and their own colleagues in science education into an integrated school site–based cohort approach to elementary teacher preparation. In each case, the conception of a small-scale, democratically influenced classroom and school is continually linked to a larger conception of a democratic profession.
- Ohio University has developed a partnership with a number of nearby schools—elementary, middle, and high schools—that emphasizes using "field experience to foster an understanding of how theory and practice are interwoven," while "requiring habits of democratic living" within a cohort to produce a generation of teachers with the knowledge, skill, and experience to produce the same democratic habits in their own classrooms. They are consciously shifting teacher education from inputs, even inputs about democracy, to a powerful experience of learning to be democratically engaged citizens.
- Long Island University began a process of "completely re-imagining" their teacher preparation programs based on a sense that the old collection of courses was not succeeding either in meeting high standards

or at offering a coherent program. A critical starting point for the Long Island faculty was a fresh look at their own students, nearly 80 percent of whom are students of color, while they built a program based on their strengths rather than trying to fit them into a preconceived mold. The effort has involved lively debates and multiple perspectives that are themselves part of a living democratic educational environment.

- In its partnership with a local urban high school, Boston College has been engaged in moving the center of gravity of teacher education from the college campus to the school while engaging the high school and college faculty as an increasingly cohesive group that is collectively responsible for an effective effort. At the same time, BC has worked hard to avoid preparing teachers for urban schools as they are and has remained focused on a democratic ideal that can animate the purpose of social justice and through constructivist means of city teaching.
- Indiana University has also relocated much of the teacher education to its Indianapolis partner schools, an important shift from an earlier era in which students selected from a very wide range of field sites and student convenience trumped in-depth experience, while recognizing the inherent difficulty of these partnerships that take years to build. In addition, Indiana University faculty have used the Interstate New Teachers Assessment and Support Consortium (INTASC) standards not as a cookie cutter but as a foundation for reflective dialogue about the development of a coherent teacher education curriculum in which courses and field assignments fit into a larger whole.
- Alverno College's faculty located the transformation of teacher education squarely within a larger 30-year effort by the whole college to reinvent itself around eight abilities that every Alverno graduate must master. The education faculty expanded this list adding five professional abilities and, over time, with significant student involvement, focused on the actions, skills, and attitudes needed to show competence in each area. Alverno reflects a long-term dialogue between the faculty, including discipline-specific and education professors and schoolteachers, and the students in a program in which students are continually pushing and faculty responding from their own position of flexibility about the means and confidence about the fundamental goals of the program.

There could be many other similar examples of equally effective efforts to transform the education of tomorrow's teachers. Only time and space have limited this volume to these particular stories. Teacher education, on many campuses, in many school districts, in the experience of many teachers and students, is a field in the midst of an exciting and productive transformation. For a sense of just how far reaching the reform effort really is, keep reading in the pages that follow in this volume.

1

PREPARING A BACKDROP

> The portraitists come to the field with an intellectual framework and a set of guiding questions. The framework is usually the result of a review of the relevant literature, prior experience in similar settings, and a general knowledge of the field of inquiry. It also resonates with echoes of the researcher's autobiographical journey—those aspects of her own familial, cultural, developmental, and educational background that she can relate (either consciously or unconsciously) to the intellectual themes of the work.
>
> (Lawrence-Lightfoot, 1997, p. 185)

Teacher preparation, much like portraiture, is a process situated socially and bound temporally in the politics and ideologies of the moment. Whereas the portraitist is concerned with recording an image of society and its actors, teacher educators are concerned with preparing future teachers to educate society and its actors. The portraitist and the teacher educator alike come to their respective places in the field with an intellectual framework, each using the framework to guide inquiry, inform decisions, and enable the individual to see society's many dimensions and reflect those dimensions in the portraitist's or teacher educator's work.

The difference between a portraitist and teacher educator is, in many ways, not that distinct. Teacher educators teach, much the same as portraitists paint, because they search, because they question, because they submit the "self" to questioning in relation to the act of teaching or painting. In this sense, the teacher and the portraitist are inquirers, continually searching and examining and reexamining their practice—inquirers concerned with the problematic nature of social issues and with their role in addressing these issues. By this act of continual inquiry, the teacher educator and portraitist intervene, and in intervening, educate individuals and society, as well as themselves. Teacher educators must engage, much the same as the portraitist, in self-critical reflection and inquiry so as to know what they do not know and to communicate and to proclaim or make public what is discovered (Freire, 1998).

The teacher educator, in understanding his or her own autobiographical journey, also recognizes the importance of enabling future teachers to learn their own autobiographical journey, to learn their responsibility as public intellectuals. As intellectuals, teacher educators and future teachers alike have to be seen in terms of the ideological and political interests that structure the nature of the discourse, social relations, and values that they legitimate in their social relations with "others" and in their struggles with challenges like youth violence, "high-stakes" testing, and growing cultural, linguistic, ethnic, and racial diversity.

Teacher educators, much like a portraitist, must learn to see the contexts and to see the subjects of their work within those contexts, to see the needs of individual students who desire to become teachers. The work ahead for teacher education is situated against the backdrop of a changing America; situated within a dramatically changing world.

The chapters in *Portraits of Teacher Preparation: Learning to Teach in a Changing America* offer insight into how teacher preparation programs can change and have changed to address the needs pressing on students, teachers, and schools today. The concept of "portrait" is adopted from Lawrence-Lightfoot and Davis's (1997) work, and therein portrait is viewed as both a metaphor and a method of inquiry. The portraits are instructed by the respective authors' intellectual frameworks, professional experiences, and understanding of the social, historical, and political contexts in which future teachers will practice their profession. The authors in part 1 prepare a backdrop for the portraits of teacher preparation, much the same as a portraitist prepares a canvas for painting the portrait. The narratives shared in the parts that follow paint rich portraits of learning to teach in a changing America.

REFERENCES

Freire, P. (1998). *Pedagogy of freedom: Ethics, democracy, and civic courage.* Lanham, MD: Rowman & Littlefield.

Lawrence-Lightfoot, S. (1997). Illumination: Searching for patterns. In S. Lawrence-Lightfoot & J. H. Davis, *The art and science of portraiture* (pp. 185–214). San Francisco: Jossey-Bass.

Overview

Patrick M. Jenlink
Stephen F. Austin State University

Knowledge emerges only through invention and reinvention, through the restless, impatient, continuing, hopeful inquiry human beings pursue in the world, with the world, and with each other.

(Freire, 1970, p. 53)

We need to help teachers attain a process for looking at the American experience so that they can raise questions. We won't know all the answers. Teachers need to understand . . . knowledge . . . [as] process. Teachers also need skills for teaching ethnic content and working with a multicultural population. They need these skills no matter where they teach because the population is changing and because ethnic content contains dilemmas and conflicts that require skills. Finally, teachers need to examine their own ethnic and cultural history, and their own ethnic journey.

(Banks, 1994, p. 5)

It is [education's] business to cultivate deep-seated and effective habits of discriminating tested beliefs from mere assertions, guesses, and opinions; to develop a lively, sincere, and open-minded preference for conclusions that are properly grounded, and to ingrain into the individual's working habits methods of inquiry and reasoning appropriate to the various problems that present themselves.

(Dewey, 1910, pp. 27–28)

> To teach consciously for justice and ethical action is teaching that arouses students, engages them in a quest to identify obstacles to their full humanity and the life chances of others, to their freedom, and then to drive and to move against those obstacles. And so the fundamental message of the teacher for ethical action is: You can change the world.
>
> (Ayers, 2001, p. 142)

The framing quotes opening this text are emblematic of teaching and teacher education concerned with making America, and in concert the world, a better place for all children to learn and grow up together, to become future democratic citizens. Teacher educators and the programs and institutions they represent are confronted with an increasingly difficult responsibility of preparing teachers to address issues of diversity, social justice, and equity as ethical and practical stances reflected in the day-to-day practices of teaching and learning. This requires teacher educators to make a firm commitment to work aggressively to address the same issues of diversity, social justice, and equity as pedagogical imperatives.

Cochran-Smith (2003), in writing on multiculturalism, validates the need for a new teacher education that works both to challenge historical ideological underpinnings of traditional programs and to situate knowledge about culture and racism at the forefront in teacher education curriculum. Included in this reimagining of teacher education is teaching for social justice as an imperative and outcome in learning to teach, as well as understanding the importance of valuing the cultural knowledge of local communities.

A CHANGING AMERICA: CHALLENGES FOR TEACHER PREPARATION

The portrait of a changing America reflects rapid societal change, which directly affects contemporary students and teachers. One element of societal change in America is population growth, which "has grown steadily, at 13 percent, but uneven among its racial/ethnic sub-populations" (Zhou, 2003, p. 209). Important markers include a stagnant growth in the White non-Hispanic population (3 percent), moderate growth in Black non-Hispanic population (21 percent), and rapid growth in Hispanic and Asian populations (61 percent and 69 percent, respectively). Accelerated immigration is a factor in the changing demographic profile (Zhou, 2003). Today in the

United States, approximately 27 percent of the population is under 18 years of age. An important marker of this population is that racial and intragroup diversity is even more pronounced than in the general population.

In urban population centers, 44 percent of all children are of non-White ethnic or racial origins, or are recent immigrants: They are Black, Hispanic, or Asian. Important to learning to teach in teacher education programs is the fact that the racial composition of the child population is reflected in public schools. "For culturally diverse children, especially those from poor, immigrant families, going to school is a daily struggle" (Zhou, 2003, p. 218).

Adding to the challenges for teacher preparation is the need for increased attention to infusing multiculturalism in the curriculum, pedagogy, and political imperatives necessary to prepare future generations of teachers. Interwoven in these imperatives are concerns for social justice and equity. The challenge, for teacher educators, in part, as Ladson-Billings (1999) points out, "is preparing students to do what they themselves do not have to do or may not be able to do" (p. 99). That is, teacher educators typically teach White middle-class teacher candidates who are able to learn successfully in conventional ways but lack experience with teaching the diverse student population found in today's schools and classrooms.

Because learning takes place in particular sociocultural contexts, learning to teach often takes place in contexts imprinted by conventional White middle-class mentalities, which creates a disconnect between the experiences in preparation programs and the cultural realities of a diverse classroom setting in schools. This is made more problematic by the pedagogical disconnect that arises as students enter diverse classroom settings and find themselves ill prepared for meeting the needs of a diverse student population.

On a societal level, September 11, 2001, is a historical marker for America and the world, a day when the perception of the safety of domestic soil was erased forever by global acts of terrorism. The significance of this act continues to reverberate throughout the country and has forced a comprehensive rethinking of domestic and foreign policy. The effect of September 11 has left virtually no social institution untouched. Schools, particularly in urban populations centers like Washington, DC, and Manhattan, were presented with the difficult responsibility of helping students assimilate the tragic event into their lives, and more importantly teachers and administrators found necessary the rethinking of their work in a democratic society no longer secure from foreign invasion.

America is changing, its identity being redefined through growing diversity and changing demographics leading to an increasing pluralism, through global events such as September 11, and through political mechanisms from within. A historical precedent for change was set in motion by the passage of the No Child Left Behind Act of 2001 (NCLB) (2002), redefining the federal government's role in education. The effect of NCLB as a legislated mandate reflects challenges to states' constitutionally delegated responsibility for education, but more important is the effect that redefining education, and in particular teacher education, will have over time on the foundation of a democratic society. The politics of highly qualified teachers, what is considered educational research, and the promulgation of standards and accountability stand as markers for constant scrutiny in years to come. How teacher educators address issues of diversity, justice, and equity must consider the backdrop of social and political tensions.

TEACHER PREPARATION AS PORTRAITURE

Portraiture as metaphor for teacher preparation reflects a concern for identity, method, knowledge, perspective, ethics, and an aesthetic and disciplined approach to learning to teach. Teacher educators as portraitists work with prospective teachers, as well as experienced teachers, understanding the preparation program as an organic medium in which the teacher is enabled to learn; making visible to students the lens through which they see and understand reality. Much the same as an artist, the teacher educator as portraitist is concerned with understanding the context in which the subject of the portrait is situated, understanding the defining qualities that give life and definition to the identity of the subject. Learning to teach in a changing America requires of the teacher educator a cultural sensitivity and political acumen necessary to examine and understand the contextualized nature of teaching and learning.

Teacher preparation refers to coherent educational experiences focused both on preparing preservice students to enter the profession for successful teaching careers and on providing continuing professional education for practicing teachers. Teacher preparation as portraiture translates the work of teacher educators into aesthetic, ethical, political, cultural, and intellectual dimensions. Returning to the framing quotes that open this text, one finds defining elements of a new teacher education that represent the field sketches a portraitist first collects in considering a subject, the preparation of the subject, and the realization of the portrait. Learning to teach, much like the portraitist's work, requires commitment to the subject and commitment to the public that will experience the product of the portraitist's labors.

A portrait may best be understood as an artist's interpretation of events and the world within which the events take place. Likewise, a teacher preparation program may be understood as the teacher educators—as portraitists—interpreting the challenges and needs of teachers in a changing America. Teacher preparation as portraiture seeks to acknowledge qualities of goodness that define the subject, while also acknowledging the realization that goodness is made visible by contrasting imperfection. Qualities of goodness in teacher education include a multiculturalism-infused curriculum, social justice–focused instruction, teacher inquiry, reflective/reflexive–guided and learning, practice-based inquiry, democratic culture, and critical dispositions of teaching.

In contrast, qualities of imperfection in teacher education include traditional or conventional approaches, cultural biases that overshadow the value in cultural knowledge of non-White populations, poor collaborative relationships with schools, a disproportionate ratio of White faculty to non-White students, disconnects between college classroom instruction and the reality of diversity and complexity of teaching in public school classrooms, the marginalization of students and faculty through normative and nondiscursive practices, and curricular and instructional processes and practices and impoverished learning experiences for preservice students. Acknowledging the imperfections of society, and the challenges these imperfections bring to teaching students in culturally diverse classrooms, requires of the teacher educator an awareness and understanding that teacher preparation is not without challenges; it is necessarily a form of social activism situated in the larger context of sociocultural injustices and inequities.

Teacher educators, as portraitists in the preparation program, must engage in innovative and imaginative approaches to learning to teach, setting aside conventional practices for new mediums of expression, and learning and constructing new and alternative pedagogies for learning. Importantly, different mediums of expression combined with different styles of teaching and learning reflect a diversity of artistic expression; in the case of learning to teach, such diversity creates a more authentic learning commensurate with life and teaching in the classroom. Multiculturalism, social justice, equity, and democracy become defining colors in the portraitists' palette as they prepare their subjects for the work of teaching in a changing America.

PORTRAITS OF TEACHER PREPARATION

A portrait is first and foremost the creation of the artist/teacher educator. It is a cultural artifact of a constructed reality in the mind of the artist/teacher educator who embeds the story within a context and centers it around selected and specific voices that give depth, dimensionality, color, and contrast to the qualities that define the subject of the portrait.

In the chapters that follow, the reader experiences portraits of learning to teach, set against the backdrop of a changing America. Importantly, the authors, as portraitists and teacher educators, bring into play the qualities signified in the framing quotes that open this text. Even more important, the portraitists present a narrative window into teacher preparation that reflects the concerns for changing demographics and growing diversity, concerns for social justice and democratic practice, concerns for preparing teachers who understand urban education and all the challenges therein, and concerns for reimagining teacher education as a culturally and ethically responsive action toward creating alternative futures for America's schools. The portraitists, through their respective portraits, offer hope for America's schools; more importantly they offer hope for America's children. In the first part, chapter 1 combines elements of multiculturalism, social justice, and democracy as qualities of goodness necessary to a portrait of teacher preparation in a changing America.

Part 2 (chapters 2 through 4) presents an exhibit of three portraits, highlighting the qualities of inquiry and social justice as defining elements of a new teacher education. Part 3 (chapters 5 through 7) bring the quality of democracy to the foreground as the portraitists examine teacher preparation in their respective programs and institutions. Part 4 (chapters 8 through 10) identifies the challenges of learning to teach in urban population centers that are rapidly growing, acknowledging the importance of diversity as a defining quality, both in terms of pedagogical methods and knowledge, as well as race and ethnicity. The final part of this book, part 5, presents a portraitist's reflective and aesthetic inquiry about the collected portraits presented in preceding parts. The closing chapter offers the reader considerations for imagining the future of teacher preparation.

REFERENCES

Ayers, W. (2001). *To teach: The journey of a teacher* (2nd ed.). New York: Teachers College Press.

Banks, J. (1994). Multicultural education for all Americans. *Catalyst*, *1*, 4–5, 8.

Cochran-Smith, M. (2003). The multiple meanings of multicultural teacher education: A conceptual framework. *Teacher Education Quarterly*, *30*(2), 7–26.

Dewey, J. (1910). *How we think*. Boston: D.C. Heath.

Freire, P. (1970). *The pedagogy of the oppressed*. New York: Seabury Press.

Ladson-Billings, G. (1999). Preparing teachers for diversity: Historical perspectives, current trends, and future directions. In L. Darling-Hammond & G. Sykes (Eds.), *Teaching as the learning profession: Handbook of policy and practice* (pp. 86–123). San Francisco: Jossey-Bass.

No Child Left Behind Act of 2001, H.R. 1 (S.R. 1), 107th Cong., 147 Cong. Rec. 1425. (2002). Retrieved April 13, 2004, from http://www.nagb.org/about/plaw.html

Zhou, M. (2003). Urban education: Challenges in educating culturally diverse children. *Teacher College Record*, *105*(2), 208–225.

1

Learning to Teach in a Changing America

Patrick M. Jenlink and Karen Embry Jenlink
Stephen F. Austin State University

The challenges facing American society are nowhere more notable than in America's schools and are mirrored in the colleges and schools of education teacher education programs. Preparing the next generation of teachers for today's diverse classrooms is a monumental task, confounded by the realization that tomorrow's teacher must be prepared in terms of multicultural imperatives for curriculum and pedagogy, culturally responsive, and critically conscious (Gay, 2002; Gay & Kirkland, 2003) to meet the needs of an increasingly diverse student population. Concurrently, in a post–September 11 climate, America is faced with the challenges of educating citizens for living in a democratic society subject to global politics enacted domestically. Giroux (2002) draws our attention to the necessity of "rethinking the role of educators and the politics of schooling" (p. 1138) as America is redefined by the "cataclysmic political, economic, and legal changes inaugurated by the monstrous events of September 11" (p. 1138).

Against this backdrop, domestic policy, such as the No Child Left Behind Act and the reauthorization of the Elementary and Secondary Education Act (ESEA), raises new challenges to education and those choosing to enter the profession. Issues of diversity further illuminate the complex and problematic nature of schools and colleges as places of cultural reproduction wherein the hegemony of controlling ideologies continues to advantage some populations while disadvantaging others. At a time when American society, and more specifically its educational system, is confronted with the challenges of preparing teachers for classrooms of students reflecting the growing diversity across the country, Dewey's (1916) concern for educating a democratic citizenry—the concern for education's role in a democracy—resurfaces with perhaps even more import.

The challenges, and relatedly the politics, of standards and accountability, state and national accreditation, teacher professionalism, and the growing needs of a rapidly changing and increasingly diverse society have created a complex milieu of problems for colleges of education, and in particular teacher preparation programs. Framed by concerns for bridging the theory of college curriculum with the pragmatic reality of teaching in the classrooms of the K–12 school, the focus on changing teacher preparation calls for authenticity in contextually sensitive and culturally responsive teacher education.

The questions before colleges and schools of education are situated within a larger discourse of social justice and democracy that has resounded across generations. These questions include the following, as well as many other that are equally important: "What is teacher education's role in preparing teachers that are concerned with social issues, and who will take a stand on preparing children as democratic citizens?" "How can teacher preparation programs prepare teachers for the complex and demanding work of teaching in multiracial and multicultural educational settings?" "What impact have standards and accountability had on teacher preparation?" "How well are we really doing in the work to rethink teacher preparation amid the challenges and politics confronting colleges of education and teacher education?"

TEACHER EDUCATION AS CULTURAL AGENCY IN A DIVERSE SOCIETY

American society is increasingly defined by its growing multicultural and multiethnic nature. We live in a time when social distinctions and ethnic, racial, class, gender, linguistic, and lifestyle differences have become increasingly political and critical to the way in which people identify themselves, experience the world around them, and make meaning of everyday life. As Guarasci and Cornwell (1997) explain, "We live in a time when our distinctions, our disconnections from one another, have become more important to some and more threatening to others than they have been at any other time certainly in the last half century" (p. 2).

Charged with the public responsibility to educate teachers to enable future generations to learn the knowledge and skills necessary to build a principled and democratic society, teacher education programs represent a significant agency for the reproduction and legitimation of a society characterized by a high degree of social and economic inequality (Giroux, 1981, p. 143). As such, teacher education programs are charged with the public responsibility to educate teachers to enable future generations to learn the knowledge and skills necessary to address social inequities and injustices, while working to build a principled and democratic society. As Maxine Greene (1986) observes, the type of community, society, and world that

> we cherish is not an endowment. . . . It must be achieved through dialectical engagements with the social and economic obstacles we find standing in our way. . . . We cannot neglect the fact of power. But we can undertake a resistance, a reaching out toward becoming persons among persons. (p. 440)

Education work at its best represents a response to questions and issues posed by the tensions and contradictions of public life and attempts to understand and intervene in specific problems that emanate from the material contexts of everyday existence (Giroux, 2001, p. 215).

In this sense, teachers and other cultural workers must be *transformative intellectuals*, working within the cultural-historical contexts in which schools are situated, intellectual and cultural workers seen through the "ideological and political interests that structure the nature of discourses, classroom social relations, and values that they legitimate in their teaching" (Giroux, 1988, p. 127). And they must address the practical consequences of their work within schools and universities in the broader society while simultaneously making connections to those too-often-ignored institutional forms and cultural spheres that position and influence young people within unequal relations of power (Giroux, 2001, p. 217). However, as Ladson-Billings argues, in too many cases prospective teachers are still being prepared to teach in "idealized schools that serve white, monolingual, middle-class children from homes with two parents" (2000, pp. 86–87).

Learning to teach in schools within a changing society—fraught with the challenges of terrorist acts, standards and accountability, federal policy, and growing diversity—reflects the complex and culturally bound nature of becoming a teacher. Wideen, Mayer-Smith, and Moon (1998), in their critical analysis of research on learning to teach, examined the question of how beginning teachers learn to teach. Their findings indicated that learning to teach is a deeply personal activity in which "the individual concerned has to deal with his or her beliefs in light of expectations from a university, a school, and society, and in the context of teaching" (p. 160).

As individuals learn to teach, they must transcend the complexity of the preparation process and situate the learning process in the often equally complex and challenging practice of teaching students in the school classroom. Therein, as Cole (1990) notes, "teaching is a complex and personal phenomenon . . . an expression of a personal and professional way of knowing that is shaped and informed by personal and professional background, experience, perceptions, attitudes, beliefs, and goals" (p. 203).

In consideration of the complex and context-bound nature of teaching, as Torres (1998) explains, "We need to prepare professionals who understand the importance and contradictions of cultural diversity" (p. 259). Educators as cultural workers must be able to "move back and forth between theoretical and applied research in real school settings" (p. 259). Moving between the theoretical and applied, and the academic and practical, accents the importance of experiential as well as academic experiences during preservice teacher education. This is particularly important if students are to become competent in matters of race, culture, ethnic, and social differences—cross-culturally competent. Students need practical, context-based experiences where one-on-one work goes on with minority students, and experience with social justice projects, for the study of the issues of multicultural education to become more than abstract concepts that fail to touch their emotional and moral lives and, therefore, lack the potential for transformative learning. Importantly, curriculum within teacher preparation must be reconsidered so as to embed both the theoretical and applied, academic knowledge and practical experiential knowledge.

Cochran-Smith (2000) provides an important exemplar in arguing that when preservice curriculum is viewed critically as "racial text," transformative learning is encouraged, for racism becomes a central issue in the course and is dealt with on close and personal levels, not just through "distant and academic" prose. Moreover, such a curriculum, evolving out of a critical philosophy, involves helping students understand that schools are always "sites for institutional and collective struggles of power and oppression, not neutral backdrops for individual achievement and failure" (p. 174).

MULTICULTURALISM AND DEMOCRACY

Current and emerging sociocultural realities about teachers and students, and relatedly teaching and learning, demarcate the importance of and need for shaping teacher preparation programs through the infusion of multiculturalism as an ethical and intellectual imperative in learning to teach. Multiculturalism is concerned with "intersections across communities as well as the simultaneous and mutual constitution of various communal identities" (Brettschneider, 2002, p. 9). As a theory and practice, multiculturalism is as much about acknowledging and working from the multiplicity of our communities in matters of national politics as it is about multiplicity within communities. It brings a critical eye to "examining what factors of human experience are considered politically salient in any given cultural and historical context" (p. 10). Multiculturalism is considered a diversity-based theory of democracy, which questions and seeks to articulate the ways that diversity and aspects of our identity situate us differently in power relationships over time.

In educational settings, theories of multiculturalism have emerged in response "to the constitution of the pedagogical subject in schools or to the interaction between the pedagogical subject and the political subject in democratic societies" (Torres, 1998, p. 3). Equally important, multiculturalism has also emerged "as a way to identify the importance of multiple identities (and hence narratives, voices, and agency) in education and culture. In short, theories of multiculturalism are intimately connected to the politics of culture and education" (p. 3), making necessary the preparation of teachers who understand the political nature of educating diverse children as well as how to engage, pedagogically, the children in a curriculum that prepares all of them for a critical, active role in a democratic society.

Bringing to the foreground pedagogical concern for multiculturalism is of paramount importance to fostering a stronger, more viable democracy.

In *Democracy and Education*, Dewey (1916) singled out "the area of shared concerns, and the liberation of greater diversity of personal capacity" as hallmarks of democracy (pp. 101–102). He noted that only after "greater individualization and on one hand, and a broader community of interest on the other have come into existence" (p. 87) could these characteristics be sustained by voluntary disposition and interest, which must be made possible by means of education. Dewey saw connections between personal voice and public space, understanding the inseparable role of education in a democratic society. Teacher education, as a process for learning to teach, has a responsibility to prepare teachers who understand the connectivity between personal voice and public space, who are activists who embrace the critical importance of helping their students—as future citizens—to pursue the realization of democracy by questioning the structural inequality, racism, and injustice that exist in today's society. Learning to teach is about learning to take action on personal, social, and civic levels, inside and outside the classroom, addressing inequities and promoting a democratic discourse.

However, as Dewey states about teacher education, and relatedly teaching practice in schools, "the conception of education as a social process and function has no definite meaning until we define the kind of society we have in mind" (1916, p. 97). When we define society as socially just and democratic, we must conceive of an educational system in that society populated by educators who embody social justice, whose pedagogical practice is concerned with

> teaching for the sake of arousing the kinds of vivid, reflective, experiential responses that might move students to come together in serious efforts to understand what social justice actually means and what it might demand. That means teaching to the end of arousing a consciousness of membership, active and participant membership in a society of unfulfilled promises. (Greene, 1998, p. xxx)

At a time when American society, and more specifically its educational system, is confronted with the challenges of preparing teachers for classrooms populated with students reflecting the growing diversity across the country, Dewey's (1916) concern for the function of education in democracy and the preparing of active democratic citizens echoes resoundingly. Fraser (1997) acknowledges this concern when he states,

A democratic society, indeed any society, will support schools for many different reasons. But at the heart of the education in a democratic polity must be a commitment to maintaining and expanding democracy itself. Any lesser goal will ultimately fail to maintain public support for the enterprise of public education or foster a dynamic and self-critical democratic society. (Fraser, 1997, p. xi)

Preparing citizens for active critical roles in America's democratic society is challenging. It requires teachers who understand the importance of fostering the principle of freedom and the human capacities of individuals to function with civic responsibility and courage. Such teachers must understand how to develop our children's individual power as citizens to their maximum, but they must also cultivate an understanding that "individual powers must be linked to democracy in the sense that social betterment must be the necessary consequence of individual flourishing" (Giroux, 1992, p. 11).

The Democratic Ideal and Education

John Dewey (1916) argues that "a democracy is more than a form of government; it is primarily a mode of associated living, of conjoint communicated experience" (p. 87). Speaking specifically to issues of difference, he further explains that democracy is the "extension of space of a number of individuals who participate in an interest so that each has to refer his own action to that of others" (p. 87). Thus democracy is the consideration by an individual of the "action of others to give point and direction to his own" actions (p. 87). Such conjoined activity is democracy, which is "equivalent to the breaking down of those barriers of class, race, and national territory which [keep individuals] from perceiving the full import of their activity" (p. 87).

Reflecting on the organization of democratic society, Dewey notes that "only diversity makes change and progress," (p. 90). Here Dewey is speaking to the uniqueness of individuals and the value such uniqueness holds for democracy. He notes "that in the degree in which society has become democratic, such social organization means utilization of the specific and variable qualities of individuals" (pp. 90–91). Dewey's concern for uniqueness—difference and diversity of qualities—plays against his primary consideration for the conception of education as a social process, a process in relationship to the organization of a democratic society. With respect to education, he argues that the "conception of education as a social process and function has no definite meaning until we define the kind of society we have in mind" (1916, p. 97).

If we determine that society is to be democratic, which is interpreted as a form of associated living and conjoint experiences, then education must necessarily foster the capacities and capabilities of citizenry toward realizing a democratic society. Dewey (1916) notes that there "are many kinds of societies," and therein a need for criterion for educational criticism and construction (p. 99). He notes two points by which to critically evaluate the worth of social life—"the extent in which the interests of a group are shared by all its members, and the fullness and freedom with which it interacts with other groups" (p. 99). A democratic society, then, is a "society that makes provision for participation in its good of all its members on equal terms and which secures flexible readjustment of its institutions through interaction of the different forms of associated life is in so far democratic" (p. 99). In a democratic society then, Dewey critically believed, education "gives individuals a personal interest in social relationships and control, and the habits of mind which secure social changes without introducing disorder" (p. 99).

A central responsibility of education in a society that chooses to be democratic is providing for its members the "habits of mind" so as to become active critical agents of that society, who utilize moral principles to prevent repression and discrimination (Pearson, 1992). Ralph Ellison (1989), in his book, *Invisible Man*, argues that fiction can serve politics by putting forth "a vision of an ideal democracy" and constructing "a raft of hope" as fellow citizens try "to negotiate the snags and whirlpools that mark our nation's vacillating course toward and away from the democratic ideal" (pp. xx–xxi). While Ellison speaks of democracy as an ideal state, he also describes it as a process imbued with transformative power, a creative process akin to fiction itself: "For by a trick of fate (and our racial problems notwithstanding) the human imagination is integrative—and the same is true of the centrifugal force that inspirits the democratic process" (p. xx). Ellison's "ideal democracy" speaks to the issues that animate the need for theories of multiculturalism in a changing America. The all-too-often cultural-political actions that make non-White individuals "invisible" are as problematic today as they were in Dewey's and Ellison's times.

Walter Parker (1996), in his *Educating the Democratic Mind*, notes that "schools are fitting places for democratic education," precisely because they "already possess easily and naturally . . . the bedrocks of democratic living—diversity and mutuality" (p. 2). Examining the historicity of educating for democracy, Parker critiques past efforts: "Beyond the establishment of free public schooling, surprisingly little has been done to educate children for democracy" (p. 11). Conventional educational practices usually constrain schools and educators from the benefit of their multicultural settings. Difference and diversity become markers of disconnection in contemporary schools, thus reinforcing the distancing and marginalizing of many students, specifically the non-White and the poor.

Democracy and Learning to Teach

James Banks (1994), writing on multiculturalism and education within the democratic project, explains multicultural education as that of helping students "develop cross-cultural competency within the American national culture, with their own subculture and within and across different subsocieties and cultures" (p. 9). The development of such competency involves knowledge of cultural and racial differences and issues; the critical examination of one's own beliefs and values regarding culture, race, and social class; and an understanding of how knowledge, beliefs, and values determine one's behavior with respect to minority groups. In its more radical or critical form, cross-cultural competency can promote the development of students who are social reformers, working for a more just and democratic society in which power and resources are more equitably distributed.

As Torres (1998) explains, "The central concern for us is education for democracy: how to build better schools, intellectually richer schools" (p. 259), wherein there is no invisibility, "particularly for those who are at the bottom of the society" (p. 259). This will require the understanding of "how to build a democratic multicultural curriculum where everybody learns from the rich diversity of the society" (p. 259). As Dewey (1916) argued, education must necessarily play a direct role in fostering a democratic way of life for all. Therein, the school "should play a central role in the constitution of democratic discourse and citizenship" (p. 259).

Learning to teach in teacher education programs is not without influence from dominant ideologies and cultural patterns, as well as political trappings of state and federal policies and professional standards proponents. The beginning teacher is often faced with moving against established pedagogical beliefs and teaching practices that are part of the "shaping" nature of schools. Teachers who first enter the classroom need to know, as Cochran-Smith (1991) suggests, "that they have a responsibility to reform, not just replicate, standard school practices" (p. 280). Teachers must learn to "teach against the grain." The critical stance of teaching against the grain provides a perspective of the beginning teacher that identifies the importance of teacher identity and the role of teacher "self" contributing to the transformation of the school culture through teacher practice. As Perry and Fraser (1993) note, education and schools should "prefigure the society we want rather than reinforce existing social and political arrangements" (p. 3).

Preparing teachers for such educational settings requires a rethinking of teacher preparation. "If the society we want is a democratic nation predicated on a diversity of racial and ethnic origins, [then] we have no choice but to revision our schools as multicultural, multiethnic, multigendered democracies" (Perry & Fraser, 1993, p. 18).

Social Justice and Learning to Teach

The challenges faced by teacher educators and the students they prepare to enter the classrooms of schools across the country are bound by a common responsibility of addressing issues of social justice. The teacher educator and the practitioner function as self-conscious, autonomous, and authentic persons in a public space where ideologically imprinted patterns of culture and the reality of life for students often leave little sense of hope. Unlike an artist or a scholar or a research scientist, the teacher educator and classroom teacher cannot withdraw to the studio, study, or laboratory and still remain practitioners (Greene, 1973, p. 290). They are involved with students, colleagues, school board members, and parents whenever and wherever they engage in the fundamental project of education. Moreover, they cannot avoid the social structures and politics beyond their classroom doors. There is always a sense in which they must mediate between those structures and politics and the young people they are entrusted with to prepare for active lives as active, democratic citizens; teachers must take a dialectical stance. As Ayers (1998) explains,

Teaching for social justice demands a dialectical stance: One eye firmly fixed on the students—Who are they? What are their hopes, dreams, and aspirations? Their passions and commitments? What skills, abilities, and capacities does each one bring to the classroom?—and the other eye looking unblinkingly at the concentric circles of context—historical flow, cultural surround, economic reality. (p. xvii)

Such a stance requires teacher educators and classroom teachers alike to prepare students in certain patterns of thinking and acting—certain social and intellectual and ethical habits of mind—while simultaneously making visible, through curriculum and pedagogy, the social injustices and inequities that mark the lives of students and preclude possible alternative futures. As teachers, they must enable students to recognize and choose among the options presented to them, as well as imagine alternative possibilities against the backdrop of cultural politics. Teachers must take a stance through their practice, a stance that recognizes the moral and intellectual responsibility of sensitizing students to inhumanity, vulgarity, and hypocrisy, while also enabling them to comprehend their society's professed ideas: freedom, justice, equality, democracy, and a belief in the rights of all members of society, regardless of race, ethnicity, socioeconomic status, gender, sexual preference, or language.

Taking a pedagogical stance on social justice involves being concerned with the effects of injustice and inequity on children; it is a political project pursued in the classroom. Social justice is not an add-on to a curriculum—whether for the teacher preparation or public school classroom. Rather, it is built into the pedagogy—the values that instruct curriculum design and curriculum delivery. The teacher must take a stand on "What should govern? An understanding of protocols, of procedures? A range of fundamental principles? Authenticity—the sense of a person one ought to be?" (Greene, 1973, p. 286), while not imposing values or virtues on the students, but rather posing questions that guide students "toward increasing awareness, deepening conviction. Granting them dignity, freedom, and autonomy (unless they are little children), he becomes a catalyst in the process of their self-identification, their learning how to learn" (Greene, 1973, p. 286). As Dewey (1922) argued, children "are not as yet subject to the full impact of established customs" (p. 89); therefore, education offers the primary means for social rectification of historical problems in society through educating the young to modify prevailing types of thought and desire, preparing a new generation "whose habit of mind have been formed" under new conditions (p. 78).

Teaching for social justice, teaching to prepare students as active critical agents of a democratic society, requires that the teacher become "highly conscious, more critical and clear" (Greene, 1973, p. 221) with respect to social conditions that work to advantage some populations of students while disadvantaging others. Teaching for social justice requires of teachers and teacher educators the need for critical praxis, for a self-critical examination of the relationships between language, culture, knowledge, and power that shape the experiences of learning to teach as well as contribute to defining teaching practice in the public school classroom. Such examination is a process of becoming self-aware that embedded in our pedagogy "is a powerful subtext about teaching and about the boundaries of race and teaching in schools and larger educational systems" (Cochran-Smith, 1995, p. 522).

Teaching for social justice must be part of a political project that is centered on issues of emancipation and empowerment. The pedagogical principles at work here analyze culture—and therein cultural identity—in relation to both individuals and classes among learners. Teachers are engaged in culturally responsive practice, consciously aware of the concrete world in which their students live, of their students' lived experiences, and social practices bound in the language, habits, beliefs, and dreams that are developed within asymmetrical relations of power. Such a pedagogy transcends "the dichotomy of elite and popular culture by defining itself through a project of educating students to feel compassion for the suffering of others, to engage in a continual analysis of their own conditions of existence," fostering a "notion of learned hope, forged amidst the realization of risks, and steeped in a commitment to transforming public culture and life" (Giroux, 1992, p. 99).

CONCLUSION

The portrait of teacher education presented in this chapter reflects a transformative cultural agency role for colleges and schools of education, a role purposed with preparing teachers who, through their pedagogy and practice, are engaged in challenging society's existing social order so as to develop and advance its democratic imperatives. Recognizing the imperatives of social justice and diversity in fostering a more democratic society, teacher preparation programs should consider curricula that bring to the foreground consideration for multicultural practices and democratic principles, integrating both theoretical and applied research as well experiential learning. Importantly, teacher education programs must reflect a democratic ideal that is guided by an understanding of the multicultural and multicentric nature of American society. Equally important, teacher preparation must reflect an understanding of the imperative for socially just practice on the part of teachers and other cultural workers, as they are charged with the responsibility of educating the future citizens of our nation.

REFERENCES

Ayers, W. (1998). Popular education—Teaching for social justice. In W. Ayers, J. A. Hunt, & T. Quinn (Eds.), *Teaching for social justice: A democracy and education reader* (pp. xvii–xxv). New York: Teachers College Press.

Banks, J. (1994). *An introduction to multicultural education*. Boston: Allyn & Bacon.

Brettschneider, M. (2002). *Democratic theorizing from the margins*. Philadelphia: Temple University Press.

Cochran-Smith, M. (1991). Learning to teach against the grain. *Harvard Educational Review*, 61(3), 279–310.

Cochran-Smith, M. (1995). Color blindness and basket making are not the answers: Confronting the dilemmas of race, culture, and language diversity in teacher education. *American Educational Research Journal*, 32(3), 493–522.

Cochran-Smith, M. (2000). Blind vision: Unlearning racism in teacher education. *Harvard Educational Review*, 70(2), 157–191.

Cole, A. L. (1990). Personal theories of teaching: Development in the formative years. *The Alberta Journal of Educational Research*, 36(3), 203–222.

Dewey, J. (1916). *Democracy and education: An introduction to the philosophy of education*. New York: Macmillan.

Dewey, J. (1922). *Human nature and conduct*. New York: Modern Library.

Ellison, R. (1989). *Invisible Man*. New York: Vintage.

Euben, P. (1994). The debate over the canon. *The Civic Arts Review*, 7(1), 14–15.

Fraser, J. W. (1997). *Reading, writing, and justice: School reform as if democracy matters*. Albany: State University of New York Press.

Gay, G. (2002). Preparing for culturally responsive teaching. *Journal of Teacher Education, 53*(2), 106–116.

Gay, G., & Kirkland, K. (2003). Developing cultural critical consciousness and self-reflection in preservice teacher education. *Theory Into Practice, 42*(3), 181–187.

Giroux, H. (1981). *Ideology, culture and the process of schooling*. Philadelphia: Temple University Press.

Giroux, H. (1988). *Teachers as intellectuals: Toward a critical pedagogy of learning*. South Hadley, MA: Bergin & Garvey.

Giroux, H. A. (1992). *Border crossings: Cultural workers and the politics of education*. New York: Routledge.

Giroux, H. A. (2001). Public intellectuals and the challenge of children's culture: Youth and the politics of innocence. *The Review of Education/Psychology/Cultural Studies, 21*(3), 193–225.

Giroux, H. A. (2002). Democracy, freedom, and justice after September 11th: Rethinking the role of educators and the politics of schooling. *Teachers College Record, 104*(6), 1138–1162.

Greene, M. (1973). *Teacher as stranger: Educational philosophy for the modern age*. Belmont, CA: Wadsworth.

Greene, M. (1986). In search of a critical pedagogy. *Harvard Education Review, 56*(4), 427–441.

Greene, M. (1998). Teaching for social justice. In W. Ayers, J. A. Hunt, & T. Quinn (Eds.), *Teaching for social justice: A democracy and education reader* (pp. xxviii–xlvi). New York: Teachers College Press.

Guarasci, R., & Cornwell, G. H. (1997). Democracy and difference: Emerging concepts of identity, diversity, and community. In R. Guarasci & G. H. Cornwell (Eds.), *Democratic education in an age of difference: Redefining citizenship in higher education* (pp. 1–16). San Francisco: Jossey-Bass.

Ladson-Billings, G. (2000). Preparing teachers for diversity: Historical perspectives, current trends, and future directions. In L. Darling-Hammond & G. Sykes (Eds.), *Teaching as the learning profession: Handbook of policy and practice* (pp. 86–123). San Francisco: Jossey-Bass.

Parker, W. (1996). *Educating the democratic mind*. Albany: State University of New York Press.

Pearson, A. (1992). Teacher education in a democracy. *Educational Philosophy and Theory, 24*, 83–92.

Perry, T., & Fraser, J. W. (1993). Reconstructing schools as multiracial/multicultural democracies: Toward a theoretical perspective. In T. Perry & J. W. Fraser (Eds.), *Freedom's plow: Teaching in the multicultural classroom* (pp. 3–24). New York: Routledge.

Torres, C. A. (1998). *Democracy, education, and multiculturalism: Dilemmas of citizenship in a global world*. Boulder, CO: Rowman & Littlefield.

Wideen, M., Mayer-Smith, J., & Moon, B. (1998). A critical analysis of the research on learning to teach: Making the case for an ecological perspective on inquiry. *Review of Educational Research, 68*(2), 130–178.

II

LEARNING TO TEACH FOR SOCIAL JUSTICE

To teach for social justice is to teach for enhanced perception and imaginative explorations, for the recognition of social wrongs, of sufferings, of pestilences wherever and whenever they arise. It is to find models of literature and in history of the indignant ones, the ones forever ill at ease, and the loving ones who have taken the side of the victims of pestilences, whatever their names or places of origin. It is to teach so that the young may be awakened to the joy of working for transformation in the smallest places, so that they may become healers and change their worlds.

(Greene, 1998, p. xlv)

There is in the United States a major effort, arguably politically motivated, now under way to create a national education system animated by standards and accountability. This effort comes at a time in American history when issues of diversity are making problematic, more and more each day, the structures and practices that define American schools, and equally as well making problematic teacher preparation programs in institutions of higher education. Importantly, America, and the world at large, is faced with the "politics of reality" (Scheurich, 2003, p. 291) that shape the lives and identities of individuals—shape the identity of children in ways that reproduce cultural oppression and marginalization and fail the children.

Teacher educators working within preparation programs are responsible for designing curricula and instructional delivery systems that foster a teacher stance of teaching for social justice (Ayers, 1998). Such a stance interprets as teaching consciously for social justice and for social change. Preparing teachers to take a critical, dialectal stance "can never be an attribute or endeavour that is achieved by the individual" (Curzon-Hobson, 2003, p. 209) teacher alone. A stance on social justice, rather, "always turns the gaze and attention of the student and teacher towards the unique potentiality of others and how one's projects impact upon the becoming nature of them" (p. 209).

Learning to teach that is premised on a stance for social justice recognizes the importance of a social justice pedagogy. This social justice pedagogy refers to a deliberate attempt to construct authentic conditions through which educators and students can think critically about what stands as knowledge, how knowledge is produced, and how knowledge is transformed in relation to the "construction of social experiences informed by a particular relationship between the self, others, and the larger world (Giroux, 1992, p. 99). A social justice stance is, in part, a disposition through which teachers reflect upon their own actions and those presented by others. Rather than passively accepting information or embracing a false consciousness, teachers take a much more active role in leading, learning, and reflecting upon their relationship with their practice and the social context in which the practice is situated.

The notion of a social justice stance is "predicated on a notion of learned hope, forged amidst the realization of risks, and steeped in a commitment to transforming public culture and life" (Giroux, 1992, p. 99). The teacher educator's work, then, in part, is to foster a sense of freedom of mind and freedom of actions. In part, the teacher educator's work is also to invoke in students entering the educational setting an understanding of the importance of retaining a sense of incompleteness and becoming. A socially just society is never achieved; rather it is in a continuous process of becoming. Maintaining a sense of incompleteness and becoming in relation to a just and democratic society is the result of the individual's will—teacher and student—and the teacher educator's encouragement to critically question, challenge, and overcome in full recognition of the imaginative possibilities of a world beyond the human will to objectify individual lives.

Teaching for social justice requires a stance realized and "imbued through and within students' and teachers' interactions with the self, knowledge, and others" (Curzon-Hobson, 2003, p. 211). The portraits presented in this part reflect a concern for social justice and teacher inquiry that guides and informs social practice.

REFERENCES

Ayers, W. (1998). Popular education—Teaching for social justice. In W. Ayers, J. A. Hunt, & T. Quinn (Eds.), *Teaching for social justice: A democracy and education reader* (pp. xvii–xxv). New York: Teachers College Press.

Curzon-Hobson, A. (2003). Higher learning and the critical stance. *Studies in Higher Education, 28*(2), 201–212.

Giroux, H. A. (1992). *Border crossings: Cultural workers and the politics of education.* New York: Routledge.

Greene, M. (1998). Teaching for social justice. In W. Ayers, J. A. Hunt, & T. Quinn (Eds.), *Teaching for social justice: A democracy and education reader* (pp. xxviii–xlvi). New York: Teachers College Press.

Scheurich, J. J. (2003). Commentary: The grave dangers in the discourse on democracy. In C. D. Glickman (Ed.), *Holding sacred ground: Essays on leadership, courage, and endurance in our schools* (pp. 286–293). San Francisco: Jossey-Bass.

2

Center X: Where Research and Practice Intersect for Urban School Professionals: A Portrait of the Teacher Education Program at the University of California, Los Angeles

Brad Olsen, with the help of Sheila Lane, Eloise Lopez Metcalfe, Jody Priselac, Gordon Suzuki, and Rae Jeane Williams[1]
University of California, Los Angeles

LISTENING TO STUDENTS' STORIES: ONE TEACHER'S PERSPECTIVE

Thirteen young teachers—some Asian American, some Latino, some White, some African American—sit around a square of tables with a university field supervisor and a faculty team leader. In one corner of the mostly bare classroom sits a table with opened bottles of soda, yellow paper cups, bags of tortilla chips, and plastic bowls filled with salsa. The large windows open out to an impressive university view: Spanish-tiled roofs of campus buildings, the deep blue evening sky, steel tables and chairs in the courtyard below. The faculty team leader, a young-looking Latino man in a pressed shirt, looks around slowly, smiles, and announces that we are here today not only to hear presentations from students' master's portfolios but also as celebration of the hard work and thoughtfulness our students have put in over the two years. Introductions are made as we go around the table because some of the teachers in the room are not UCLA graduate students but colleagues who teach with the students—they came both to support their friends and to listen to the teaching stories to be told. One student begins. She has blond hair and a small diamond stud in her nose (we learn later that she drives race cars as a hobby). She clears her throat and then narrates for us an agonizing but ultimately empowering struggle she imposed on herself this year as she critically confronted some of what her dominant culture upbringing had taught her and found ways to listen differently—listen better, really—to her third-grade students:

> I've had to question the stories I told in the classroom and the examples I used. Sure, the children listened to the stories—I was their teacher—but I realized that those stories, my stories, don't always have much to do with the lives of these students. . . . It's hard not to revert back to what I grew up with, not to impose my culture on my kids—hard because I came to teaching with stereotypes I've had to recognize. My view of the community where I teach was formed by movies like *Boyz in the Hood* or other aspects of Hollywood, and I've had to get past that—to become a good listener to the students, to their experiences. It's taken me all year, but now everything I do in our classroom I try to make relevant to their own lives, not only as I see them, but as they see them.

TEACHER PREPARATION AT UCLA

Center X was first conceived in 1992 out of the upheaval and self-examination stemming from Los Angeles's Rodney King verdict uprisings (Oakes, 1996). Two years and countless marathon Friday meetings later, Center X came into being in 1994–1995 as an integrated, experimental, two-year urban teacher preparation program for both elementary and secondary teachers in the Graduate School of Education and Information Studies at the University of California, Los Angeles. Previously, the UCLA teacher education program was a highly regarded but conventional one-year MEd program that prepared teachers by emphasizing constructivism and practitioner reflection. The newly formed Center X—named as such to highlight experimentation and the intersection of theory and practice—put forward an activist commitment to social justice, grounded itself in sociocultural learning theory, and embedded teacher apprenticeship inside urban school community partnerships. Center X consciously reconceptualized teacher preparation as dialogical inquiry and guided social practice about what it means to be a transformative social justice educator in urban Los Angeles.[2]

The new program, under the guidance of Jeannie Oakes and Lynn Beck, recruited diverse groups of faculty and teacher candidates interested in social change, put students and instructors in small learning teams, and extended the one-year MEd program through a scaffolded, "resident" year of full-time teaching after the novice year. We began small, with 90 teachers in each of our first few years, and have slowly grown to twice that size. We conduct outreach to recruit teacher candidates from urban Los Angeles communities and attempt to attract candidates of color into the profession, and, though limited in our success, our efforts are beginning to show: The first Center X graduating class was 40 percent White, 12 percent Latino, 30 percent Asian American, 3 percent African American, and 5 percent "other" or "declined to state." The entering class for 2004 looks different: 19 percent White, 31 percent Asian American, 28 percent Latino, 8 percent African American, and 15 percent "other" or "declined to state." Figure 2.1 illustrates the racial/ethnic demographics of the total of all our students, past and present.

The Center X curriculum stresses views of inequity as structural, activism as necessary, multiculturalism as central, and the critical study of

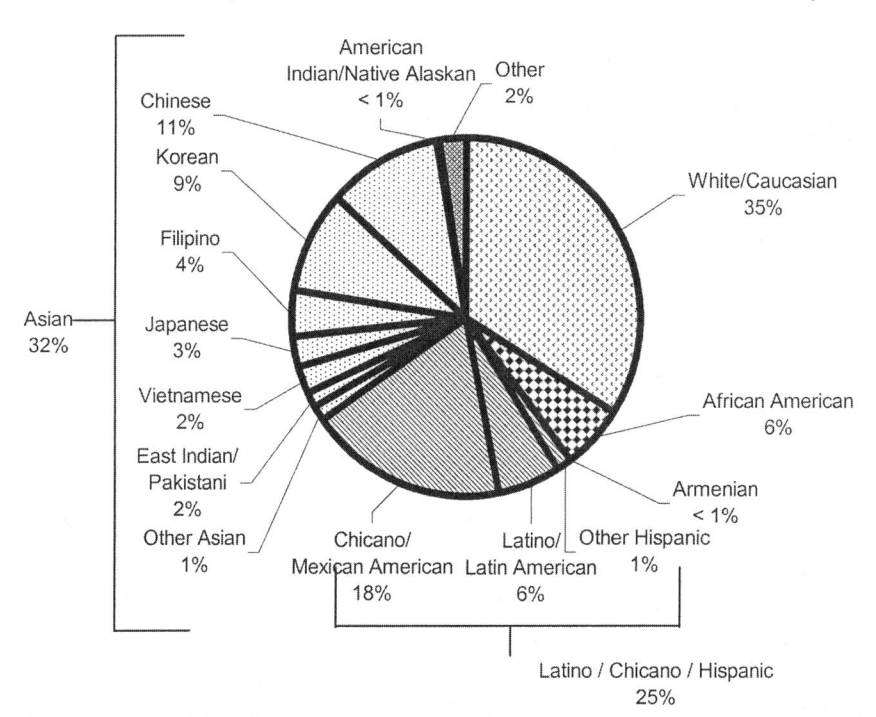

Figure 2.1. Ethnicity of Center X Students/Graduates, 1995–2003 ($n = 913$)

race and culture as crucial to preparing teachers to teach successfully for social justice in urban schools. The program rejects purely technical, social efficiency models of teaching and learning in favor of culturally relevant pedagogy, sociocultural learning approaches, and moral-political dimensions of teaching. Teacher candidates are now likely to engage around notions of social learning (Lave & Wenger, 1991; Vygotsky, 1978), asset mapping (e.g., Richman, n.d.), funds of knowledge (Moll, 1988, 1998), language acquisition (Cummins, 1996, 2000), and cultural identity (McIntosh, 1998; Tatum, 1997). Our candidates participate in inquiry sessions, curriculum design courses, and teaching projects embedded in schools, classrooms, and community centers with groups of peers, K–12 students, professors, and veteran teachers. This set of ideas and practices has become the program presented in these pages.

For the sake of this chapter, we have selected three questions that we believe currently shape, and are shaped by, Center X. We use discussion of them to illuminate some of the contours and concerns of our program:

- How does this program emphasize social justice?
- How does this program honor its commitment to teacher preparation as an integrated whole, occurring over time, in social contexts?
- How can this program maintain the integrity of its principles in the face of increasingly rigid political climates of standardization and high-stakes testing?

Data Collected for This Chapter

Since any portrait is shaped as much by how it is produced (and who produced it) as by any inherent essence of the subject, it seems important to briefly describe the research for this chapter. The six authors work at Center X: Brad Olsen is a postdoctoral researcher affiliated with Center X; Eloise Lopez Metcalfe is the director of the Teacher Education Program; Jody Priselac is the executive director of Center X; and Sheila Lane, Gordon Suzuki, and Rae Jeane Williams are teacher education faculty members. For data, we relied on our own experiences and on interviews with a purposeful selection of program participants we considered, in the aggregate, to be a fair sample of the available range of positionings, experiences, and attitudes in Center X. We interviewed four graduates currently teaching, four Center X program administrators, and four Center X faculty past and present, asking all of them to describe their experiences with and perspectives on Center X. We also relied on program documents such as grant proposals and research studies written by in-house researchers. To analyze, we coded and discussed what the interview transcripts and other data revealed. We realize that our own particular locations in, and perspectives on, this program certainly affected the ways in which the data were used—as paints, to belabor the portraiture metaphor: Both the colors we chose for a palette and they way we brushed them onto this canvas probably reveal us as painters as much as the program as an uneasily sitting subject.

How Do We Emphasize Social Justice?

Interviewer: What would you want others to know about the program?

A recent graduate: I want them to know that social justice is its goal. That it still is and it will always be, hopefully. I want others to know that Center X is one of the few that will still maintain this position, no matter what happens. That whenever in doubt, whenever in fear, whenever isolated, UCLA and Center X will always be there. I felt fear and isolation two years ago, at the school I began working in. One of the ways in which I was able to understand that things are not insurmountable was by going back to UCLA.[3]

A Diversity of Conceptions around Social Justice

Center X is committed to preparing teachers as agents of social change. Given this, we foreground social justice. Ideas and readings from related domains informed the creation of the program and guide our practice still: multiculturalism (Banks, 1994; Darder, 1998; Nieto, 1999), critical pedagogy (Freire, 1970; Giroux, 1992; hooks, 1994; McLaren, 1997), culturally responsive teaching (Cochran-Smith, 1997, 2000; Ladson-Billings, 1995; Oakes & Lipton, 2003; Sleeter, 1993), second language acquisition (Cummins, 1996, 2000; Gutierrez, 2001), and community organizing (Alinsky, 1989). We have adopted a view of teaching that moves us outside traditional frames of classrooms into larger examinations of societal inequity and conditions of schooling. The program attempts to link macro perspectives of society (coming from sociology, cultural anthropology, and political science) to micro analyses of students, schools, and classrooms (including student motivation, tracking, and curriculum design). Through participation in seminars, projects, and inquiry classes, our candidates use theory and research to create curricula that integrate learning goals with the students' homes and communities. The goal is to encourage, scaffold, and support our candidates so that they can raise awareness in and empower K–12 students to identify and challenge inequity at the same time these students learn the academics of their school's official curriculum.

Though this may sound clear on a page, in practice our principles are mediated by the contexts in which we work and by the wide variation in the ways participants interpret their views in relation to our program. We asked the 12 people we interviewed how they defined social justice, and what role Center X played in those definitions. Unsurprisingly, we found that there are both differences and similarities among conceptions and that there is tension around differing conceptions of social justice. The primary commonality was this: Social justice is recognizing and working to change unequal structures and practices extending inside and outside the schools. One program faculty member put it this way:

> I guess I look at social justice as a passion to right society's wrongs—to be an active community member, where you're especially drawn toward those places or those aspects of society where individuals are not given full access to what society has to offer. "Social justice" really refers to this notion of supporting those individuals, and changing—on a more basic level—the policies and the organizations of society, so that those individuals have more full, active participation in society.

Another faculty member said this:

> I believe that in this country and in this world there are serious inequities, and those inequities are based on class and race and ethnicity and language. And what that does to our educational system is that there are a huge number of the population who are taught to comply, and are taught to labor, and are not taught to be educated. And the minority in this country who are taught to rule and to profit—it's usually they [who] profit from the lives that they can exploit.

We found a continuum of social justice conceptions that ranges from the belief that social justice is primarily about providing high-quality education to students in high-poverty, urban communities by supplying those schools with well-trained, equity-minded teachers, to a more politicized stance advocating active disruption of schooling practices considered corrupt and therefore illegitimate. Though most believe social justice includes parts of both components, our students and faculty are located at different places on this continuum and sometimes clash over "who's more socially just." It is a tension we struggle with—one that emerges in comments such as these:

> And of course, you know this is free speech—our students certainly have a right to be a [committed social activist], but they also have a social justice responsibility to be a teacher. And I think that there is some conflict in this because it's hard for them to do it all. Sometimes, our most, quote-unquote, "socially active" teachers have to realize they still have a lot to learn about effective classroom teaching.
>
> There are those faculty advisors and instructors who are very traditional. And then there are those who, I think, really do live what the [social justice] philosophy says. . . . It's not consistent throughout the program.

Social Justice: Theory Into Practice

A few years ago, in response to a governor's initiative, Center X was required to prepare more teachers. As well, our social justice principles guide us to prepare more teacher candidates of color. Therefore, as the program has increased in size and deepened in diversity, we have tried to learn from and manage the tension around "What is social justice?" without stifling it. This is a difficult task because size, diversity, and consensus sometimes coexist uneasily. In response, we have tried to privilege inquiry and dialogue as ways for students and faculty to explore the whole range of social justice conceptions and differences among them. We are learning how to better facilitate conversation around the difficult topics of oppression, inequity, and privilege. We try to emphasize socially just teaching as a developmental process. The faculty tends to place the daily exigencies of classroom challenges (pedagogy, student-teacher-classroom relationships, curriculum, etc.) in the context of open themes like the social justice implications of practice; the teacher's respectful participation in helping students construct knowledge; the unspoken, ignored, or unintended lessons about themselves and society that students learn; and so on. Students (and faculty) are often frustrated to find that these dialogues do not produce firm answers—that it is the constructive participation itself that may, ultimately, be most liberating and productive. That said, however, such pedagogical practices can be deeply unnerving in the short run.

Many of those we interviewed discussed the importance of viewing diversity positively: the need for Center X itself to be diverse, and the need to see the value and resources in the cultural and linguistic diversity of those urban communities with which we partner. Partly, this leads our desire to have teachers and program faculty more closely resemble our partnership communities. As the director of teacher education said, "[We want to] mirror the diverse, caring communities we hope to serve. That's an important goal for us: How do we look more like where we're working, bring in a more diverse group of people to work here?" And partly, this positive view of diversity relates to our perspective of difference as an asset, not a deficit. A story by one faculty member illustrates our programmatic emphasis on combating deficit-model thinking:

> We move our candidates away from having a deficit view towards students, [instead] having high expectations as a bottom line—looking at students in a positive way and trying to find the strengths in the community. At Center X, there has always been some kind of community project or case study. And the goal was always for the students to discover the strengths in the community. The very first year, I was working with a student who absolutely didn't want to go visit the neighborhoods to do a case study—she was afraid to go to the homes. But afterwards, she was astonished to see that parents were very interested in what their kids were doing. They really wanted their children to learn. That was a big eye-opener for her. And after that, she is, I think, our alum who's done the most with parents. She got a grant at her school, worked on Saturdays, built the community garden. She did this going-to-college [project for] the kids and parents.

Center X attempts to build partnerships in the urban school communities with which we work, though considerable effort remains. After a few years and one particularly vocal cohort of activist students, Center X decided to partner only with hard-to-staff schools in low-income urban neighborhoods of color—those Los Angeles communities most in need of highly qualified teachers. Center X teams often hold their seminars in the local communities, not on the university campus. As part of the coursework during their first year, candidates complete a community project in which they form groups to investigate the particular community in which they will student teach: They identify and map community assets; interview parents and other community members; research the history, demographics, and culture of the neighborhoods; and present findings in portfolios and community presentations. One of our graduates said this:

> The community research project's one of the program's strengths. It makes us work in cooperative groups and it exposes us to that community variable that's so important in education—especially once we come back and bring cooperative learning into our classrooms. . . . I remember going in as an ethnographer—researching people, questioning and interrogating them in the streets like I was an actual scientist-reporter-historian. It opened my eyes . . . not only talking to the people but talking to teachers, professionals in the area. . . . It allowed me to see the great potential I have as an individual to bring positives into a community, not as a savior or someone who is going to save the world, but as someone who can learn from the community and, basically, take what the community has to offer, and put it into practice.

Our second-year students—now full-time teachers—teach in partner schools in pairs or small groups and work closely with each other, Center X alumni and faculty, and veteran teachers to continually embed social justice in their practice. Additionally, we are working to establish several formalized partnership structures and projects to better integrate Center X with community features and school district realities. Our director of teacher education said this:

> I feel really good about the partnerships we have now. There's a reason why we're there. There's a commitment to the districts. Not all, but most faculty advisors are getting very close to saying, "This is my home, this is where I live, this is where I work."

These community partnerships, however, are still a work in progress. It has proved difficult to dislodge the traditional hierarchy of university-school (or expert-subject) relations; full buy-in from communities and district administrators has proved elusive; pushing forward with our social justice agenda of transforming schools poses obvious challenges; charges of elitism and favoritism linger; and many Center X teachers report a wide gap separating university conceptions and L.A. school realities, finding it hard to build pedagogical bridges between them. One of our graduates said this:

> Sometimes in teaching, you're looking for the ideal—it's what we hope to create in our classroom. And then when you get to school, it's not ideal. I

had to travel and teach every period in a different classroom, so the idea of the "classroom environment," [or having] a classroom library—those things were just completely undoable. And this year, I'm finding a big challenge between my high expectations . . . and the school culture, where I have been asked to lower my expectations for students.

Finally, Center X attempts to guide its own practice with social justice principles. As our director pointed out, "We had to realize that, if we were going to keep talking about social justice, as we were doing, it was not just about saying that we're putting our students in low-income schools. We had to have an attitude about that—why were we doing that—and that attitude had to be pretty deep within each of us." With varying success, the program recruits diverse groups of students and faculty. We established a professional development faculty committee that led a faculty workshop on racism. Recently, we became involved with the Paulo Freire Institute on campus. By no means perfectly democratic, Center X favors collaborative decision making, a flattened hierarchy, and governance by committee. Since 2001, every faculty member joins one of four committees—focusing on student development, faculty development, community, or curriculum—which meet regularly to research and revise the program (see UCLA TEP Case Research Group, 2002). These components allow us to remain self-renewing and responsive to our students' needs and the needs of the school communities we serve.

The Paradox of Promoting Critique

One interesting—and inadvertent—result of our attention to student concerns is something we might call the paradox of promoting critique. Since we consciously recruit, admit, and prepare critical educators, in a way we obligate them to critique the very program that has spawned them. Because we encourage critical looks into educational practice and because we privilege voice, we are sometimes criticized by our students. For us, this paradox means three things: The program benefits from a built-in feedback mechanism that (sometimes painfully) keeps us honest; we must constantly negotiate between dual desires to be responsive to students and maintain our principles; and some people find us too flexible while others find us not flexible enough. For example, some students and staff applaud our responsiveness to students:

I've never seen a program so concerned about what the students wanted and needed, and so willing to change. It's one of the reasons I love teaching Teacher Education Program classes, because I just think the program is very sensitive and open to feedback from the student population, which I've really never seen to that degree. They're always changing. I mean, every time I talk to a [Center X] faculty, they're always trying to improve and be very conscientious.

Others worry about this same responsiveness:

Because the program promotes students having a voice, part of the critical pedagogy—students really become empowered to change or to challenge inequities. But within that, because of their age, and their development, they want to practice that—and sometimes they practice it to the point where they want to challenge everything, and they want to have the major voice. And sometimes the department . . . maybe they listen too much, and change policies or procedures because students have questioned them, rather than negotiating with the students and saying, "We want to keep this policy because of [such-and-such]."

HOW DO WE HONOR OUR COMMITMENT TO TEACHER PREPARATION AS AN INTEGRATED WHOLE, OCCURRING OVER TIME, IN SOCIAL CONTEXTS?

Conceiving of learning as embedded inside students' and teachers' social interactions and contexts, the program embraces sociocultural learning perspectives (Cummins, 1996; Lave & Wenger, 1991; Moll, 1988, 1998; Tharp & Gallimore, 1988; Vygotsky, 1978). Center X believes learning emerges from the multiple identities, knowledge, purposes, prior experiences, and combined perspectives any group of people relies on in a collective endeavor like schooling. Since we view teachers and teaching holistically, the program stresses that teacher development is about identity changes as much as constructing new skills and understandings. This stance leads us to instruct candidates in the same ways we urge them to conduct their own teaching: in teams and using inquiry and dialogue as the primary pedagogical tools. Students remain in the same team (of usually 18 candidates) for two years, and typically have the same faculty team leader for both years. Team leaders and students develop relationships that personalize the preparation process and allow them to attend to frequently neglected aspects of professional development, including moral, political, social, and affective dimensions of becoming a career urban educator. The team structure and the pedagogical emphasis on personal relationships emerged often in the interviews we conducted. Representative of that are these comments by two of our graduates:

> I think the program's cohort system, the system of families and teams, is very well done. I think students really do develop a very strong relationship with one another, and that becomes a community of practice, and so in that respect I think the program really works well to establish a community of practice, and a solid relationship with the more expert facilitator, whoever the faculty advisor is.
>
> [I like] that you have one team and you stay with that team for two years, and have most of your classes with that team.... The bonds that you make with your team members, for me, were so important because that space for team seminar every week became a really safe place to explore the challenges of teaching as well as the successes, and to build friendships that I still gain strength from in my teaching.

To evaluate candidates, we tend to rely on authentic, embedded forms of assessment such as collaborative projects, portfolios, ongoing conversation, and field supervisors as teaching coaches. Candidates participate in inquiry-based courses such as Cultural Identity and Social Foundations and Cultural Diversity in American Education, and they choose one of three cultures of emphasis (African American, Latino, or Asian American) for an inquiry group linking culture, curriculum, language, and pedagogy. Our methods and curriculum design courses try to integrate questions about social justice into the discussions about classroom teaching and learning.

A Community Perspective on Teacher Preparation

The sociocultural principles that prepare teachers for classroom work also guide our efforts to structure teacher learning communities in schools. Center X tries to recruit faculty from partner districts. Center X maintains close working relationships with like-minded teachers and administrators from the schools with which we partner, using those relationships to re-create schools as productive places of collaboration and inquiry toward social change. However, it has sometimes been difficult to find sufficient numbers of school personnel whose education philosophies match that of Center X (Lane, Lacefield-Parachini, & Isken, 2003).

The program has adopted an iterative view of teacher development, believing that our preservice candidates and in-service graduates should continually revisit the theories and principles of Center X practice. During the novice year, students grapple with the perspectives and issues (related to language, race, culture, and schooling) that our program emphasizes; during the resident year, Center X faculty guide them in another cycle of reflection on these notions that are now embedded in their full-time teaching practice. These investigations take place as the teachers continue to meet in teams and prepare their master's portfolios. These portfolios are a major part of the resident year, and we use them to encourage second-year students to personalize, identify, and analyze ways in which they rely on theory to guide and understand their own practice. One graduate explains:

> The portfolio epitomizes the program because it's where students are expected to take academic and theoretical information and apply it and think about it during a whole year in our classroom, through reflection. And I think that's really what the program is about—really trying to identify what's going on in my classroom, how do I apply social justice, how do I apply learning theory? One of the stories I wrote about was a story of a student who wanted to commit suicide, and, for me, discussing the aspect of being a teacher and a counselor and a lifesaver—sometimes literally. Writing about it, being able to step back from it and think about and process it, share it with other people, reflect on what it means. That's what's helpful about the program. We start doing that kind of thinking in the program and it becomes what keeps us teaching well after we graduate.

Once they graduate, the beginning teachers are invited into our Urban Educator Network (UEN)—a series of professional development opportunities, inquiry groups, and graduate networks created to establish additional sites of collaborative practice for teachers within the school-university partnerships. For example, one component of the network is CIRCLE (the Consortium of Urban Schools Involved in Renewal and Committed to Leadership in Education), a set of district-based groups of teachers, administrators, university faculty, and community leaders who meet quarterly to strategize ways to better integrate school, district, and university. Another example is *Teaching to*

Change LA (www.tcla.gseis.ucla.edu), an online journal publishing articles, essays, and news about and by Los Angeles students, teachers, and parents, as well as work by educational researchers from UCLA and around the country. A third UEN effort, Critical Teacher Inquiry Groups for Growth and Retention, brings activist-minded teachers from a school together to collaborate on ways to continually embed social justice in their teaching practice (Quartz, Olsen, & Duncan-Andrade, in press). The UEN network also provides grants to graduates interested in pursuing research and development. For example, one alumna interested in assisting African Americans and non–English speakers to become more comfortable using academic English received UEN funding to develop a handbook of instructional strategies and then work with our student teachers in her spare time.

Although those who participate in UEN activities find them helpful and often invaluable (Quartz et al., 2003), only a few dozen teachers participate regularly. And, even though some non–Center X teachers participate, the groups are sometimes perceived as closed-door UCLA enclaves. Moreover, as Center X has grown, its view of professional development for graduates has had to change: with over 900 graduates, the goal of reaching everyone has been replaced with the more research-oriented goal of understanding how best to embed continual professional development in urban schools. At their best, these professional development structures act as a kind of collective apprenticeship that facilitates our teachers viewing their practice as an integrated, coherent whole that deepens over time. In this way, we attempt to support urban teachers to build activist communities at their teaching sites; consider themselves as researchers, school leaders, community liaisons, and coalition builders; become public intellectuals; and find strength in the sharing of their stories and challenges. Though not always successful, we are committed to the effort. One graduate of Center X who has been teaching for seven years now reported this:

> The teacher ed. program doesn't just end at the end of two years: "OK, bye." I've been involved with Center X ever since I graduated, with the inquiry [group] and the collaboration [group]. We started a mentoring project that became Voices for Change. . . . I know not all graduates take advantage of it, but if you want that connection, if you need support for your teaching, because it can seem isolating at the school site. Center X alumni are different than other alumni, have a different perspective—so that connection to

Center X and other social justice educators is really important for keeping you thinking about issues of social justice.

HOW CAN WE MAINTAIN THE INTEGRITY OF OUR PRINCIPLES IN THE FACE OF INCREASINGLY RIGID POLITICAL CLIMATES OF STANDARDIZATION AND HIGH-STAKES TESTING?

Interviewer: What are some of Center X's current challenges?

Center X faculty member and district administrator: In 30 years of being in the field of education, this is the most conservative, constrictive, dogmatic, far-right-wing time I've ever experienced, and I think it's diametrically opposed to the principles of the program. When we really emphasize learning theory, critical pedagogy, and sociocultural theory, it cannot be played out within the prescriptive programs being mandated by the state, and an assessment system that pits teachers against one another and students against one another. I think it's a horrible time—the testing and the way students are tested, the way they're looked at, the way they're compared, and that they're thought of through the deficit model of thinking. Our kids—mostly African American and Latino students—are really at the low end of the totem pole here, and so they're receiving all the directives and constrictive programs. . . . And teachers are treated the way the kids are, as if they were incompetent, as if they had no intelligence . . . [no] critical thinking or critical voice at all. And so our teachers struggle over how to make a program that they're mandated to do fit with the theory and the practice they know are best for children.

At the time of this writing, Center X finds itself inside the throes of city, state, and federal pushes for standardization and high-stakes testing for both K–12 schools and university teacher education programs. The Los Angeles school district mandates a scripted reading program in all grades; the No Child Left Behind Act requires strict allegiance to standardized tests and produces a climate of competitive distrust among many school stakeholders; urban bureaucracies typically promote behaviorist, managerial views of schooling and students. One graduate put it this way:

> We're in schools as social change agents trying to do all these different things . . . but when you come out here to a school district, your administrator really just sees you as a worker—like a cog in the machine—that you're going to turn

out certain types of curriculum, certain types of tests and meet these standards, and that's it. The *Open Court* reading program is a perfect embodiment of that. You [follow it], and you don't need to think too much about it, just make sure that everybody is just following right along, and that's it. . . . That's really, really different from the way we frame teaching and learning [at Center X].

Additionally, a recent California senate bill, SB 2042, requires all state-accredited teacher preparation programs to adopt various standardized features for preparing, evaluating, and credentialing teacher candidates. As our director of teacher education described, this creates a context difficult for social justice educators committed to personalizing, deepening, and reframing the learning-to-teach process:

> How do you maintain the kind of program that we want to have, which is a very rich, diverse, multiperspective program, that runs smoothly and one in which everybody values each other? I think that's very difficult when everything becomes systematic. You know, you give a teaching credential based on this new performance assessment which comes from elsewhere. [Senate Bill] 2042 has made everything more standardized. You can easily fall into being captivated—your energies go into meeting all the compliance issues, rather than staying open to our set of social justice goals. . . . How do you keep your own agenda going, while at the same time making sure the compliance issues are met?

Policy Tensions That Shape Our Work

Political demands for formulaic teacher education structures carry two kinds of concern for us. One is that, largely, the city and state standards are not aligned with our principles of social justice. The second is that *any* pressure to standardize constrains our ability—our mission, really—to tailor Center X education experiences to the unique characteristics of our students, our partner school communities, and our social justice commitments. Bureaucratically and philosophically, we currently find ourselves trying to conform to standards that do not fit who we are. Additionally, alongside these policy demands, the governor's office and state legislature have cut significant amounts of our state funding. We are therefore compelled to do more, with less, while we simultaneously struggle to implement program reforms misaligned with our contours. We are obligated, therefore, to prepare more teachers, do it in standardized ways that do not fit, and carry on amid dramatic funding cuts. This exists inside the already difficult task of deepening our own views of how to successfully prepare transformative social justice educators who stay in urban schools. To better understand our own work within these kinds of policy realities, we have instigated several research projects. For example, we are three years into a longitudinal, multidisciplinary study of urban teacher retention and the careers of our graduates (Quartz, Barraza-Lyons, & Thomas, in press). The curriculum committee has begun a study examining how one state mandate around literacy within teacher preparation is changing the teaching practices of our faculty. And we have just embarked on a yearlong, ethnographic study to investigate the various ways our graduates experience the Center X Urban Educator Network professional development efforts.

Even though we sometimes find ourselves demoralized and overworked, we try to find ways to persevere. We are fueled by the power of our commitment; we are humbled by knowing we still have much to learn and ways to improve; and we are energized by the sight of our graduates building meaningful careers in Los Angeles, committed to improving the structures and practices of schooling while assisting K–12 students toward success. It seems appropriate to end this portrait with the words of that graduating teacher whose personal story opened this chapter. She told us that

> I want to provide educational experiences that validate my students' lives and experiences—that start where they are and move them toward their own successes. Center X has taught me that education can't be a cookie-cutter social process that decides who does or doesn't have the right to succeed. I've had to move past my own background—to confront just how "natural" it can seem to emulate the dominant practices and systems that are ultimately oppressive because they divide us. That kind of schooling writes off my students as failures. [Center X] showed me these realities and showed me how to challenge and think about my practice as an urban teacher who wants to make change.

NOTES

1. We are also indebted to Martin Lipton for his editing assistance.
2. "Social justice educator" in this chapter refers to teachers who see their work as part of a broader agenda for social change and justice—one that embodies activism and active engagement with communities. The specifics of just what

that means in practice are open for discussion and are, in fact, part of what continues to shape Center X.

3. Here, and in all quoted passages, we have edited speakers' words for flow, excising most false starts and pause fillers unless directly relevant.

REFERENCES

Alinsky, S. (1989). *Rules for radicals: A practical primer for realistic radicals.* New York: Vintage Books.

Banks, J. (1994). *An introduction to multicultural education.* Boston: Allyn & Bacon.

Cochran-Smith, M. (1997). Knowledge, skills and experiences for teaching culturally diverse learners: A perspective for practicing teachers. In J. Irvine (Ed.), *Critical knowledge for diverse teachers and learners* (pp. 27–88). Washington, DC: AACTE.

Cochran-Smith, M. (2000). Blind vision: Unlearning racism in teacher education. *Harvard Educational Review, (70)*2, 157–190.

Cummins, J. (1996). *Negotiating identities: Education for empowerment in a diverse society.* Los Angeles: CABE.

Cummins, J. (2000). *Language, power and pedagogy: Bilingual children in the crossfire.* Clevedon, UK: Multilingual Matters.

Darder, A. (1998). Teaching as an act of love. In J. Fredrickson (Ed.), *Reclaiming our voices: Emancipatory narratives and critical literacy, praxis and pedagogy* (pp. 25–42). Ontario, CA: CABE.

Freire, P. (1970). *Pedagogy of the oppressed.* New York: Continuum.

Giroux, H. (1992). *Border crossings: Cultural workers and the politics of education.* New York: Routledge.

Gutierrez, K. (2001). So what's new in the English language arts: Challenging policies and practices, ¿y que? *Language Arts Journal*, 78(6), 564–569.

hooks, b. (1994). *Teaching to transgress: Education as the practice of freedom.* New York: Routledge.

Ladson-Billings, G. (1995). Toward a theory of culturally relevant pedagogy. *American Educational Research Journal*, 32(3), 465–491.

Lane, S., Lacefield-Parachini, N., & Isken, J. (2003, Spring). Developing novice teachers as change agents: Student teacher placements "against the grain." *Teacher Education Quarterly*, 30(2), 55–68.

Lave, J., & Wenger, E. (1991). *Situated learning.* Cambridge: Cambridge University Press.

McIntosh, P. (1998). White privilege, color and crime: A personal account. In C. Richey Mann & S. Zatz (Eds.), *Images of color, images of crime* (pp. 207–216). Los Angeles: Roxbury.

McLaren, P. (1997). *Life in schools: An introduction to critical pedagogy in the foundations of education.* New York: Addison-Wesley Longman.

Moll, L. (1988). Some key issues in teaching Latino students. *Language Arts, 64*(5), 465–472.

Moll, L. (1998). Funds of knowledge for teaching: A new approach in education. Keynote address: Illinois State Board of Education, February 5, 1998.

Nieto, S. (1999). *The light in their eyes.* New York: Teachers College Press.

Oakes, J. (1996). Making the rhetoric real: UCLA's struggle for teacher education that is multicultural and social reconstructionist. *Multicultural Education, 4*(2), 4–10.

Oakes, J., & Lipton, M. (2003). *Teaching to change the world* (2nd ed.). Boston: McGraw-Hill.

Quartz, K. H., Barraza-Lyons, K., & Thomas, A. (In press). Urban teacher retention. In N. Bascia, A. Datnow, & K. Leithwood (Eds.), *International handbook on educational policy.* New York: Kluwer.

Quartz, K. H., Olsen, B., & Duncan-Andrade, J. (In press). The fragility of urban teaching: A longitudinal study of career development and activism. In F. Peterman (Ed.), *Resiliency, resistance, and persistence in transcending traditional boundaries: Communities partnering to prepare urban teachers.*

Quartz, K. H., & The TEP Research Group. (2003). "Too angry to leave": Supporting new teachers' commitment to transform urban schools. *Journal of Teacher Education, 54*(2), 99–111.

Richman, N. (n.d.). Neighborhood Knowledge California (NKCA)—a project of the Advanced Policy Institute (API) at the University of California, Los Angeles. Retrieved September 15, 2004, from http://nkca.ucla.edu.

Sleeter, C. (1993). How white teachers construct race. In C. McCarthy & W. Crichlow (Eds.), *Race, identity and representation in education* (pp. 157–171). New York: Routledge.

Tatum, B. (1997). *Why are all the black kids sitting together in the cafeteria?: And other conversations about race.* New York: Basic Books.

Tharp, R., & Gallimore, R. (1988). *Rousing minds to life: Teaching, learning and schooling in social context.* New York: Cambridge University Press.

UCLA TEP Case Research Group (A Joint Product of Center X and IDEA). (2002). *Teaching for social justice: The successes and challenges of preparing urban educators.* Los Angeles: University of California.

Vygotsky, L. (1978). *Mind in society.* Cambridge, MA: Harvard University Press.

3

Collaboration and Inquiry: Learning to Teach at the Lynch School of Education

Kelly Donnell, Andrea J. Stairs, and Nicole Guttenberg
Boston College

With my experience at Brighton [High School] I can say that I have a strong realization of what urban schools are actually like and the injustices that occur within the school system. . . . I will end up teaching in an urban setting because I want to help solve these problems, I want to become an active member of the community, and I want to give urban students the same chances I had.

(Adam,[1] a sophomore in Urban Immersion, 2003)

I am constantly asking myself questions and seeking ways to improve as a teacher. I feel that inquiry is an extremely important part of teaching and improving. No classroom is the same and you will have to reflect on your practice to make changes to accommodate student learning.

(Survey response, Graduate Inquiry Seminar, 2001)

These student voices highlight two important commitments of the teacher education program at the Lynch School of Education at Boston College: collaboration and inquiry. The teacher education program at the Lynch School draws much of its identity from a constructivist view of learning and from preparing educators to teach for social justice. The program's theoretical commitments to constructivism and social justice stem, in part, from an understanding that America's public school population is increasingly more diverse in race, culture, ethnicity, language, and ability. Meeting the needs of all learners can easily become a platitude unless educators grapple with its complexity in the daily work of teacher education. Two key elements within the field-based teacher education program best exemplify the Lynch School's commitment to accommodating diversity through constructivist and socially just teacher preparation. The first is the development of multiple layers of collaborative relationships, and the second is inquiry as a stance toward teaching and learning.

In creating this portrait we considered our insider and outsider perspectives on preservice teacher education at the Lynch School. We are currently doctoral candidates in curriculum and instruction at the Lynch School and have assumed the roles of students, teaching fellows, and research assistants in our time at the university. We have been particularly involved in the Boston College/Brighton High School Partnership and Inquiry coursework. These roles provide us with an insider perspective into teacher education at the Lynch School. Our roles as former classroom teachers, school-based consultants, and adjunct faculty at other institutions lend us an outsider perspective as well. We write this portrait drawing on both our insider and our outsider perspectives. In this portrait, we have selected examples of the Boston College teacher education program's collaborative and inquiry practices that will illuminate the program's commitment to diversity, constructivism, and social justice.

THEORETICAL COMMITMENTS AT THE LYNCH SCHOOL

The Lynch School teacher education program is built on a foundation of five themes, addressed throughout teacher education courses and experiences: promoting social justice, constructing knowledge, inquiring into practice, accommodating diversity, and collaborating with others. As is evident in these five themes, teacher education at the Lynch School is built upon several assumptions: American public schools are increasingly diverse and inequitable, teaching is a political act, classrooms are places where teachers and students construct knowledge, and education is a collaborative endeavor that challenges the status quo. The themes are emphasized throughout all of the Lynch School teacher education courses and form a common template at the beginning of every syllabus, though one course may not address all five themes evenly. These themes are important as they encompass both the theoretical and practical frameworks for teacher education at the Lynch School.

Theoretical commitments to constructivism and social justice inform collaboration and inquiry, the two characteristics highlighted in this portrait. These theoretical commitments are seen as critically important considering the diverse nature of America's public school population. To varying degrees, teacher educators at the Lynch School recognize the importance of accommodating for diversity and meeting the needs of all learners and see constructivism and social justice theoretically supporting this mission. First, constructivism rejects traditional transmission models of teaching and learning and views knowledge as being co-constructed by teachers and students in the classroom. The "knowledge base" in teacher education becomes knowledge for preservice teachers only when they are provided with authentic learning experiences from which they construct meaning in conjunction with their prior knowledge and experience. Therefore, each preservice teacher will construct his or her understanding of course material uniquely and contextually. In an era of prescribed standards and learning outcomes and high-stakes tests at all levels in education, Lynch School teacher educators remain committed to constructivism and teach their students how to negotiate policies and practices that ultimately perpetuate transmission models of teaching and learning. In this way, Lynch School preservice teachers are prepared for the current realities of education and schooling, yet continue to explore constructivist knowledge as knowledge that is personal, meaningful, and long lasting.

A second theoretical commitment of Lynch School teacher educators is learning to teach for social justice. A commitment to social justice means viewing teaching as a political act and teachers as activists, challenging the status quo. In America's increasingly diverse public schools, it is more important than ever for teachers to understand their power to either perpetuate current inequities in education or to promote more inclusive, accessible, and equitable learning opportunities for all students. The Lynch School honors its commitment to social justice by addressing issues of teaching for social justice across coursework and experiences in the teacher education program.

AN OVERVIEW OF THE LYNCH SCHOOL

Boston College (BC) is a coeducational Catholic institution situated on a hilly 116-acre campus in Chestnut Hill, an affluent suburb just a few miles west of Boston. Of the 13,500 students attending the college, two thirds are undergraduates. The student body is predominantly White, Catholic, and from middle- to upper-class backgrounds. As a Jesuit university, Boston College is grounded in Ignatian spirituality and is committed to improving the human condition. At the Lynch School of Education, the mission emphasizes both excellence and ethics in aspiring to make the world more just. The Lynch School is committed to preparing its students to serve diverse populations in a variety of professional roles, as teachers, administrators, human service providers, psychologists, and researchers.

The Lynch School offers a range of National Council for Accreditation of Teacher Education (NCATE) and state-approved teacher education programs at the undergraduate and graduate levels. Undergraduates enrolled at the Lynch School may select from among four major areas of study: early childhood education, elementary education, and secondary education, which lead to teaching licensure, and human development. Graduate students can earn a Master of Education in curriculum and instruction, early childhood education, elementary education, reading/literacy teaching, secondary teaching, and special education, or earn a Master of Arts in teaching in a content area. Exemplary students may participate in a fifth-year program, obtaining both their bachelor's and master's degrees in education in five years. There are also two specific graduate teacher programs that focus entirely on urban schools in Boston: the Donovan Teaching Scholars Program, where students experience extended student teaching placements in Boston's public schools, and the Urban Catholic Teaching Corps, where students prepare for careers teaching in urban Catholic schools. The graduate students in both programs participate as cohorts in additional seminars specifically designed to meet their unique needs. All education students are required to participate in prepracticum field experiences, primarily observation and initial teaching opportunities, in suburban, rural, and urban schools. All education students are also required to complete an inquiry study as a part of their practicum (full-time student teaching) experience.

COLLABORATION AT THE LYNCH SCHOOL

Multiple levels of collaboration and partnership exist at the Lynch School. Nationally, BC is a member of the Holmes Partnership and the Urban Network to Improve Teacher Education (UNITE), organizations that bring together people from across the country to improve the quality of teaching and research and make an impact on policy. The Lynch School is engaged with these organizations because of their emphasis on partnerships and urban education. On a statewide level, the Lynch School serves as the lead institution of the Massachusetts Coalition for Teacher Quality and Student Achievement (MassCoalition). Formed in 1999 with the awarding of a Title II Teacher Quality Grant from the federal government, the MassCoalition comprises seven school-university partnerships situated throughout the commonwealth of Massachusetts. Together with their urban public school partners from Boston, Springfield, and Worcester, and their community and business partners, the MassCoalition works to improve the quality of teacher preparation and professional development with the ultimate goal of improving overall student achievement in urban areas. It is not uncommon for cross-fertilization and adaptation of teaching practices to occur among participating institutions. As a result of their participation in the partnership, the Lynch School has implemented new teacher education practices, such as teaching courses at the partner school sites and totally immersing preservice teachers in the day-to-day activities of schools. Spurred on in part by participation in the MassCoalition, and in part by the internal drive of Lynch faculty to better serve their students, the Lynch School made a determined effort to build on a previously existing collaborative relationship between Boston College and Brighton High School, a Boston public school.

Urban Immersion: Collaboration Between the University and an Urban School

The Lynch School has always had a strong relationship with Brighton High School, our partner high school in the Boston public schools, particularly through student teacher placements and individual faculty members' work with classroom teachers around professional development. Beginning in the fall semester of 2002, the collaboration advanced to another level. It was in response to a need expressed by Brighton High School administrators in the spring of 2002 that the Lynch School's Urban Immersion program was instituted in the fall. The administration needed more Boston College student presence in their building to aid teachers and students during class time. The

Lynch School was ready to move a required course on-site to Brighton High for the fall. So, in conjunction with Boston College students' first field experience (prepracticum), the combined undergraduate/graduate course Secondary Curriculum and Instruction (ED 211/407) met in the high school's College and Career Center every Thursday at the start of the school day. This was followed by preservice teachers teaching individuals, small groups, and whole classes of students all day before reconvening for the second part of the university course after school, which was cotaught by BC and Brighton High School faculty. The essence of true collaboration is evident in this example. The university, which had held graduate courses on-site after school hours, provided consultants, technology, and other materials for classrooms, and placed student teachers at Brighton High School for many years, listened and responded to the school's need in a way that also improved the Lynch School's teacher education program. Now Boston College students see the possibility of teaching in an urban school as a reality. They mediate theory and practice by conducting the course on-site and breaking up into inquiry groups in the afternoon session so that students may pose difficult questions and learn how to negotiate dilemmas in classrooms, dilemmas for which there are no "right" answers.

For nearly half of the Boston College students, this is the first time they have been in a public school, and for some it is their first time in a coeducational school. For all but a few, it is their first time in an urban school. They express their anxiety at the first class meeting, asking, "Do I have to do my prepracticum here? Is this required?" and the answer is "Yes." A commitment to collaboration and social justice meant the Lynch School taking the leap with primarily White, privileged, monolingual students and requiring them to have an "urban immersion" experience as an introduction to the secondary teacher education program. Though the students are initially uncomfortable about not being at a school just like the high school they attended, their assumptions about urban schools and urban students are challenged, and they begin to understand why teaching for social justice is important.

Jenny, a junior in Urban Immersion during the initial semester of the program, shared her assumptions about urban students in a reflection paper for the course.

> All I knew of urban students was what was fed to me through the media in films such as *Dangerous Minds* and Lifetime Original Movies about the an-

gry city kid who completely spits in the face of authority and eventually brings a gun to school. . . . I thought urban kids were scary, that they never listened to authority, that they did not care about school or much of anything else, and that they were all hardened by their various emotional problems that were rooted in their homes and neighborhoods.

Jenny's perceptions and beliefs about urban students were rooted in media influences, and she had to face her fears in the Urban Immersion program. Jenny said at the end of her experience that she felt "ashamed" about these assumptions, but that working with individuals and small groups of Brighton students helped her to gain confidence. She admitted, "I still have a lot to learn about urban schools and the students in them," and that she still felt "uninformed" at the end of the semester. However, Jenny, like many of her classmates, were afforded new experiences through Urban Immersion that challenged their assumptions and helped them to expand their understanding of the urban school context.

Rebecca, a sophomore in Urban Immersion during the spring of 2003, felt ready to commit to urban teaching after her experience at Brighton High School. She said in her reflection paper, "Not only did I become more confident in myself and my desire to teach, but above all I developed a desire to go into urban education and work to change the system." Other students, now committed to teaching in the urban context, expressed sentiments similar to Rebecca's. In fact, most of the students who have gone through Urban Immersion say that they will teach in an urban school when they graduate. Whether they make the choice to do so when the time comes remains to be seen. However, the Lynch School has institutionalized a feature of the secondary education program that supports its social justice mission. It will be important to build off the successes of the Urban Immersion program to create other systematic ways of encouraging preservice teachers' commitment to urban schools.

The preservice teachers note the importance of having a cohort going through the Urban Immersion experience together. They note the connection between theory and practice that occurs by conducting the university course on-site in conjunction with the field experience. They also note the discussion and reflection that can occur immediately while their concerns and dilemmas are fresh on their minds. These are features of the program that help the preservice teachers' development as reflective practitioners and professionals. As Gina, a junior in the fall of 2002, explained in an interview with a course instructor,

> I thought it was really beneficial to have the class on-site. I really liked being able to share my experiences right after they happened, or taking care of my concerns right before I taught. I also enjoyed that the people who were [student] teaching at Brighton were the ones who were in my class; we were all sharing the same experiences. . . . I felt that the fact we were learning about teaching essentially while we were teaching was really helpful.

Sara, another junior in 2002, shared similar feelings about the integrated experience: "It was good to be able to talk about theories and concepts in class and then be able to apply them in the classroom and after that to be able to discuss them and how applicable they are in the classroom." The integrated and site-based nature of the course and field experience were seen as real strengths of the Urban Immersion program by nearly all of the preservice teachers.

The Urban Immersion program has continued every semester since the fall of 2002. Most of the Brighton High School teachers have found that having a pair of Lynch School preservice teachers in their classrooms every Thursday is helpful for facilitating cooperative learning activities, and they plan for their day accordingly. These teachers are also empowered to share their local knowledge with the preservice teachers who are conducting their first field experience. The Lynch School is committed to maintaining this successful, on-site Urban Immersion program for the foreseeable future, especially in light of the positive responses the preservice teachers have shared about their experiences, as well as the support it provides Brighton High School teachers and students.

Though the Urban Immersion program has been successful in many ways and supports the social justice mission of the Lynch School, the collaboration has also presented challenges. Some basic logistical challenges include the large number of preservice teachers placed at Brighton High School on Thursdays and the confusion around course and field experience requirements. The large number of preservice teachers enrolled in the program was manageable for the course instructors but felt overwhelming for the classroom teachers who needed to accommodate these preservice teachers every Thursday. So the course has been separated into undergraduate (ED 211) and graduate (ED 407) sections, with only the undergraduates enrolled in Urban Immersion. This change, begun in the fall of 2003, has eased the tension between the BC course instructors and the Brighton classroom teachers. However, the graduate students are not in a combined course/field experience model because ED 407 now meets on campus at Boston College. The course instructors feels like this is a step backward in the Lynch School's commitment to collaboration and social justice, one that needs to be examined carefully and for which other high school partnerships will need to be forged. The separate requirements for the course and for the field experience also presented a challenge, especially during the first semester of the program. Students often expressed their concerns about their uncertainty around what "counted" for course and what "counted" for their prepracticum experience. The course instructors and prepracticum supervisors now regularly explain expectations for the course and the field experience, while maintaining the interconnectedness of the two.

Other challenges have resulted from resistance on the part of Boston College preservice teachers and Brighton High School teachers. Some preservice teachers were simply not interested in urban education at the beginning or by the end of the experience. Others are only beginning the process of considering the inequities in American public education when the semester ends. Though other Lynch School courses will ask them to rethink their assumptions and promote social justice, these preservice teachers can easily remain resistant or merely pay lip service to the ideas for the duration of the teacher education program. Even a few Brighton High School teachers can also undermine the critical stance taken in Urban Immersion. Simple resistance is evident in the occasional teacher not planning for the BC preservice teachers to interact with the students in the classroom and asking them regularly to sit and observe. Though this is the exception, it is a reality that must be addressed by all involved.

Through the Urban Immersion program, the Lynch School is developing its collaboration with a local high school. This collaboration is further strengthened through the participation of BC Arts and Science faculty in teacher education. The Collaborative Fellows program provides an opportunity for the Lynch School to further its commitment to social justice by promoting the preparation of highly effective teachers committed to urban schools.

Collaborative Fellows: Collaboration Within the University

During an NCATE evaluation of the teacher education program at the Lynch School, a small group of Lynch School and English department faculty met to discuss the English Language Arts teacher education program. Participants agreed that significant misunderstandings regarding the purposes and rationale of their respective programs must be resolved in order to work together to prepare prospective teachers. In addition, they thought that public school teachers possessed a wealth of local knowledge that could be an immensely valuable asset in bridging the gap between the English and education professors. As a result of this perceived lack of collaboration, an English professor from the School of Arts and Sciences teamed with a teacher education professor from the Lynch School and responded with a "Collaborative Fellows" program titled "Preparing the Best Secondary English Teachers." The stated goal of this collaboration, begun in the spring of 2002, follows:

> To facilitate and enhance collaboration among faculty from the English Department, Lynch School of Education, and Brighton High School English Department toward the goal of adapting, changing, or modifying curriculum and instruction to prepare the very best secondary teachers of English Language Arts who will commit to teaching in urban schools. (Kowaleski-Wallace & Friedman, 2002, p. 1)

Twelve invited participants and volunteers met biweekly for two hours, for a total of eight times, during the spring semester of 2002 to read current literature and discuss how they could meet the goal of curriculum and instructional modifications. Each Collaborative Fellows meeting had a focus upon which readings and discussion were built, such as "Organization of Existing Fields," "The Everyday High School Classroom," and "The Role of Assessment." Participants shared their understanding of the topics and their point of view, working toward some tangible steps they could take in each of their respective roles in the fall.

Based on themes that emerged from the first year of the program, English faculty committed to advising their students as to the most relevant coursework for secondary teaching raising their awareness of and modeling effective pedagogy in English Language Arts. They agreed to better accommodate diversity in their own classrooms and to be explicit about the literary theory that informs their instruction. The Lynch School faculty determined to further integrate literary theory into their own teaching, to assume a stronger voice in advising secondary English majors, to spend more time in the field observing student teachers, and to respond to the preservice teachers' desire to complete their prepractica and full practicum in the same site. The Brighton High School teachers expressed how they had been suggesting this kind of collaboration for years, but they had never been invited into the conversation before. These teachers want to be more involved with teacher preparation in other integral roles, not just as cooperating teachers. They recognized how much they continue to learn from the Lynch School students and faculty who work onsite. The high school teachers felt that Boston College student teachers were extremely well prepared to teach in urban schools, with the exception of classroom management, an area in which the classroom teachers are versed and able to share strategies with their student teachers.

Specific changes occurred as a result of the cross-school collaboration. A university course open to all English majors and required of secondary English certification students titled Theory and Pedagogy in the English Language Arts is cotaught by teacher education and English faculty. An additional example of cross-disciplinary collaboration to come out of the first year was a new design for year two, which reflected more direct involvement with preservice teachers and their students. In the spring of 2003, the participants from the School of Arts and Sciences, the Lynch School, and Brighton High School worked in clusters. Three English student teachers who were completing their full practicum at Brighton High School were observed by and regularly met with their cluster of content, theory, and pedagogy support, including their Brighton cooperating teacher, a BC English professor, a BC education professor, their clinical supervisor, and a Collaborative Fellows grant leader. The clusters also met four times during the semester as a whole group to reflect upon their learning and identify changes to be implemented to better prepare secondary English teachers for the urban setting. All participants deemed the cluster model a success despite the challenges faced in bringing multiple perspectives together. The Collaborative Fellows are currently discussing how to increase the number of student teachers impacted by this supportive program.

The Urban Immersion and Collaborative Fellows programs are just two examples of the Lynch School's determination to embody their theoretical commitments in practice. Through these collaborations, the Lynch School has recognized and acted upon the notion that effective teacher education requires the co-construction of knowledge and experience regarding education and schooling by multiple constituents. Like collaboration, the Lynch School's emphasis on inquiry as a stance toward teaching reflects its efforts at embodying its theoretical commitments in practice.

INQUIRY AT THE LYNCH SCHOOL

At the Lynch School, *inquiry* is defined as reflecting on and documenting the relationships among teacher learning, student learning, and professional practice across the professional lifespan (Cochran-Smith & Lytle, 1999). In contrast to the traditional assumption that knowledge about teaching is generated solely by university researchers, inquiry encourages a constructivist perspective in which teachers develop local knowledge in their educational settings. Through inquiry, teachers generate knowledge about teaching and learning by engaging in self-critical and often collaborative research about their own schools and classrooms. Inquiry is seen as a significant opportunity to learn from and about teaching through systematic exploration, documentation, and analysis of important questions in practice.

Students at both the undergraduate and the graduate levels of teacher preparation participate in inquiry, also known as teacher research or action research. The Lynch School has set the goal of encouraging beginning teachers to use the process of inquiry to develop high standards for all students, as well as a commitment to professional growth and social change. This conception of learning to teach involves viewing teaching as an intellectual rather than a technical process and teacher learning as a lifelong process of systematic investigation into elements of teaching and schooling within local contexts (Cochran-Smith, 2002). The inquiry approach is designed to help prospective teachers bridge the learning that takes place in the academic environment with what they learn in field placements in an effort to avoid the common disconnect between theory and practice. Preservice teachers at the Lynch School are encouraged to connect and expand their professional knowledge by examining their own narrative knowledge of teaching and learning.

An inquiry approach to learning to teach paradoxically makes teaching and learning more complicated rather than simpler and more uncertain than certain. As faculty member Dr. Marilyn Cochran-Smith (2002) notes,

> Although an inquiry stance makes teaching more complex and hence more difficult in a very real sense it also serves as a way to document and make sense of the inevitable uncertainties and dilemmas of teaching and thus makes it richer and more intellectually interesting. (p. 29)

These uncertainties and dilemmas are not unique to the preservice teachers. The faculty at the Lynch School are continually reworking the design, development, and implementation of inquiry in coursework and field placements, a process that highlights the reflexive nature of posing questions about and studying teaching practice. For both prospective classroom teachers and teacher educators, the inquiry orientation is intended to problematize teaching and learning to teach, and also to help teachers become problem solvers and generators of new knowledge to meet the challenges of constant change in schools and classrooms.

Graduate Inquiry Seminar

At the Lynch School, the teacher education curriculum is intended to bridge the gap between research and practice by fostering critical reflection and by treating classrooms and schools as sites for teacher research and other forms of practitioner inquiry. All master's degree students participate in a required yearlong, 3-credit course entitled Inquiry Research Seminar. By posing fundamental questions, conducting investigations, and constructing and developing local knowledge over time, prospective teachers understand that learning to teach is an ongoing process that is contextually specific.

Each preservice teacher chooses a question, issue, problem, or wondering that has emerged during their prepracticum and full-time student teaching to explore in depth through a classroom-based teacher research project. Problems posed by preservice teachers include questions such as "What happens when I use collaborative learning in my ninth grade Latin class to increase students' translation fluency?" "In what ways do questioning strategies affect literature circle discussions in my fourth grade classroom?" "What's going on with J—? How can I work with him to develop his English skills and enable him to establish his own voice?" "What happens when I make various accommodations to increase ESL learners' participation in my general education class?" These questions form the impetus for prospective teachers to conduct systematic and self-critical inquiry into their own schools and classrooms in order to increase teachers' knowledge, improve students' learning, and contribute to social change.

Throughout the inquiry process, preservice teachers are asked to discuss, reflect on, and write about how who they are as a person impacts their role as a teacher and a researcher. They are encouraged to consider their own frame of reference and to address their biases, assumptions, beliefs, and values about teaching, learning, and their students. One student, who had already been teaching for several years, reflected on the growing role of inquiry in his thinking about teaching:

> I wonder how many teachers question their practices and teaching. What do I do every day? How do I do it? Am I teaching to the [state achievement exam] or am I just following the same notes and lesson plan that I have followed for the past five years? Do I look to the individual student and observe him or her for who they are? Do I get bogged down with the number of students in the room and do I assume things based on prior test scores? I think many teachers confine themselves to a pattern, a safe position from where to give out the knowledge in their head to their students. (Preservice teacher's written reflection, Spring 2001)

Preservice teachers are also asked to consider the impact of the culture of the school in which they teach with respect to the school mission, the social-historical context, demographics and resources, teaching, and learning as well as the lenses of teachers, students, administrators, and parents through which the school culture is experienced.

The final project in the graduate inquiry seminar is a culminating paper designed to document growth in teacher learning, student learning, professional practice, and social justice. Preservice teachers connect their questions about daily teaching practice to the larger social, historical, cultural, and political issues embedded in education at the same time that they make the scholarship of their teaching public and open to critique within an inquiry community. This final paper not only fulfills the requirements for the graduate inquiry seminar, but also addresses requirements for NCATE, the students' master's comprehensive exam, and the field placement office. While many of the aims of the different constituencies overlapped, the need to fulfill the demands of each left many students feeling overwhelmed and frustrated.

Through the examination of their own beliefs and assumptions about teaching and learning, as well as the assumptions that are often taken for granted in traditional school practices, preservice teachers grapple with issues of equity, justice, and learning opportunities for all children. Encouraged to explore the idea that teaching is an inherently political act, preservice teachers at the Lynch School use their inquiry project questions to make connections between larger issues of social justice and their daily practice.

Undergraduate Inquiry

Like their graduate counterparts, undergraduates at the Lynch School also participate in an inquiry approach to learning to teach. Several years ago, most constituents saw the weekly seminar for seniors in their full practicum field placements as a "moan and groan" session or an opportunity for group therapy. While preservice teachers were able to share their successes and frustrations, there was little curricular focus or content in the seminar. As a result, a new course entitled Teacher Research was developed in which students had an opportunity to explore issues in their teaching using an inquiry approach. However, this seminar lacked consistency as it was taught by a variety of instructors without a common syllabus or approach. As a result of continued feedback and discussion, the course was again reworked with an emphasis on developing a consistent syllabus across all sections of the course, strengthening the links between theory and practice, making the facilitation of the course more grounded in the daily life of schools, and pairing two clinical faculty or a teacher education faculty member with a practicing classroom teacher to collaborate in teaching the course.

Currently, the development of the inquiry approach for undergraduates has moved even closer to realizing the Lynch School's commitments to constructivism and social justice as well as addressing the realities of today's schools. The goals of the seminar continue to include helping prospective teachers work through the reciprocal relationships of theory and practice; pose questions for inquiry; learn through reflection and discussion; learn from their students and colleagues; construct critical perspectives about teaching, learning, and schooling; and improve teaching and learning. Compared to graduate students, who participate in the inquiry process over a full year, seniors complete their inquiry projects in one semester.

While this course for seniors has been deemed highly successful by both faculty and students, it was determined that students needed additional involvement in the inquiry process earlier in their teacher education program. The developmental needs of sophomores and juniors in their prepracticum field placements were considered by the teacher education and field office faculty. As a result, sophomores, who need more explicit instruction and early involvement in the inquiry process during their first prepracticum teaching experience, now participate in three weeks of roundtable discussions before going out in the field. They are presented with the concept of inquiry, the categories of reflective judgment, and opportunities to reflect on their own beliefs and assumptions during two-hour seminars five days a week for three weeks. The roundtable discussions are facilitated by teams of trained graduate assistants who will eventually become the students' prepracticum supervisors. Juniors, who participate in two prepracticum field placements, do not attend a seminar but are engaged in increasingly sophisticated activities required in their prepracticum that draw on their developing knowledge of the inquiry process, as well as their knowledge of education and schooling. Like their graduate counterparts, juniors at the Lynch School are asked to examine their personal assumptions, reflect on their own learning experiences, and consider the different lenses through which school culture is experienced.

The continual evolution of this course exemplifies the Lynch School's commitment to collaboration and constructivism as well as the challenges inherent in the collaboration and execution of a complex and often controversial orientation. Through feedback from students, faculty, supervisors, and school-based cooperating teachers, the relationships between field placements, coursework, and supervision have been strengthened, and the role of inquiry has become stronger and clearer over time.

Collaborative Faculty/Student Inquiry at the Lynch School

Just as students are required to engage in reflective teacher research, the faculty at the Lynch School have also made collaborative inquiry a part of their teaching and learning. Several years ago, a group of 10 faculty members conducted a multiyear collaborative self-study. They used inquiry to address the ways in which they understood social justice and how those abstract understandings were translated (or not) into daily practice (Zollers, Albert, & Cochran-Smith, 2000). Over the course of two years, the participating faculty met repeatedly to discuss, reflect, write, and analyze data. Although faculty members' conceptions of and commitments to inquiry and social justice vary, their work as a collaborative team engaged in inquiry "provides a 'proof of possibility' for faculty groups attempting to emphasize or infuse social justice into preservice teacher education despite profound differences in politics, disciplines and perspectives" (Cochran-Smith et al., 1999, p. 230). Practices and policies such as course development and the hiring of new faculty at the Lynch School were influenced by this inquiry project on social justice.

Another example of collaborative inquiry in action at the Lynch School comes from the work of a professor and doctoral student facilitators of the graduate inquiry seminar. During the academic year 2000–2001, this group met for thirteen 2 1/2-hour sessions in order to plan, document, reflect on, and inquire into the practice of the inquiry seminar and the experiences of the preservice teachers. In the same way that the graduate students in the seminar were being asked to pose questions about their own teaching practices, the professor and the facilitators also posed significant questions about their teaching and facilitating of the inquiry course. Questions such as the following framed their discussions: How do our agendas as teacher educators interrelate or collide with their agendas as student teachers? How do our agendas clash with the agendas of their cooperating teachers? Which comes first when people are learning to be teachers—the day-to-day stuff, the know-how for getting through the day, or the inquiry approach, the reflection? How are we as teacher educators reflecting and demonstrating the notions about inquiry that we are trying to teach to the students? In trying to understand the preservice teachers' initial resistance to inquiry and their deep desire for practical teaching tips, one facilitator reflected,

> If most of the participants have never been in a teaching context, it would be logical that they would think they needed "how to" advice on how to "do" teaching before they were introduced to the concept of looking critically at their emerging practices. From their perspective there was no reference point to begin looking critically at. . . . It was like a person taking a first step in a life-long journey saying the scenery hadn't changed much yet. What else would they have to base their experiences on? Probably not much more than the "12-year apprenticeship" of being a student in school. (Doctoral student facilitator's written reflection, Fall 2000)

These meetings helped the instructors of the inquiry seminar address some of the problems, dilemmas, and confusion of planning and teaching the course, as well as discuss the progress being made by the student teachers in the course.

At the Lynch School, inquiry is seen not only as the province of preservice teachers, but as an important approach to growth, learning, and teaching for social justice for all educators regardless of level of experience.

CONCLUSION

The Lynch School of Education at Boston College is committed to addressing the realities and complexities of teaching. The faculty, as do we, believe that classroom teachers and teacher educators should be held accountable for their work. However, while standardized test scores can provide useful information, the Lynch School wants to develop a broader view of learning, utilizing multiple measures of outcomes rather than just test scores. Addressing the complexities of teaching at the Lynch School includes a deep commitment to improving the human condition, particularly through learning to teach for social justice. Through collaboration and inquiry, the Lynch School strives to fulfill its mission by resisting static and standard teacher education practices and engaging in more generative learning processes. By inquiring and collaborating together in learning communities, educators at the Lynch School strive to construct deep and rich understandings of learning and teaching that challenge the status quo. This portrait reveals what it looks like to translate theoretical commitments into practice at the Lynch School. The ultimate goal for teacher educators preparing the Lynch School's preservice teachers is to improve the education of each and every student in America's diverse public school population. Through collaboration and inquiry, among many other practices, this goal toward social justice may ultimately be realized.

ACKNOWLEDGMENTS

We would like to acknowledge the support of Dr. Marilyn Cochran-Smith and Dr. Audrey Friedman for their suggestions regarding an earlier draft of this chapter. For more information on the MassCoalition and the BC/Brighton High School Partnership, contact Dennis Shirley at shirleyd@bc.edu; for Urban Immersion, contact Andrea J. Stairs at stairsa@bc.edu; for Collaborative Fellows, contact Audrey Friedman at friedmaa@bc.edu; and for Inquiry, contact Gerry Pine at pineg@bc.edu or Marilyn Cochran-Smith at cochrans@bc.edu.

NOTE

1. All student names have been changed.

REFERENCES

Cochran-Smith, M. (2002). Inquiry and outcomes: Learning to teach in an age of accountability. *Teacher Education and Practice, 15*(4), 12–34.

Cochran-Smith, M., Albert, L., Dimattia, P., Freedman, S., Jackson, R., Mooney, J., Neisler, O., Peck, A., & Zollers, N. (1999). Seeking social justice: A teacher education faculty's self-study. *International Journal of Leadership in Education, 2*(3), 229–253.

Cochran-Smith, M., & Lytle, S. (1999). Relationship of knowledge and practice: Teacher learning in communities. In A. Iran-Nejad & C. D. Pearson (Eds.), *Review of Research Education, 24* (pp. 249–306). Washington, DC: American Educational Research Association.

Kowaleski-Wallace, B., & Friedman, A. A. (2002). *Yearly report: Preparing the best secondary teacher*. Unpublished report, Boston College.

Zollers, N., Albert, L., & Cochran-Smith, M. (2000). In pursuit of social justice: Collaborative research and practice in teacher education. *Action in Teacher Education, 22*(2), 1–13.

4

Reimagining One Urban Teacher Education Program: Transformation Through Inquiry, Difference, and Field Experience

Valerie Lava, Laurie Lehman, and Cecilia Traugh
Long Island University

> Can we decide to act in a certain manner, choose a better order of things, and thereby bring values into being, as Sartre suggests?. . . What might we begin imagining for our pedagogies, using the "education and reflection" required to move us toward what is not yet.
>
> (Sartre, 1956, p. 435)
(Greene, 1995, p. 48)

Maxine Greene challenges educators to make their work transformation for social change, a re-creation of "reality." In her terms, this is about the interaction of what is and what might be possible, staying in touch with the world as it is while naming alternatives to the "given," bringing the new into existence by going beyond ordinarily accepted limits to create it.

In the fall of 1998, faculty and administrators in the department of Teaching and Learning[1] of the School of Education at Long Island University [LIU], Brooklyn, took up Greene's challenge to "choose a better order of things." Our teacher education programs were no longer meeting the educational needs of our students. We were offering a collection of courses and not a coherent program organized around a set of educational values and commitments. In addition, we were a school struggling to meet New York State's test score standards as many of our students fall into those categories of test takers who often do poorly. The question we faced was how to renew our programs and ourselves in ways that emphasized the possibilities of our urban circumstances, helped us see and develop the strengths of our urban students, and recommitted us to helping create a more democratic society. In a time when educators can allow the standardizing technology of testing and other mechanical forms of accountability to drain dry their vision of possibility—students' and theirs—and of the role of education in our democracy, we needed to make it possible to think about education generally and teacher education specifically as a transformational adventure, a "bring[ing] values into being," a moving "toward what is not yet."

Now, in 2003, we have strengthened our commitment to educate teachers of color for the public schools by completely reimagining our undergraduate and graduate teacher education programs. In so doing, we gained the approval of the New York State Department of Education (NYSDOE), implemented and began to graduate students from the new programs, and helped students raise their test scores and remove the program from state review. Through this re-creation, we brought a set of values into being programmatically.

We, the authors of this chapter, are members of the faculty and administration who participated in the five-year process of reimagining our teacher education program. Our description is one of insiders immersed in a transformational project. This portrait describes two layers of an effort to "move us toward what is not yet" by infusing difference, field-based knowledge making, and inquiry throughout the program. First, we tell elements of a story of a faculty who reimagined their entire teacher education program to make it one that educates teachers who can transform classroom and school life. Second, we give windows into this program in action through pictures of classroom and student work.

LIU is located in Brooklyn, a multicultural and multilingual part of New York City, and is only blocks from the courthouse and bustling life of downtown commerce. The university's mission, "to open the doors of the city and the world to men and women of all ethnic and socioeconomic backgrounds who wish to achieve the satisfaction of the educated life and to serve the public good," set the stage for our reform efforts.

Students in the Department of Teaching and Learning (TAL) are urban dwellers and members of a variety of racial and ethnic groups that represent different communities of Brooklyn. About 80 percent of our students are students of color, and 82 percent are women, and many are married with children. Many are immigrants, speakers of other languages, first-generation college students, and middle-aged, nontraditional students. Our undergraduate students often work in offices and other business establishments or as paraprofessionals in public schools.

IT MATTERS WHERE YOU BEGIN

Part of regenerating our program was creating a space in which that work could be done. We are a group of scholars representing different areas of interest and educational values. Using the structures of collaborative and descriptive inquiry to study critical issues, we disciplined ourselves to describe, not evaluate or judge. In so doing, we created a conversation in which we all speak and try to listen to each other, allow differences to sit alongside each other in an effort to let new ideas emerge, and come to know what is at the center of our attention from the various perspectives we all bring.

Initially a beginning place for our program development, this inquiry work is now a defining feature of our work together as a faculty, of our work with students, and of what we educate students to enact in their own classrooms. We meet once a month to study our work as teacher educators. The inquiry engages us as a faculty in the ongoing process of creating and reworking a democratic and generative space in which we collaboratively create knowledge about teaching and learning through reflecting on our teaching experience and in nurturing the reciprocal relationship between action and thought. The inquiry helps us make real the necessity that our program be one that is both implemented in actuality and in process, growing through the continuous reworking needed to more fully enact the values and ideas at its base.

As we edged into the hard work of re-creating the undergraduate program, faculty talk would often spill over into deep concerns about students. These concerns centered on reading, writing, and what faculty perceived as a thin knowledge base. With such concerns percolating and with the reality of a low standardized test passage rate facing us, it seemed possible that we would go down the road of building a program based on remediation. This seemed a bad choice to almost everyone, so when the person leading the inquiry, Cecelia Traugh, suggested we begin the work of program regeneration by laying out the strengths of our students as we saw them, people entered into that inquiry conversation energetically. In this way, our students, their differences and their capacities became the second starting place for our work.

In January 1999, responding to the focusing question about the strengths and capacities that LIU students bring to their work in education and that have strong potential for contributing to their studies of teaching, faculty described their students as (1) Having important life experience. For example, they often have a firsthand awareness of racism and discrimination. They can have understanding of and concern about the challenges faced by families in underserved communities. (2) Bringing knowledge of their native languages and cultures. (3) Often being disaffected with the ways they were taught and the failure of their teachers to include them and respect diversity. (4) Being persistent and knowing how to stand up for themselves. This was more than an exercise. Through describing our students more deeply, we used inquiry to establish a base on which we could build. We acknowledged publicly the myriad of strengths our students bring to college and urban school classrooms and stated our respect for cultural differences. We expressed our belief that they, like the children they would be teaching, are capable learners.

Committing to a structured process for working together and establishing value ground in our students' strengths gave us our starting points and enabled us to take on the heavy-duty thinking (and feeling) needed for program transformation and its ongoing strengthening. In this portrait of our program, we describe two intermingled layers: (1) the faculty's use of collaborative inquiry to develop the ideas of difference and field-based knowledge making as important threads in the program, and (2) the way these threads live in the program as it is enacted by faculty and undergraduate students. The portrait needs them both because an important aspect of our program is that we faculty engage in the same kind of ongoing and searching learning that we expect of our students.

USING COLLABORATIVE INQUIRY TO DEVELOP A PROGRAM

Differences in Constructions of Difference

When the department began to reflect on the role that "difference" would play in our undergraduate teacher education program, we turned to two elements of our KEEPS Mission[2] as agreed-upon statements of value: pluralism and social commitment.

> Pluralism: LIU/Brooklyn educators value the sociocultural and sociolinguistic pluralism of New York City's children and communities. We strive to acquire the different experiential knowledge that diverse communities have, to find commonalities in human experience, and to shape a transcultural learning context, a third space, that is inclusive of differences.
>
> Social Commitment: LIU/Brooklyn educators are committed to making sure that all students, regardless of race, class, gender, language, sexual orientation, or capabilities/disabilities, receive equitable educational services. We value the importance of inclusion in education and the merits of children from diverse educational and ethnic backgrounds learning together.

Tackling how to address the theme of difference in our vision of teacher education and to represent it as an asset, we faced our own differences in vision and thinking. Maxine Greene's ideas about transformation became real as we were asked to value colleagues' ideas and think in new and different ways about teacher education. The grappling is ongoing. A telling conversation happened in the fall of 2001 (several years after the start of our process) when a small group was given the charge to review the narrative inquiry notes[3] and find the framing questions and issues about difference that wove their way through our program development process. Each person wrote about the role of difference in our teacher education program and shared their reflections with the group. As a member of that group, Laurie Lehman recalls the considerable struggle to identify the full range of difference—from disability, language, and culture to race, class, and ethnicity. The group also noted families and communities as well as educational preparation of students and faculty and the theoretical and philosophical orientations of faculty and staff as defining elements of difference. A few asked to include religion, gender, and sexual orientation. This collaborative inquiry brought to light the multiple meanings and perspectives and divergent thinking about difference that continue among our faculty.

Difference as Asset and Strength

However differently we think about difference, we continue to ground ourselves in the insight that emerged from our initial description of our students.

Our students bring to the classroom a rich and varied array of family, ethnic, linguistic, cultural, and experiential differences. These differences are resources, a strength to build on, and a foundation for learning.

The curriculum of our undergraduate childhood program encourages students to bring their differences into the college classroom so they can learn the value of encouraging the children they teach to do the same. Our students are asked to consider their diversity as a strength and a defining element throughout their studies of schools, teaching, and learning. We have made the idea of difference an integral part of all courses rather than offering add-on courses. Our approach of integrating diversity throughout our curriculum has required radical rethinking of approaches and pedagogy, and we have used inquiry to support us.

One example is the rethinking of our coursework in development, a field in which multiple perspectives are rarely presented. In the fall of 2000, Laurie Lehman was creating a new course—The Developing Child—for the undergraduate program. This course was taught for the first time in spring 2001. As part of the planning process, Laurie thought about the degree to which she should shift the point of view from which the new course would be taught. In a graduate course that covered some of the same ground, she had experimented with incorporating nondevelopmental points of view into the mix of ideas that students considered. We brought her questions and some of her students' work to the inquiry group as a way to further her thinking with colleagues and as a way for members of the faculty to learn more about the approaches to development Laurie was considering.

The focus question for the session was "How do I take a nondevelopmental point of view on the developing child and not throw the baby out with the bath water?" Laurie told the story of the journey of her own thinking about child development and described the development of her realization that childhood is a socially constructed idea; theories of development were largely based on samples of White, middle children, and there are valid questions to be asked about the given-ness of the biological roots of theories of development. Then the faculty group read and discussed Laurie's graduate students' papers that evidenced the ways these students were making sense of these new ideas.

This review made a faculty member's grappling with new ideas public and discussable among members of the inquiry group. For some faculty the ideas about development Laurie presented challenged their learned understandings. For others, these ideas were an opening to consider the cultural implications of the points of view we present in our courses and the need to at least consider some radical choices. For some of us, the review and the ensuing conversation strengthened our hope that we were on the way to developing a pluralistic curriculum. The group gave Laurie thoughts about the course and so supported her rethinking of its content. And, importantly, the group's members now knew more about the direction of the new course and so expanded their understandings of the content of the new program. If they taught in the undergraduate program, they could begin to imagine how Laurie's work fit with their course purposes. This conversation has continued among several of us around questions on the role of theory in observing, describing, and interpreting children and the ways theoretical knowledge can make a child less visible to the observer.

Alongside our belief that all children can learn is the commitment to teaching all children. The rainbow of children in New York City includes recent immigrants, students who are labeled disabled, those from different cultures and languages, those who are poor, those from nontraditional families, and those with different sexual orientations. Our focus on all children extends to a vision of inclusion as a value commitment; that is, valuing knowing our students and the children they will be serving, helping teachers make commitments to all children, and helping students of teaching value heterogeneity. Through an inquiry session in January 1999, we developed an organizing principle that helped us envision inclusion as provision of equity for all, as grounded in belief in pluralism and social responsibility.

Later that semester, we invited Dr. Gerald Mager from Syracuse University to speak with us about inclusive education. One important idea running through our discussion was that inclusion is grounded in our beliefs about society and social justice and in our belief that all children can learn together. We noted that inclusion had the potential of broadening the definition of multicultural education. On the other hand, members of the group also saw some dangers of going "full bore" into inclusion. Does this commitment fit this faculty and the schools it serves? (notes from 3/18/99, p. 1). The last phrase reflects the tension within the faculty when they are faced with taking a stance in favor of full inclusion. Some indicated support for this new model for addressing difference, and others were not so willing to forge ahead with curriculum reform that reflected that principle.

The idea that inclusion is a value commitment led some to describe inclusion as requiring "the re-imagining of classrooms and so of the ways teacher education is conceived. Moving in the direction of preparing students to teach in inclusion classrooms could mean being part of the transformation of the structures of education generally" (notes from 3/18/99, pp. 1–2).

Through our collaborative inquiry, we expanded our vision of inclusion to go beyond the integration of general education students with those receiving special education services to also include English language learners (García, 2002). Alongside the actuality of the distance we have come, this commitment is also one of the unfinished edges of our program, a place that offers the promise of new discoveries and further transformation.

Making Knowledge Through Work in the Field

From the earliest conversations in the transformation process, the value of hands-on experience in schools was a repeated theme. As one faculty member articulated early in the transformation process,

> Knowledge of teaching comes from interaction of work in the field, (in schools) and coursework (reading). That knowledge comes from being able to spend a span of time in schools to observe and participate in the daily life of teaching and to begin to see oneself as a teacher. That knowledge also comes from having good opportunities to practice and reflect. (Notes from 11/19/99, p. 1)

It seemed clear from the start that our new program would have a strong fieldwork component with or without the mandates from the NYSDOE.[4] Ultimately, the program's fieldwork component exceeded the state's minimum requirement of 100 hours. Although there was consensus on the necessity of the fieldwork in the program, through our inquiry there were many conversations and debates regarding the specific model we would adopt. A review of the notes from the inquiry revealed several critical issues that we addressed in creating the fieldwork component. We describe here the issues and the process as they pertain to the transformation of our undergraduate program.

Selecting Schools

After naming the initial course in the program Teaching: Imagine the Possibilities, it became apparent that we had different ideas about the possibilities that the students should experience through fieldwork. There seemed to be two differing points of view on the types of schools our students should be exposed to in their undergraduate teacher preparation program. Phrases used to characterize this dichotomy were "reality versus progressive" and "traditional versus innovative." The reality/traditional camp advocated that the students be placed in a broad range of settings that translated into a continuum from the worst schools in NYC (those under review by the state education department) to some of the best, particularly a coalition of small schools. As one faculty member articulated, "Early in the program, students should be in a range of places and should be talking about what worked and didn't work. . . . Then they move to more positive models and philosophies" (notes from 11/19/99, p. 2). The rationale for providing the students with the range in public schools was to allow them to make an informed decision about a career in teaching in an urban setting. There was a sense that we would be deceiving these future teachers if we were to offer a view of only successful and healthy schools. An underlying assumption of the reality theory was that we needed to toughen up the undergraduates so they would succeed as urban teachers because it was more likely that they would be hired to teach in a challenging school. Also at question was our commitment to improving urban education. Shouldn't our students be placed in the neediest schools?

The people committed to placing students in progressive/innovative schools for fieldwork wanted the students to be hopeful and excited about the prospect of a career in teaching. Spending time in dismal schools would not heighten students' interest in becoming urban teachers and might deter them from the field of education entirely. In terms of the reality argument, many of the teacher education students are products of a large urban school system, and they are well acquainted with its foibles. Spending time in schools that demonstrate best practices provides the students with reserves to draw on if and when they are teaching in an urban school with minimal resources and support. We can support the work of urban schools by providing them with a well-prepared teaching force based on a belief that "transformative pedagogies must relate both to existing conditions and to something we are trying to bring into being, something that goes beyond a present situation" (Greene, 1995, p. 51).

In selecting schools for fieldwork sites, the idea of fit was a theme in the discussions. Fit needs to go both ways; students' experiences in schools need to fit course content, and course content needs to reflect what the students are seeing and learning in schools. We described this relationship between fieldwork and course content using words such as "link, congruence, and inter-relatedness." Was our new teacher education curriculum compatible with the work being done in traditional or progressive schools? This question contributed to the conversation about the type of schools that should be selected for fieldwork.

After much debate and discussion, the majority of the faculty supported the idea of choosing progressive and innovative schools for the fieldwork component. As one faculty member who originally advocated for fieldwork in traditional schools shared, "We debated about placements. I wanted them to see "reality" but we are sending people [students] into more "progressive" schools, places where students are not beaten down. This has worked well. I have learned from that" (notes from 4/10/2001, p. 2).

Wedding Ideas and Practice

The idea of relating theory and practice in teacher education was one of the big ideas that recurred in the transformation process at LIU. The idea took various forms but had a shared meaning evident in some of our questions: What is the relationship between experiential knowledge and book knowledge? How are theory and practice related? How do we link the fieldwork to the classes? This is certainly a critical issue for teacher education particularly in light of Dewey's (1938) thoughts that experience at times can be miseducative. There must be ways of drawing meaning from experience.

This slice of conversation between two faculty members about student field observations and how they are responded to exemplifies the LIU stance toward integrating theory and practice:

B: I am wondering. When students make their observations, do they return to them or have the chance to look at them from another perspective?
K: I have had to create space for them to return to re-see and re-listen.

Questions about what the students see and hear in the field are incorporated into coursework, and they have the opportunity to put these observations alongside the theoretical frameworks and ideas they are learning through reading, discussion, and written assignments. This relationship between knowledge and practice is consistent with the model Cochran-Smith and Lytle (1998) refer to as *knowledge-of-practice*. "This model is a departure from the false dualism of knowledge and practice; it is a more fluid and unified experience than thinking about these two things separately or even side-by-side. Provided with the knowledge-of-practice model, the students have the capacity to reflect on both at once. It is a unity of experience not one based on a defined difference between knowledge and practice" (notes from 3/1/00, pp. 5–7).

PORTRAITS OF LIFE IN THE PROGRAM

Portrait of Fieldwork Issues—Valerie Lava

As an instructor of TAL 301, Observing and Describing Children, the second course offered in the undergraduate teacher preparation program, I can describe elements of this particular course that give life to the fieldwork issues discussed above, namely, selection of schools and relating theory and practice.

Several schools that belong to a coalition of small progressive schools were selected as the fieldwork sites for the students enrolled in TAL 301. The majority of the administrators and teachers in these small progressive schools are experienced with the process known as the Descriptive Review of the Child[5] that is the basis of the curriculum in TAL 301. Personnel in these small schools are able to provide meaningful guidance and support to the LIU students who are learning to look closely at one particular child. LIU students are assigned to the schools in cohort groups so that they can provide peer-to-peer support and create their own learning community within the public school.

These cohort groups or school groups meet periodically in the university classroom to share their experiences and make meaning of what they are observing in the schools. Although these discussions are generally focused on the needs and ideas of the LIU students, I often give several questions or issues for them to ponder. My ideas for framing the conversation have come from teaching the course several times and identifying recurrent themes from the different classes I have encountered. During their initial meeting, I focus the conversation on their entry into a public school classroom with the following questions: How were you introduced and/or welcomed into the public school classroom? How and why did you select a particular child to observe throughout the semester? What surprised you?

All three of these questions yield interesting, important, and necessary discussion; however, the last one (What surprised you?) has become my favorite. Although each new semester there may be a novel response to this question, for the most part the LIU students are initially surprised and challenged by several issues in these progressive classrooms: multilevel/multiage groupings, child-centered curriculum, the physical environment (i.e., no individual desks for students or teachers, easels replace blackboards, etc.), and the children calling the adults by their first names. This last practice results in the most lively and heated discussion. Many of the undergraduate students initially view the teacher role as one of authority, and this discussion reveals deep-rooted ideas about power, position, and respect often grounded in cultural mores. Disrespect seems to be at the core of the students' consternation. I challenge the students to describe instances of disrespect between the children and their teachers at their field sites. To date there has not been any incidence reported of a disrespectful interchange between students and teachers despite the first name policy.

As I work to debunk the relationship of formal titles and respect between students and teachers, I recount my own initiation into the progressive schools movement. A decade before teaching at LIU, I entered a progressive school as a consultant with expertise in educating students with disabilities. Having been educated myself in parochial schools where discipline and formality were the norm, I was awestruck by the children's use of first names with their teachers but quickly became impressed by the easy relationship that was obvious between them. I too struggled with the idea of respect but recalled from my early days as a student that a child publicly addressing an adult with the title Mr., Mrs., or Sister could easily add a whispered phrase under his or her breath that was not kind or respectful. My recounting of this particular memory always gets a chuckle and affirming head nods from my LIU students. I came to learn that respect was an attitude, not necessarily a title, and I share this revelation with my students.

Through such discussions and readings centered on creating relationships with students, respectful teaching practices, and learning environments where students feel comfortable and secure, the students of teaching have many opportunities to meld theory and practice. I attend to the practice of children calling teachers by their first names in hopes of challenging some preconceived notions and developing new ideas about teaching and learning. My success with this task is variable as some students clearly begin to see the value in being familiar with their students, others can't defend the formal titles but are still unwilling to incorporate such informality into their future teaching practice, while still others do not budge. As one of my students in this last category articulated at the end of the semester while shaking her head back and forth vehemently, "It just isn't right."

Although students vary in their ability to draw meaning from their fieldwork experiences, both students and faculty alike would agree that the intensive fieldwork component of the LIU undergraduate program provides a rich, authentic, and necessary background for the development of well-prepared urban educators.

Developing a Descriptive Inquiry Stance: Learning from the Field—Cecilia Traugh

Jeannette[6] was introduced to observing and describing as modes of inquiry and knowledge making in Observing and Describing Children, a course she took her first semester in the program. Through the Descriptive Review of the Child exercise, the course offered a way of seeing and thinking about children and of making sense of direct observation that was entirely new to her and to her classmates. The work laid the ground for becoming an observer and student of children in a way that helps her understand them in their terms. It also laid ground for her to reconsider the role of the teacher and to include inquiry in that role.

Jeannette's first effort to describe was of a natural object, a branch.

> Drawing the branches was pretty simple but it became difficult when I tried to draw the individual leaves. The leaves took on different shapes, shades &

fullness. In sections where I had most difficulty drawing exactly what I saw, I drew what I felt would be closest to what I saw. At first I believed I wouldn't have great difficulty drawing the branch, but then I realized that I was incorrect. Half way through the drawing I knew that I would not be able to draw it exactly as I saw the branch, but I would come as close as possible. The drawing turned out all right but it taught me that I shouldn't be so quick to judge. (Journal entry, 9/11/00)

Jeannette names here some basic truths about knowing and representing what we know. What seems simple, a branch, in reality is complex. In her effort to capture what she sees, she is not able to do it exactly. Her drawing must be an approximation, as any effort to capture reality and not oversimplify it must be. Jeannette also notes that she needs to resist judgment. It is not clear if she means judgment of her own work or of the difficulty of a task, but either way judgment made too quickly seems to have taken her down a wrong path.

In her Descriptive Review of the Child, Jeannette evidences her many efforts to see and describe the child's multiple sides, her complexities. While she judges Carol as "outspoken," she provides much support for her interpretation. And, later in the Review, Jeannette offers the possibility that "for an instant I could actually mistake her for being a shy and insecure person," a judgment mitigated by making room for another possibility. In her final statement in the Review, "My Thoughts," Jeannette connects not judging with developing understanding. In addition, she includes here a new idea, one that becomes a thread for her thinking about teaching—it is okay to have questions and to keep them open.

It is strange, but the thought that keeps coming up to my mind is the answer that I had given on the first day of this teaching and learning course. . . . And my answer to the question was, "I have a habit of having to know the answers. If there is something that is left unanswered then I am not content and it will eventually get the best of me. I need to learn to accept the fact that I will not always have or get an answer." And this is actually what this descriptive review has helped me to learn. I have become better at dealing with questions left unanswered. I have come to realize that not all unanswered questions are a sign of inability. Instead, I can now look at a question as a foundation on which to build. The process has taught me not to strive for short conquests (categorizing a child) by trying to answer all questions, but instead to gain greater triumphs (understanding a child). (Descriptive Review, 12/07/00)

Jumping ahead two years to Jeannette's student teaching semester, we can see how this ground fared over time. As part of her student teaching seminar, Jeannette writes another Descriptive Review, which she uses as a place to think about a child who poses problems for her.

> The main reason why I chose to write about Franky was that I found him to be a challenge. I could have written about other students in the class, but Franky made me wonder as a future teacher, how can I or will I ever be able to reach this child? My first instinct when it came to writing this paper was to avoid any students that may pose a problem for me, but this I realized was simply being a coward. How can I avoid a child who needs help? Whether or not I find the process of trying to reach a child difficult should not be the cause for not attempting to do what the child expects and needs of me. (Descriptive Review, 4/15/02)

In this inquiry, she works to capture this child's complexities. Even though he is "difficult" to work with, Jeannette wants to see his various sides and uses description to lay out a complicated point.

> As for the adults, I find that Franky is at most times more helpful than co-operative. What I mean is that he is usually easier about helping an adult set up things or put away things than he is about having to behave a certain way. He simply doesn't appreciate being reminded what he should or shouldn't be doing. If he is being asked by the teacher to sit down and listen or don't do that, at times he'll get angry and yells, "Oh my God!" and he'll stump off without permission and doesn't return even when he's being asked to do so by the teacher. "Franky, I am going to count to five and you need to be here." After the teacher counts up to five, he'll slowly walk back and then do what he's being asked to do. ("Connections with Other People," Descriptive Review, 4/15/02)

Through her program—coursework integrated with fieldwork—Jeannette developed her descriptive inquiry stance. The elements of that stance are the importance of trying to go beyond the simple surface of things to capture the complexity of reality, working to understand rather than falling back on quick judgments by aiming to see multiple facets and so more than one possibility in children and in events, finding courage in the possibilities, and keeping questions open as an element of the development of understanding.

Facing Difference: One Student's Efforts—Laurie Lehman

To illustrate how our program attends to difference, I think of two particular courses and how they stimulated the development of one undergraduate student, Beverley.[7] At the beginning of her coursework in teacher education, Beverley took the course Teaching: Imagine the Possibilities, where she read about the importance of race, language, culture, and other social dimensions in the life of a teacher. The following passage captures her reckoning with the role of difference in education:

> I have never had a more agonizing time in my life writing and reading.... The more I read, the more distance I realized that I had mentally removed myself from the issue of race and racism.... Just as I've struggled through these exercises I know now that I have to struggle as a teacher along with the children to ensure we will be able to discuss racial and cultural differences intelligently, that I can lend a voice to making schools and ... what is being taught there more democratic. I just know that I cannot be silent any longer. (Reflection on writing assignments 19 and 20)

Beverley confronted her "silence" around race and how important it would be to make it more present in her life. Just as the faculty had worked to make difference a visible and vital part of the program, Beverley struggled in the first course to bring social differences into the light of day. She projected herself as a teacher realizing that racial and other social differences would need to be given voice in her classroom.

The next semester Beverley took a course, The Developing Child, that I was teaching at the time. That course is an extension of the rethinking I had done on human development courses (see the earlier discussion of my inquiry) that led me to incorporate multiple perspectives on childhood into the course curriculum (e.g., sociological and political analyses, autobiography, teacher research, student reflections as well as developmental theories). Course assignments including double-entry journals, autobiographical reports, and recollections of childhood provided venues for writing about difference.

From one book chapter, Beverley compared her experience to the lives of children with learning disabilities. "I know just like the word 'black' identifies and projects an image of me, which often leads to discrimination, so too does the label, LD, identify and project an image of the child, which leads to discrimination" (Double-entry journal #5, 3/12/01, p. 2). Later in the same assignment, Beverley reacted to this quote—"Where and when a child is born has a tremendous impact on whether the child will be labeled as having a learning disability"—by telling a story about her son.

> The counselor . . . told me that [my son] will need special help and for the time being, she will put him in a special ed. class where he would receive expert help. Her argument was so convincing that I almost signed the forms until I looked down at S. and saw that he was crying. Through tears, he told me that he didn't want to be like T. (his sister who was in a special ed. class) because everyone will laugh at him. So I refused to sign the forms. (Double-entry journal, #5, pp. 2–3)

Situating her own story in the consideration of learning disabilities, Beverley realized the varied meanings of this label and developed a more critical consciousness (Freire, 1998).

Students were exposed to the perspective of the "insider" by reading an autobiography of a person with a disability. The following is an excerpt from Beverley's book report on Helen Keller:

> I was just cheering her on and at the same time coming to understand that disabled persons just want to be treated as "people"—as persons who are capable, competent and independent. They are not childish, nor are they mindless objects, and Ms. Keller demonstrated this idea to us by graduating from Radcliffe, cum laude, in 1904. (Book Report, 2/28/01, p. 4)

Her thinking about disability, with the help of the autobiography, was changed from stereotypes to an understanding of a person's capabilities and humanity.

Beverley examined her youth and that of a classmate for one assignment, Recollection of Childhood, as shown in this excerpt:

> It would appear that only those children who have exhibited changes that will help them to be socially fit, can and will be accepted into society, while those who have not achieved these determined changes could be labeled

developmentally slow or perhaps mentally retarded. An implication for me, therefore, is to see myself as a transformational teacher, to develop an instrumental plan that would provide the best education to both the retarded child and the rest of the children in the class. To this end, I now appreciate the fact that both Randi and I were able to meet those predetermined standards for development. (Recollection Paper, 5/1/01, p. 11)

Beverley saw her younger days as significantly different from those of other children who didn't fit society's expectations and realized they too deserved "the best education." The recollection assignment was, in a sense, field based and made one's personal history relevant material for study.

As a teacher educator, my review of one student's writing on difference has helped me to answer the question "Why is the incorporation of difference into the curriculum so valuable for students of teaching?" Beverley's work shows how one student, through an attention to differences, can take pains to locate herself as a learner and teacher willing to change herself to make student differences visible. Situating herself in the mix through examining her own field experiences and making personal connections with the experiences of people she read about allowed her to build bridges across social differences, deepen her understanding, and change her view of the world. Paulo Freire's words explain Beverley's reflections about differences: "A deepened consciousness of their situation leads men to apprehend that situation as an historical reality susceptible of transformation" (1970, p. 73).

How does such a "difference" curriculum support transformation for social change? I have learned that attention to difference is central to both student and educator work. As Paulo Freire pointed out, "One of our greatest mistakes as educators and politicians is not perceiving that our 'here' is the student's and the people's 'there'" (Escobar, Fernandez, & Guevara-Niebla, 1994, p. 55). Through looking at differences in people and ideas, we become vigilant in the reality that our perspective is not the same as others'. We become more cognizant of the need to listen to others and to learn from others about their own experiences. Through learning about people who were different from her, Beverley took attention to difference one step further, seeing it as a positive, and through that realization, she committed herself to take action to make education more equitable and inclusive for all children. Beverley helped me to be awake to student and faculty differences and how the "here" and "there" can work together for social change.

FURTHER THOUGHTS

Writing this portrait has done what writing is supposed to do; that is, help us think more deeply about the work we are immersed in. Through the process of creating this piece, several points clarified themselves or emerged that we briefly describe here. One was about who we are as a faculty. Largely White, middle-class, and female, we illustrate the continued need for more teachers of color in education. We do have colleagues of color who bring some racial, ethnic, and language diversity to our department. However, the differences between the predominantly white faculty and the predominantly African American, Caribbean, and Hispanic students are important and create a tension that often goes unspoken and that requires further attention.

As we described the interwoven nature of the three threads we chose to highlight, the importance of the reciprocal relationship between thought and action—for example, thought feeds action and action feeds thought— was underlined for us. For example, our ideas about social differences reframes our field experiences, and our field experiences bring meaning to and a deepening of those ideas. We also see how critical the collaborative inquiry is as the methodology that allows us to move back and forth from idea to action and back again while recognizing that there is no clear division between idea and fieldwork. They are part of each other.

We see more clearly what learning from the field means for us, and there is a double nature to our frame. For our students, learning from and through the field means learning how to learn from children as they live in schools and classrooms and from the work of teachers. In addition, however, we think we have extended the idea of learning from the field by creating the opportunities we have for students to bring who they are culturally, linguistically, and racially into our classrooms and making these experiences part of our shared experience.

Of course, the work of "moving toward what is not yet" is never-ending, and having enacted a set of values in our programs means only that we have embarked on an ongoing journey of exploration. We have had to recognize that "the very essence of real actuality . . . is process" (Whitehead, 1958, p. 274) and to let our work help us continue the imagining process and open up more possibilities.

NOTES

1. This department includes faculty in a variety of fields: childhood and adolescent education, special education, bilingual education and TESOL, and language and literacy education. Everyone participated in the discussions described in this chapter.

2. KEEPS is an acronym for knowledge, enquiry, empathy, pluralism, and social commitment. Our mission is an elaboration of these five ideas.

3. Narrative notes are the main documentation of the work done through the SOE inquiry. They are written after each inquiry session and form a record we can return to periodically. They were an important resource in the writing of this chapter.

4. At the time we were reinventing our teacher education programs, personnel preparation programs throughout the state were being revised in direct response to new guidelines from the NYSDOE requiring 100 hours of supervised fieldwork prior to student teaching.

5. The Descriptive Review of the Child is an inquiry process developed by the Prospect Center in Bennington, Vermont. It requires the presenter to describe a child around five headings: physical presence and gesture, disposition and temperament, relationships with others, interests, and modes of thinking and learning. See Himley and Carini, 2000, for more information.

6. Jeannette is a Puerto Rican American mother of two who entered her studies of teaching when she was about 40. She is a graduate of New York City public schools.

7. Beverley, a Caribbean student in her 30s, immigrated to New York City in 1992 and was raising three stepchildren with her husband while being a full-time undergraduate student.

REFERENCES

Cochran-Smith, M., & Lytle, S. (1998). Relationships of knowledge and practice: Teacher learning in communities. *Review of Research in Education, 24,* 249–305.

Dewey, J. (1938). *Experience and education*. New York: Macmillan.

Escobar, M., Fernandez, A. L., & Guevara-Niebla, G. (with Freire, P.). (1994). *Paulo Freire on higher education: A dialogue at the National University of Mexico*. Albany, NY: State University of New York Press.

Freire, P. (1970). *Pedagogy of the oppressed*. New York: Continuum.

Freire, P. (1998). *Pedagogy of freedom: Ethics, democracy, and civic courage*. Lanham, MD: Rowman & Littlefield.

García, O. (2002, April). *Teacher education reform at LIU-Brooklyn campus*. Paper presented at the meeting of the American Educational Research Association, New Orleans, LA.

Greene, M. (1995). *Releasing the imagination*. San Francisco: Jossey-Bass.

Himley, M., & P. Carini. (2000). *From another angle: Children's strengths and school standards*. New York: Teachers College Press.

Satre, J.-P. (1956). *Being and nothingness*. (H. Barnes, trans.) New York: Philosophical Library.

Whitehead, A. N. (1958). *Modes of thought*. New York: Capricorn Books. (Originally published 1938).

III

LEARNING TO TEACH IN A DEMOCRACY

> A society which makes provision for participation in its good of all its members on equal terms and which secures flexible readjustment of its institutions through interaction of the different forms of associated life is in so far democratic. Such a society must have a type of education which gives individuals a personal interest in social relationships and control, and the habits of mind which secure social changes without introducing disorder.
>
> (Dewey, 1916, p. 99)

As teacher educators, our first context for the development of a "democratic imperative" in teaching is our family and our K–12 experience. Relatedly, as teacher practitioners, the cultivation of a disposition of democratic practice, the cultivation of an active voice begins in teacher preparation and carries forward into the classroom where the teacher practices—the public space of our collective classrooms. The development of a "democratic imperative" premised on fostering classrooms as democratic publics rests on the understanding and valuing the role of teaching in the development of wide-ranging, critical, engaged democratic citizenry. Greene (1981) argues the importance of a "democratic imperative" in teacher preparation when she states,

> There is an obligation, I think, on the part of all who educate to address themselves, as great artists do, to the freedom of their students, to make demands on them to form the pedagogy of their own liberation—and to do so rigorously, passionately, and in good faith. (p. 303)

Ensuring the freedom of students requires democratic experiences in classrooms and schools, experiences enriched by teachers who understand the democratic imperative equally in relation to the responsibility of preparing teachers who embrace this imperative. Teaching that embodies the "democratic imperative" provides for imaginative and cognitive contexts in which students may experience the world differently from a world that, as Maxine Greene (1986) characterizes it, "is palpably deficient: there are unwarranted inequities, shattered communities, unfulfilled lives" (p. 427). Such a world is reified by the absence of a democratic imperative in our schools and in our teacher preparation programs.

Learning to teach in a democracy requires, first and foremost, that the teacher preparation programs in which learning occurs embrace the basic ideals of democracy. The notion of teacher preparation that works to foster democratic teaching practice is underpinned by a valuing of diversity and honoring of voice. Importantly, the teacher preparation for democratic teaching practice recognizes the value that is gained within a social context that is exploited by all in order to reflect upon and imagine anew what is presented and the perceptions of our interrelationships (Freire, 1985, p. 44). The democratic teacher often brings to question and introduces conflict to bear on the object of inquiry through her or his practice. Relatedly, teacher preparation programs that engage students authentically in democratic experiences provide enriched learning experiences that prepare future teachers to act responsibly in creating democratic cultures in classrooms and schools through democratic social practice. Such social practice works to create and sustain democratic cultures and democratic practices, and equally if not more important to foster the development of teacher identities—identities as critical, democratic practitioners concerned with the well-being of all children in a changing and problematic world.

Teacher preparation as a transformative process, and therein the teacher educator's work, must embody a concern for conditions that affect just and democratic practices that foster conditions necessary to self-identity and self-respect, self-development and self-expression, and self-determination and self-democratization. This means the teacher educator's work is that of arousing a consciousness of democratic membership, a consciousness of socially just membership that recognizes all individuals as valued and contributing members of society.

The authors in this part bring to the foreground considerations for democratic pedagogy, democratic learning community, and the role of self as reflective inquirer. Embedded within each portrait are patterns of social justice, equity, and democratic practice.

REFERENCES

Dewey, J. (1916). *Democracy and education*. New York: The Free Press.

Freire, P. (1985). *The politics of education: Culture, power, and liberation*. South Hadley, MA: Bergin and Garvey.

Greene, M. (1981). The humanities and emancipatory possibility. *Journal of Education, 163*(4), 287–305.

Greene, M. (1986). In search of a critical pedagogy. *Harvard Education Review, 56*(4), 427–441.

5

Keepers of the Flame: The CARE Program for Democratic Education

Rosalie M. Romano
Ohio University

In ancient times, people lived in villages, eking out their existence through hunting and gathering. The most important role was given to a wise person who was responsible for making sure the flame of the fire was always aglow. Fire to cook food and keep the villagers' bodies alive was critically important to the future existence of a village. The keeper had to forage for wood to feed the fire, learn what kind of wood that fire needed, and then sustain the flame at the best level for the village needs. Each keeper of the flame was required to find the fuel to feed the flame, no matter how scarce the resources. The keeper of the flame held the village's health and future because she had to be responsive to both the flame and her village community. I view teachers as the keepers of the flames when they become active, engaged educators in democratic life.

THE CARE PROGRAM

Set in the southeastern foothills of Appalachia, Ohio University is the oldest university outside of the original 13 states. Established as a university in 1803, one of Ohio University's missions is to serve the community. Today, one significant aspect of that service is through education, in numerous forms. Ohio University serves teachers around the region who attend the university to earn master's degrees or to provide continuing education for professional development. The College of Education also has large undergraduate teacher preparation programs that lead to licensure in Early Childhood, Middle Childhood, and Adolescent Young Adult. Additionally, the college has a Center for Partnerships that supports four distinctive school-university partnerships. The oldest of these, the CARE Program, was established in 1987 as a collaborative model of classroom teachers, principals, and a superintendent and university faculty. CARE is the acronym for "creating active, reflective educators" for democratic education.

The CARE Program is a partnership between Ohio University's College of Education and local schools. CARE is founded on the assumption that one of the fundamental purposes of schooling is to prepare young people to be active participants and citizens in their democratic communities and in the world. Today, the CARE Program partners with five schools (one elementary, two middle schools, one high school, and a multigraded community school), where CARE students spend the field component of their three years of taking education coursework. CARE emphasizes field experience to foster an understanding of how theory and practice are interwoven. The CARE faculty act on the concept that preparation based on promoting educational practices explicitly tied to theories can assist preservice teachers in their development of democratic ideals and values, such as respect, tolerance, equality, justice, and community.

In the CARE Program, we offer an intensive, rigorous three-year program that begins in the sophomore year when students apply for the CARE cohort. Within a CARE cohort, students take a three-year sequence of courses together as a group, where they learn to observe and practice, reflect, and write on what they are learning in their courses and what they are learning as they participate in the field. In the best case, CARE sophomores work with a partnership teacher in their junior or senior year, and enter into a mentor/mentee relationship where all subsequent fieldwork is in the mentor's classroom.

CARE PEDAGOGY FOR STUDENTS

The CARE Program's aim is to cultivate interwoven ideas of democratic theory and approaches to teaching, and to make explicit the underlying principles that animate democratic practices. The CARE faculty seeks to model democratic approaches in university classrooms, making their pedagogy transparent and an explicit part of the course. CARE students are encouraged to see and question pedagogy, and to structure their own lessons. In this way, CARE students learn to think out loud about teaching and learning. CARE students develop curriculum early in their program, building on what they are reading and doing at the university to develop experiential and discovery learning, active engagement, cooperative organization, and community building, to name a few.

Our aim in the CARE Program is to foster educators who seek new forms of human possibility, new ways of being and constructing a world of justice and equity (Romano & Glascock, 2002). This is a challenge for new teachers because of the ways in which schools tend to be structured. The CARE Program seeks to uncover the hidden curriculum of school and reveal its unexamined impact on teaching. Through course readings and classroom field experience, CARE students analyze the differences between a student who consumes knowledge and one who produces knowledge; one passive, the other active. As awareness is raised, CARE students are afforded actual experiences in classrooms to seek new ways of conceptualizing educational practice through epistemological complexity. This, in turn, uncovers how multiple perspectives of a topic or lesson are grounded in a tolerance for ambiguity and complexity. When CARE students articulate the need for tolerance for ambiguity and complexity as part of what it means for their own students to produce knowledge and understanding, they are introduced to the principle of civic courage. Civic courage is required to be a teacher who is an active, ethical, reflective decision maker, for there are moral choices a teacher must face every day in the classroom. CARE aims to prepare teachers who can see the moral landscape of the classroom and prepare to live an engaged life of educator (Palmer, 1999).

FIVE ELEMENTS OF THE CARE PROGRAM

The CARE Program identifies and integrates five elements into the CARE coursework and field experience. These elements are social and cultural considerations, nature of the learner, curriculum design, pedagogy, and praxis and partnership. The five elements conjoin in democratic teaching and learning and represent the underlying assumptions and beliefs of the CARE Program.

Social and Cultural Considerations

In a democratic society, a primary role of the school is to develop in students the habits of the heart and mind that make active and full democratic citizenship possible. As teachers in democratic classrooms, responsibilities go beyond preparing students with a subject content area or for future careers. Democratic teaching is far more than this. Education is not a neutral endeavor. It is both a social activity and an institution that is embedded in an always-changing sociocultural context. People are not born knowing how to be democratic. Hence, schools become a key place for developing the attributes that are part of being a democratic citizen. In the United States, we believe that the promises of democracy belong to all citizens. A democratic education aims to foster ideals such as equity, social justice, freedom, responsibility, community, and tolerance.

Nature of the Learner

Who are our students? What is their nature? How does their psychological, emotional, cognitive, social, and physical development impact their learning and our teaching in the classroom? This element is a critical one if we are to prepare teachers to develop a pedagogical relationship with students. Our focus in CARE goes beyond the psychological and social development of youngsters. In addition, we interrogate those societal forces that impact young people today such as poverty and prejudice.

We encourage CARE students to learn how to take on other perspectives and viewpoints, so that their own assumptions do not make them blind or deaf to those many students who come from backgrounds different from theirs. We use literature as well as research articles to frame the field experience. Therefore, in CARE, we ask students to explore how to keep this natural wonder and curiosity alive throughout all grades by opening a window to the world. While CARE students examine an array of child development theories, we pay attention also to how social, cultural, and economic factors impact the learner and the learning (and hence, the teacher and the teaching) within the school experience. In CARE, we are committed to education for all children, regardless of issues of difference that so frequently lock youngsters out of the educational system.

Curriculum Design

Curriculum can be defined as the sum total of experiences that a youngster has in school. How teachers and others choose to structure and organize the curriculum is a key element in teaching for understanding and engagement. A teacher must be aware of the complex layers of curriculum, both the explicit standard curriculum as well as the implicit hidden curriculum. Each has its own impact on student understanding and engagement. The choices that teachers make should, we argue in CARE, be predicated upon enhancing the intellectual, moral, and social development of all students within the context of a democratic society. CARE students gain pedagogical knowledge on how the curriculum can be organized with particular aims that include the social and moral development, as well as intellectual growth of students.

Pedagogy

Dewey argued that education must prepare our young for democratic living, and this involves learning to live conjointly in association with one another (Dewey, 1916/1944). The role of the teacher in the democratic classroom goes beyond transmitting official knowledge or providing information that is supposed to help students grow intellectually and socially. Teachers must understand their students enough to know how to use different strategies and approaches to engage them in knowledge work. To say we must construct knowledge is one thing, but to implement with our students is quite another. CARE teachers explore and experience different educative processes that promise to provide a more authentic and holistic experience for their students. As such, nothing is more critical to this than learning how to forge an educative community (Romano, 2000). Classroom culture and climate are key components of powerful pedagogy but, like the invisible aspects of curriculum, are often hidden from view. Hence, given that culture and climate are so instrumental in helping students want to learn, it is critical to make explicit the intentionality of creating a classroom community as part and parcel of what is educative.

Critical aims of such a pedagogy of relations, which we will call a pedagogy of associative living, emerge from Deweyan notions of democracy and education. Associative living for teachers means they are aware of how to forge an inclusive environment in the classroom where respect and a sense of belonging are as privileged as understanding and knowledge construction. This pedagogy of associative living is central to the CARE Program's mission and aims because democracy in the classroom or in society brings with it stated ideals that include respect for others that is the foundation for learning to dialogue.

Relations are central to dialogue and learning to be able to listen with respect to the ideas of others. A pedagogy of associative living places relationships with students as primary to the teaching-learning process. Such a pedagogy places relationships at the center of classroom life, animated by the question "How shall a teacher foster the conditions in her classroom such that students want to be there and want to participate?"

Praxis and Partnership

The CARE Program adheres to three basic commitments in teacher preparation: praxis, partnership, and citizenship. First, praxis is the blending of theory and action. Reflexively, theory and action inform each other iteratively to create a stronger sense of teaching and learning.

The second commitment is partnership. The CARE Program strongly respects and values the high involvement of classroom teachers in the preparation of teachers. As such, CARE classroom teachers also teach some of the CARE courses at the university, while at the same time directing their field experiences in partnership school classrooms. Bringing classroom teachers into the university setting affords opportunities to collaborate with university faculty researchers as part of a team. Additionally, classroom teachers are in touch with the local community in a variety of ways. As such, they are invaluable in pointing to community resources and issues that could be used for exploration of a topic in the classroom.

This leads to the third commitment of citizenship: to explore the democratic notion of the "common good amidst diversity" as it applies to one's local, national, and global citizenship. The CARE Program's aim is to prepare teachers to be active and valuable educational leaders-as-citizens in the classroom, their school, and community. For purposes of a broader and integrated discussion of teacher preparation, in the next section I will focus on democratic education as a significant component of teacher preparation. If we take democracy seriously, we must pay attention to how we foster discrimination and judgment in teachers as democracy's keepers of the flame.

DEMOCRACY AND EDUCATION

In 1918, Mary Parker Follett, a social reformer of the progressive era, wrote that the preparation for the

> new democracy must be from the cradle—through nursery, school and play, and on and on through every activity of our life. Citizenship is not to be learned in good government classes or current events courses or lessons in civics. It is to be acquired only through those modes of living and acting which shall teach us how to grow the social consciousness. This should be the object of all day school education, of all night school education, of all our supervised recreation, of all our family life, of our club life, of our civic life. (p. 363)

What I think Follett is describing is the work of teachers in our public schools, who are also engaged in an active civic life. Acquiring habits of democratic living is a continuing process, begun in our early years learning how to be with one another. Teachers are in a position to foster young people to "grow the social consciousness" necessary for the continuation of a democratic society, with full participation of its citizens in public life. However, as Follett warns, such a social consciousness cannot be trained, dictated, or taught in lessons. Rather, this social consciousness must be learned through daily life with others, such as in a school.

John Dewey (1916/1944), social philosopher and educational reformer of the progressive, argued for a rich understanding of democracy when he stated,

> A democracy is more than a form of government; it is primarily a mode of associated living, of conjoint communicated experience. The extension in space of the number of individuals who participate in an interest so that each has to refer his own action to that of others, and to consider the action of others to give point and direction to his own, is equivalent to the breaking down of barriers of class, race, and national territory which kept men from perceiving the full import of their activity. (p. 87)

Dewey reminds us that democracy is far more than casting a vote, or being able to live wherever one can afford to, or all the other actions we take for granted today. He reminds us that we, the public, constitute democracy through our associations, from our responses to one another, and for a commitment to equity, such that barriers are diminished that would hinder our speech and activity. Yet, are we paying attention to how we are to constitute this democracy, this mode of associated living?

Walter Parker (2003) argues this point in *Teaching Democracy: Unity and Diversity in Public Life* when he points to our society's historical and current struggle to work with both Pluribus and Unum (manyness/oneness). Parker points to the work of democratic society to rework a robust political framework to sustain the Pluribus, a "strong cultural pluralism" necessary for a robust democracy (p. 29). He calls for a particular kind of education that fosters participation within Pluribus. This education cultivates among the young the process for becoming democratic citizens who re-envision public life, constituting it anew with each generation, through public participation, "community service, social action, and deliberation" (p. 30).

Building on Parker's robust view of a citizen who is actively engaged in public life, we can engender this vision through the people who cultivate the new citizens: teachers who are themselves conscious of living deliberately a public life of engagement. This chapter is about one program that is specifically and intentionally committed to fostering teachers who constitute this public life of political, intellectual, and social engagement in their classrooms.

TEACHER PREPARATION WITH A VIEW TOWARD ROBUST DEMOCRACY

In many teacher preparation programs today, the dominant model is based on turning out a "finished product" of a professional teacher, and, as such, assumes coursework in theory will be carried over into classroom. Little or no attention is paid to the social and political context of teacher education, save for one or two required foundations courses. Further, the social and political context is focused outward from the teacher, rather than inward.

New teachers are filled with the "what" and "how" of teaching, perhaps even the "why" of teaching. Who are we who call ourselves teachers? Who are the students we teach? What is the nature of how we relate? Such questions give voice to the complexities of teaching, in fact, to new ways of conceptualizing educational practice that honor new forms of human possibility. Reconceptualizing educational practice is the vision that Parker (2003) argues we need, that each generation learns to be politically engaged citizens. This is required if each generation is to reconstitute robust democracy. Therefore, teachers themselves must re-envision the world so that they teach their students for a world that does not exist: a world of justice, of peace, of such deep connectedness that it is unthinkable to hurt another. This is the Oneness/Manyness, the Unum and the Pluribus, Parker argues for, "the pluralist conception of democratic citizenship" (p. 30).

SERVICE LEARNING IN PARTNERSHIP SCHOOLS

During the three years of cohort experience in the CARE Program, CARE teachers engage in a variety of service-learning experiences. In at least two CARE courses, service learning is either a major part of the course or, in the case I will focus on, a particular type of service learning that I call "service-learning expeditions." In this sense, service learning is used as a pedagogical structure to foster student learning and development through active participation in carefully organized experiences that serve the community in some way. Because all service learning is specific to the contextual aspects of a community, CARE uses service-learning expeditions to introduce CARE students to unique situations that vary depending on the setting, fostering problem solving and negotiation within that specific context. In other words, like teachers, CARE students must learn to think on their feet, to make decisions in real time, increasing their understanding of the complexity of teaching (Zlotkowski, 1998).

Planning for Service Learning

There are multiple aims for a service-learning expedition beyond the stated objectives of the inquiry topic. Once subsidiary questions are posted and the most important ones agreed upon, the children self-select by their question choice. Focus groups form organically, and then CARE teachers pair up to become the "teachers" for a specific focus group. This group will remain together throughout the quarter, exploring the question and examining their research.

This is a reciprocal event that allows for a collaborative model so preservice teachers can work in focus groups with fourth and fifth graders. Working out a schedule of meeting times becomes a problem-solving activity in itself, and this schedule must be worked out with the children and CARE teachers together. In trying to find a time to meet during the week, students and CARE teachers have to plan and problem solve. This is how each begins to learn about the other. For CARE teachers, it means balancing between their other university coursework and the meeting times with their focus group in school. For the youngsters, this affords an opportunity to glimpse the work and schedule of university students. For our partnership schools in southeastern Ohio, students see the university as a place far away from their daily lives or aspirations. Getting to know their CARE teachers as people who often have different lives than they do allows the children to ask questions or simply share common stories with their CARE teachers. Wrestling with the joint schedules engages both children and CARE teachers with real work in real time. This is the prelude to the work that will be done all quarter—with CARE teachers learning to listen to the children, and the children learning how to state their ideas.

Students and Teachers in a Collaborative Model

In their junior year, CARE students take a course that provides them with an extended opportunity to bring together the theory and ideas from their CARE coursework, the field experiences they have had for six prior quarters working with CARE mentor teachers in their classrooms, and practice their pedagogy for themselves.

Mr. M and Ms. E, two teachers, teach fourth and fifth grade, respectively, in one of the CARE partnership schools. They both were involved in the conflict resolution program at their school, which they instituted shortly following September 11. In rural southeastern Ohio, the response to 9/11 by school districts was varied. In this school district, the teachers were asked not to discuss the events or watch the unfolding story on TV while in school. Yet, as teachers everywhere experienced, the repercussions of that tragedy infused discussion. Classroom doors could not shut out the world. But these teachers were not supposed to have discussions specifically about 9/11 in their classrooms.

When Mr. M, Ms. E, and I, the course instructor, met in the fall, we began our conversation about what they were noticing in their fourth and fifth graders. Mr. M noted that there seemed to be more conflict on the playground, or an increased need for peer negotiators in the conflict resolution program. Students seemed more aggressive and, added Ms. E, more apprehensive. As we talked, questions began to work their way into our discussion. We spoke of children's apprehension as of great importance, because this revealed some sense of insecurity, even in the safety of the teacher's classroom community. Our conversation kept coming back to the effects of violence, specifically the diminishment of human dignity.

At the end of that first meeting, we were close to a question that did not directly address 9/11 but had potential to address the resultant effects. The question was honed to "What should we do about violence?" Our overall aim was to invite the students to examine and analyze expressions of violence as the negation of human dignity. Because the district curriculum required state and United States history to be taught in these grades, we included historical expressions of violence as part of our inquiry. We wanted the students to discover how violence manifests itself during different time periods (looking first at state and national history since 1850, the time period to be addressed in the district curriculum). Our objectives included an exploration of how different people have experienced violence in the state and nation since 1850 (women, people of color, children, those of different ethnic/cultural/religious heritage, etc.).

At our first meeting at the start of spring quarter later that year, the CARE students (whom we call CARE teachers during the service-learning expedition), Mr. M's fourth grade, and Ms E's fifth grade class meet together. We had a few minutes to find places to sit in the small classroom, each constituent feeling excited and curious. Since fall quarter, the teachers had shared that in spring the children would be working with the CARE juniors on a project about violence. The teachers had asked the students to create a question/topic bulletin board where questions and ideas about violence could be posted as they came up in class or as someone thought about it. The CARE students were also alerted to the topic of violence. They knew that this quarter was devoted to praxis: putting theory and action together, and they were looking forward to it.

On the first day as we came together as an entire group, there was a buzz of excitement in the room. A CARE teacher stood up and led the group through some introductions before turning to the chart with "What should we do about violence?" written in bold letters at the top. "What other questions come to mind?" asked the CARE teacher. Hands were raised. Each comment or question was written on chart paper: What is violence? How does violence affect people? Why do people do violent things? Does violence happen to all of us? Is there a history of violence? Is violence the same, or are there different kinds of violence? What can we do about violence and whose problem is it? What happens when something violent happens to you? These questions provided an inquiry path for further exploration by participants.

Service-Learning Outcomes

Focus group projects that students developed and CARE teachers facilitated over the 10 weeks included a number of cooperative groups, which I will briefly sketch to give an idea of what resulted from the service-learning expedition. One group decided that it was important to begin with their peers. The fourth and fifth graders developed a school survey protocol, went into other classrooms to describe what they were studying, administered the survey, organized the data, tabulated the data, and created a chart/graph to find frequencies and the mean. Another group turned their attention to discovering what the perspective of the local community was and developed their own survey. Students went out into their community and asked people if they were willing to fill out their survey on violence. CARE students accompanied the children into the community during school hours. Surveys were organized and analyzed as above. This afforded the students the opportunity to compare and contrast their findings from two populations. Yet another group decided that school leaders' viewpoints were necessary. Therefore, students interviewed the building principal and the district superintendent on issues of violence in the school and district. Using state and district data reporting expulsions, detentions, and hearings, students compared the past three years of district reporting to discover that the schools in their district with a conflict resolution program had significantly lower expulsions, detentions, and hearings than other district schools. Since their school was one of the schools with such a program, the students became aware that active participation toward conflict resolution seems to have an effect on misbehaviors of students.

A cooperative group composed of fifth grade boys chose to investigate war as violence. As part of the district course of study, students were to focus on U.S. history. This focus group decided to look at WWII as an expression of violence. They developed a newscast that gave historical facts and chronologies of violence that led to the outbreak of war, and compared primary source documents of different reporting of the war. Additionally, they located community members who served in WWII and interviewed them for their perspectives.

A group of fifth grade girls decided to study violence as a form of oppression, investigating immigration, both voluntary and forced, and the attitudes of people toward new immigrants over time and history. They researched the biographies of different immigrants and then created and retold in their own words those life stories to illustrate the social, political, and, often, racial or gendered barriers that a person had to struggle against to be part of society. The students brought their biography to the primary grades and read them to the classes. A cooperative group of fourth graders chose to view violence as the loss of human dignity. This was an interesting group of youngsters who had some identified reading difficulties. They wanted to learn more about slavery and in their initial discussion hit upon the notion of human dignity as the absence of violence. The CARE students worked to adapt, assess, and craft the topic for maximum participation of all members of the group. The students went to the children's book section of the library and checked out books about life for Blacks during slavery. Each student chose a book to read aloud while other members of the group took notes. They then created a readers' theater from their readings. This readers' theater was presented to the school.

CONCLUSION

This is not all that was done during the work the CARE students did with their fourth and fifth graders. Nevertheless, the service-learning expedition, with focus group inquiry, gives a flavor of what was accomplished. A public presentation to the school and community was done the last week of school, where each focus group shared with the audience the understandings they acquired in their study of violence. The multiple forms and myriad faces of violence that the children discovered set the stage for audience discussion at the end. Schoolchildren, administrators, teachers, and community members (many of whom had been interviewed or were guest speakers) engaged in public deliberation of the social issue of violence. The topic once "owned" by the students became a public forum, owned now by those who participated in the deliberation. I posit that this was in itself a form of reconstituting our civic life together, in one small town, in a rural setting. We start where we are, and in so doing, bring the judgment and discrimination for how to fuel the flames with us where we go.

I view teachers as the keepers of the flame when they become active, engaged educators in democratic life. When associative living is placed at the center of our work as educators, teaching and learning look and feel different from the predominant utilitarian model imposed and propelled by privileging test scores over how we learn together to be one as part of many, Parker's (2003) Unum/Pluribus. Yet like the flame keeper, we cannot force or demand the flame into existence. We must coax and invite it, nourish it and tend to it time and again and again. Moreover, when we focus on the flame, we are also nourished by our work, our kinship with it and with the villagers it sustains. Our vision requires literate action: careful discrimination and judgment, for this is our work as keepers of the flame.

REFERENCES

Dewey, J. (1916/1944). *Democracy and education.* New York: New Press.
Follett, M. P. (1918). *Mary Parker Follett.* Retrieved July 15, 2004, from http://www.infed.org/thinkers/.
Palmer, P. J. (1999) *The courage to teach: Exploring the inner landscape of a teacher's life.* San Francisco: Jossey-Bass.
Parker, W. (2003). *Teaching democracy: Unity and diversity in public life.* New York: Teachers College Press.
Romano, R. (2000). *Forging an educative community: The wisdom of love, the power of understanding, and the terror of it all.* New York: Peter Lang Press.
Romano, R., & Glascock, C. (2002). *Hungry minds in hard times: Educating students of poverty for complexity.* New York: Peter Lang Press.
Zlotkowski, E. (Ed.). (1998). *Successful service learning programs: New models of excellence in higher education.* Bolton, MA: Anker.

6

Cultivating Democratic Learning Communities: Three Portraits of Roosevelt University's Department of Teacher Education

*Nona Burney, Andy Carter,
Elizabeth Meadows, and Tom Philion
Roosevelt University*

The story of the founding of Roosevelt University is truly inspiring. Appalled by a quota-based approach limiting the number of minorities to student admissions, a group of activist professors walked out of the old Chicago YMCA College in 1945 and started their own institution of higher learning. Initially named Jefferson College in honor of Thomas Jefferson, all qualified students were accepted for admission regardless of their race, creed, or national origin. When Franklin Delano Roosevelt died suddenly in August 1945, the college renamed itself, and shortly thereafter acquired a permanent home in the Auditorium Building, a Chicago landmark designed by Louis Sullivan and Dankmar Adler. With its identity and location firmly secured, the faculty at Roosevelt College dedicated themselves to developing innovative educational programming for first-generation college students and members of Chicago's thriving union workforce community.

Today, Roosevelt University continues to have one of the most socially diverse student bodies of any private university in the nation and retains its commitment to educate nontraditional students who work full time in order to support families and pay for their learning. The university's mission statement sets the goal of being a "national leader in educating socially conscious citizens" and notes that the university is "deeply rooted in practical scholarship and principles of social justice expressed as ethical awareness, leadership development, economic progress, and civic engagement." However, like most colleges and universities, Roosevelt has grown and changed over the last half century. Over 8,000 students are now enrolled in five colleges located on two campuses, in downtown Chicago and northwest suburban Schaumburg. Tuition is inexpensive compared to other private universities but is significantly higher than most public institutions. Most important, perhaps, Roosevelt competes energetically for top-notch, traditional-aged students, and is adding a new dormitory and other amenities to attract and retain them.

These changes and a recent National Council for Accreditation of Teacher Education (NCATE) review have led us to reflect carefully upon some important questions related to our mission and goals as teacher educators for the 21st century: What does it mean to educate "socially conscious citizens" in a metropolitan environment in which economic opportunity and access to higher education are largely taken for granted, but economic and social stratification remain enduring characteristics? Within this complex context, how do we sustain the activist commitment that has been a hallmark of Roosevelt University graduates? In particular, how do we foster this commitment and at the same time prepare prospective teachers to negotiate the many social, academic, and bureaucratic challenges that they can expect to face in contemporary K–12 schools and classrooms?

These questions, we believe, are very important to consider and discuss. Like other teacher educators across the United States, we are fully committed to the practice of reflective teaching. Given the important role that we play in shaping the learning and classroom experiences of America's youth, we believe that it is incumbent upon us to think deeply about the relationships and learning environments that we collaboratively build with teacher candidates, and to engage others in productive dialogue about our practices, assumptions, and aspirations. More provocatively, we believe that recent developments in teacher education—the No Child Left Behind Act, alternative certification programs, and high-stakes testing—are creating challenges and pressures like never before for teacher educators committed to democracy and social justice in teaching and learning. Rather than ignore or hide from these challenges and pressures, we have decided to interrogate our work, and to think critically about how we might respond productively to the dynamic social context in which we are situated. We hope that our insights are useful to others and catalyze meaningful learning and growth not only within our own teacher education department, but also within the broader context of state and national public policy decision making.

At the core of our effort to think critically about the role of democracy and social justice in teacher education are three succeeding "portraits" of current pedagogical practices. Taking our cue from Lawrence-Lightfoot and Davis's (1997) work with portraiture as a research method, each of our portraits represent different dimensions of teaching and learning and our department's identity as an emerging leader in educating socially conscious citizens. The first portrait in this chapter summarizes the Department of Teacher Education's efforts to orient cooperating teachers to the responsibility of guiding teacher candidates through the challenge of student teaching. The second portrait represents the instructional methodology and impact of a science methods course for elementary education majors. And the third portrait provides insight into a special cohort program within the elementary education program. As Paulo Freire (1984) has written, codifications such as these are important first steps toward *rewriting* the world. In the pages that follow, we invite you to join with us in reflecting carefully upon the social justice–oriented teacher education initiatives that we have undertaken, and the multiple ways in which we might refigure these initiatives in order to breathe new life into our goal of fostering democracy and equality in K–12 teacher education and in the world.

CULTIVATING DEMOCRATIC LEARNING COMMUNITIES

Before we present our portraits, we will describe some key elements of the context of our work and the conceptual framework that guides our efforts.

Roosevelt University's Department of Teacher Education consists of initial teacher preparation programs in Early Childhood, Elementary, Secondary, and Special Education. In addition, the department houses advanced certification and graduate degree programs in Teacher Leadership and Language and Literacy. Approximately 1,200 undergraduates and graduate students are currently enrolled in these programs. Although students are evenly distributed across both the Chicago and Schaumburg campuses, the Schaumburg campus is less socially diverse—although the surrounding area is growing rapidly in its diversity. In addition, Schaumburg students and the campus as a whole are perceived as having more resources for learning, whereas the

Chicago campus and students are perceived as having more challenges. Paradoxically, the Chicago campus is still seen as the flagship campus, and faculty are sometimes disproportionately assigned to teach at this site.

Despite the economic and social tensions encompassing these two campuses, faculty aim to achieve the vision outlined in the conceptual framework of Roosevelt University's College of Education. Revised in 1999 and 2000 in response to an NCATE review, the conceptual framework challenges faculty, students, staff, and all associated community members to "enlighten the human spirit through the cultivation of democratic learning communities."

Like most mission statements, this one is informed by different and sometimes conflicting discourses, assumptions, and aspirations. The phrase "enlighten the human spirit," for example, comes from a dedication speech by Eleanor Roosevelt (1945) at the time of the founding of the university. It embodies an overarching commitment to Enlightenment ideals about education and self-improvement, which posit that it is the responsibility of the educated and well-to-do to lead society to knowledge and self-discovery. The word "cultivation," on the other hand, emerged from faculty discussions during the recent NCATE review and indicates the prevailing orientation of today's College of Education faculty members toward postmodern, constructivist concepts of teaching and learning, which posit that knowledge is not so much "discovered" as it is shaped and co-created by equal contributors to a learning process.

Although the conflict here is a function largely of tradition and public relations (i.e., the desire to make a connection between Eleanor Roosevelt's founding statement and more current epistemological assumptions), other tensions are not so easily explained away, and indicate better the unresolved tensions embedded within the department's overarching commitment to the social justice mission of the university. Within the full-length version of the conceptual framework, John Dewey's (1916) ideas are cited repeatedly, especially his assertion that democracy is a multilayered process of social dialogue on problems of significance. However, the framework also acknowledges the existence and value of more nationalistic understandings of democracy ("allegiance to representative government"), as well as understandings representing a more radical or egalitarian epistemology ("To be genuine to Roosevelt University's charter and the College of Education's commitment to . . . democratic learning communities, we advocate for social equality with special attention to educational resources" [Roosevelt University, 1999]). In addition, the framework calls attention to the importance of passion, skill, and academic expertise in teaching. Since there is no single view of democracy or teaching that is true or absolute, the conceptual framework posits a range of possibilities and suggests that all are integral to the achievement of meaningful learning.

The conceptual framework informing the work of the Department of Teacher Education, then, provides not so much a definition of democratic learning communities as a description of paradoxical dispositions that contribute to their formation. Democratic learning communities result not only when people pay attention to multiple ways of perceiving and understanding, but also to traditional disciplines or pursuits of knowledge. They emerge not only when people empathize and inquire, but also take action in the world to ameliorate social injustices. They develop when individuals are given opportunities to speak and hear without a need to find consensus—although this goal is generally valued and understood. In the words of Peter Elbow (1986), the conceptual framework guiding the Department of Teacher Education "embraces contraries," or recognizes that dialectical or outside-the-box thinking and behavior are sometimes necessary for the achievement of democracy and education. Of course, faculty are free to ignore or overlook these paradoxical dispositions, but they are always called back to the importance of constructing in some manner productive educational responses to social, intellectual, and political inequalities. These responses might occur in a variety of venues and forms, but they must take place, and they need to be undertaken not only by faculty, but also by students, teachers in the schools, staff, and all others who participate in the process of preparing teachers at Roosevelt University.

NAILING JELL-O TO A TREE: A PORTRAIT OF COOPERATING TEACHERS ORIENTATION

It has been said that trying to teach a cooperating teacher to be a good cooperating teacher is like trying to nail Jell-O to a tree (Frerichs, 1997). The same might be said of a private university's teacher education program effectively collaborating with several urban and suburban schools and school districts in order to make manifest its conceptual framework and national teacher education standards. Roosevelt University's Department of Teacher Education has approached this quixotic challenge through the implementation of a Cooperating Teachers Orientation.

We began this project with "insider information" from members of the faculty of Jones College Preparatory High School, an academic magnet high school with which the College of Education (COE) has a professional development school relationship. A team of three veteran Chicago public school teachers, all of whom had served as cooperating teachers for RU teacher candidates, met with the college's liaison to the school and a COE administrator over three sessions during the summer of 2000 to revise the department's student teacher evaluation form. This dialogue enabled us to reduce a 60-item document to a "user-friendly" instrument half that size, containing helpful explanatory bullet points for each element.

We had already been admonished by the last team of NCATE examiners about not effectively including school personnel in the design and process of our field experiences. In fact, when Mari E. Koerner (1992) studied the journal entries of eight RU/COE cooperating teachers, she noted the recurring theme that

> All of the teachers thought the university would provide a clear and explicit outline of their job, and all were disappointed because the university not only failed to meet that expectation, but also often turned out to be a source of conflicting or unclear directives and unstated, unspecific goals. (p. 51)

In light of these comments, we decided to seek out our most trusted cooperating teachers for advice about how best to inform other cooperating teachers about the changes that we were making in the student teacher evaluation form and the conceptual framework that undergirds it. Their recommendations led to the pilot of a Cooperating Teachers Orientation: a two-hour overview of the student teaching process, roles, responsibilities, and evaluation that was first held in August 2000. Growing from 12 attendees for that first session to 48 at the spring 2003 event, we believe we are getting closer to "nailing Jell-O to a tree."

The organization of the spring 2003 orientation, and the feedback that we received on it, revealed some important connections to our conceptual framework and especially the notion of cultivating democratic learning communities. This orientation started with an exposition of our conceptual framework, not in the form of a lecture, but in the form of a PowerPoint presentation detailing the student teacher evaluation form and its complementary rubric. As in previous orientations, this approach proved advantageous because several of the participants were new to the role of cooperating teacher and needed specific information about their role and our expectations. In addition, this presentation grounded the conceptual framework in a highly purposeful context. One teacher commented, "This was very informative. This is my first experience as a cooperating teacher. I am looking forward to working with my student teacher and you." Another commented that the orientation was "well organized, and most important, questions were already thought of and answered for me. I love the addition of the rubric." It seems that we have created something like a shared dialogue on issues of significance, and addressed the "need to know" that Whaley and Wolfe (1984) describe as an untapped motivator of cooperating teachers: "Cooperating teachers are, first and foremost, *teachers*, and applying this role with student teachers is simply an extension of an original career concept and motivation" (p. 47).

Fully "knowing" requires reciprocity and inclusion in an open-ended conversation (Freire, 1984). Consequently, university-based faculty were, at times, on the receiving end of the information sharing that took place during the spring 2003 orientation. Veteran educators, now "retired" to the role of university supervisors, shared the podium with full-time faculty to explain the process, roles, and responsibilities of the student teacher, cooperating teacher, and university supervisor. In addition, the orientation's climax was a series of small group discussions, with questions and answers for and from university supervisors and other faculty. Half of the attendees in the spring 2003 orientation made specific comments about this activity as the best part of the workshop, reaffirming our belief that providing all members of our teacher education community with a voice in teaching produces quality learning and enhances motivation to achieve shared goals and objectives.

Although cooperating teachers appreciate opportunities to dialogue and share authority, they also appreciate the more practical or material benefits that flow from their participation in our orientations. Whether through "earning CPDU's" or "learning how to evaluate student teachers, how to assist them, the role of the university supervisor, and the philosophy and goals of this program," to quote participants, the orientations empower our school-based colleagues to grow as professionals as well as better assist our teacher candidates (Hamlin, 1997). Typically, the orientation is a Saturday morning affair, held simultaneously on RU's Chicago and Schaumburg campuses using video conferencing rooms. We provide a continental breakfast, a small honorarium, and all the materials that explain the processes and expectations of this capstone experience in our initial teacher preparation programs. The responses to our evaluation questions at the spring 2003 orientation give us some confidence that the materials and external incentives that we provide for participation are useful for creating an environment that is perceived as consistent with our mission to foster social justice.

Though we believe the orientation is a powerful initiative to fulfill our mission to cultivate democratic learning communities, we recognize that it has its limitations. Except for our PDS relationships, we are still very much at the mercy of schools and school districts when it comes to identifying cooperating teachers (Giebelhaus & Bowman, 2002). They have the exclusive option to accept our teacher candidates as student teachers and to choose the respective cooperating teachers, which sometimes leads to relationships and student teaching experiences that are far from optimal. We also remain aware that our Saturday morning overview is not the equivalent of the seminars, courses, or self-study modules that have been employed or recommended (Frerichs, 1997; Giebelhaus & Bowman, 2002; Koerner, 1992). As a department, we still have a long way to go to achieve the long-term, systematic immersion in democracy and learning that is envisioned in our conceptual framework.

However, as we continue to move along the road toward democracy, social justice, and program improvement, we will continue to seek out the expertise of our "insiders"—our colleagues in professional development schools and our best cooperating teachers. Engaging this more broadly defined teacher education community, which includes school-based teacher educators, is the primary way by which we will continue to enact the foundational coda of our conceptual framework: "Enlightening the human spirit through the cultivation of democratic learning communities."

TEACHER DISPOSITIONS: A PORTRAIT OF MULTIPLE PERSPECTIVES IN A SCIENCE METHODS COURSE

As stated earlier, the sharing and interrogation of multiple perspectives is a fundamental principle of our conceptual framework. In line with this, students in my science methods class share and question their contrasting viewpoints with one another as they work together to investigate scientific phenomena and enhance their teaching skills and abilities.

My own commitment to the exploration of multiple perspectives is informed by several beliefs. First, I think that if teacher candidates practice listening to and valuing viewpoints different from their own, then they will be more open minded and welcoming of their future students' scientific observations and reasoning, thus helping nurture their own students' scientific abilities. Second, I know that when teacher candidates experience the benefits of sharing and discussing multiple viewpoints in their efforts to find answers to questions that they care about resolving, they become more enthusiastic about having their future students collaborate in ways that further scientific inquiry and the creation of knowledge. Third, I believe along with others that the pursuit of knowledge through science depends upon individuals in communities thinking for themselves about the world around them and communicating with one another to come up with explanations that are generally accepted. In science, one person can and often does see the world in a fresh way that meaningfully forwards others' understanding. An important goal of my teaching is nurturing people's scientific abilities so that they can persuade others while being open minded about others' contrasting views.

Activities that I use to create this collaborative environment for teaching and learning include growing plants, exploring how to build a sturdy, weight-bearing structure out of drinking straws, and experimenting with substances that do and do not dissolve. In the plant-growing activity, students choose from a variety of materials to formulate and enact an investigation into one or more questions that they find interesting. Materials include dry seeds, seeds soaked overnight, seeds soaked for fours days, three types of bean seeds, soil, pots with and without drainage, and large and small pots. Each group of three or four discusses the available options and, more important, which question(s) they want to explore. Some students' questions have been, "What happens if we try to grow plants in the dark and some in the light?" and "Do seeds need soil to grow into plants or can they grow in water only?" After tending their experiments for the week, students share their observations and interpretations in a class discussion. Often, more than one group has investigated similar questions. In discussions after a week's growing time, these groups compare what they find and what they think it means.

That these activities produce the dispositions described in our conceptual framework is borne out by what students say in the context of their learning in this course. Not long ago, a student described in her journal her reaction to an investigation into solubility:

> Today we did a very interesting experiment. We went to the lab and experimented on mixing and dissolving candy.... I never did any of this in grammar school or high school. I think it is important for children to be able to do these kinds of things in class. These experiments bring out their curiosity, and make them want to learn about science. It also brings about class discussions. Everyone has his or her own ideas and opinions, and everyone's are so different.

This student asserts that when a teacher engages students in scientific investigations that they find interesting, they want to share their "ideas and opinions." When their curiosity is piqued, students want to learn science. Furthermore, this student conveys the value she places on hearing others' varied perspectives and ways of thinking about the world of scientific phenomena. Hearing these multiple perspectives helped her learn more about science and how to teach it.

Another student shared a similar perspective after completing this course and her student teaching. She also added that science demonstration lessons in class gave her and her peers multiple perspectives about all the ways that a teacher can approach the teaching of science.

> I really liked doing everyone's experiments in their units, their projects, because that gave me a really broad idea of how things could be presented.... You modeled listening to everyone's opinions when ... each group was doing an experiment. You know, why they think that's happening, what did you do that's different from what they did ... it gave me a different perspective as a teacher in connecting science in my class.

This student emphasizes how much she learned from experiencing other students' science lessons and how these impacted her views on science instruction. She also says that the instructors' modeling of listening closely to and valuing everyone's opinions was a helpful way of looking at teaching science to K–8 students. These views are consistent with my underlying assumption that finding value in classmates' ideas helps preservice teachers see the importance of welcoming their future students' scientific reasoning. These students' comments demonstrate that they have cultivated the ability to listen closely to viewpoints that differ from their own and to value them as well. I believe that having these abilities and attitudes will allow them to listen closely to their students and to follow up on their ideas, in the process of helping their K–8 students take their own scientific thinking seriously.

Most people reason scientifically through experiences. For example, we figure out what worked well (or not so well) in a recipe or in an effort to repair a car. Students need to have their scientific thinking recognized and affirmed by their teachers in order to learn more science. By discussing their findings and interpretations with one another, students learn how to build convincing arguments about what happened and why. Further clarification of their arguments can occur as classmates ask them questions in a genuine effort to make sense of the same phenomena.

Embodied in the fundamental principle of sharing multiple perspectives in science education is the need for teachers to find out about their students' backgrounds in order to use their learning from outside of school as a foundation for their school learning of science. After reading a chapter from *Classroom Diversity* in which teachers write about how they respond to students' background knowledge and interests in ways that help students learn school science and create democratic communities, a student asked what the authors meant by students' "funds of knowledge" (McIntyre, Rosebery, & Gonzales, 2001). Although the following student responds with comments about the lack of flora that reveal her inexperience with inner-city environments, nonetheless, her comments powerfully illustrate that all learning needs to be connected to prior learning and knowledge.

> When teaching in the inner city, you are not talking about tress and leaves and everything else because there are not trees and leaves. Maybe you're talking about congestion and walking and . . . families living together in buildings. It's bringing lifestyles and interests inside and outside of the school back into the school so that they can relate to what you're trying to teach. So that the teacher can get what they [already] know. The teacher really understands. (p. 2)

This student describes how a teacher needs to learn about what interests a child and the experiences of that child in order to enrich and deepen the child's learning of science. She emphasizes the robust knowledge, "what they ... know," that all children have that begins and thrives in their home and community contexts. She states how important it is for teachers to recognize and build on a foundation of scientific knowledge in order to help students continue to learn science in and out of school. Her experience of this science methods course is in accord with our conceptual framework's commitment to "social justice and global responsibility," whereby it is of utmost importance to nurture the scientific abilities and understanding of all people.

I have learned from my preservice teachers how highly motivated they are to learn all that they can in order to help all of their future students learn science. As one student summed up, he wants to reach a student before she or he concludes that "science is not for them." These future teachers respond with a passion for bringing this equitable and democratic science learning into their future classrooms, and they raise this as a social justice issue. They emphasize the critical importance of allowing students to directly experience and think about the world for themselves, as in taking them outside to see the autumn leaves, rather than having them only read about them or listen to someone else's experiences. They understand in a powerful way that a teacher's acts of valuing the perceptions and thinking abilities of all children is fundamental to democratic learning because it affirms and nurtures every person's abilities to think for themselves. This kind of teaching supports students in trusting in their own perceptions, ideas, and reasoning and in listening to those of others. This is a core aspect of a democratic learning community. My students are committed to bringing the kind of collaborative and democratic science learning that they experience in this methods class to their K–8 students and wish that they could have experienced more of this in their own elementary school years.

DEMOCRATIC LEARNING COMMUNITIES IN META: A PORTRAIT OF FIELD-BASED PREPARATION

The Metropolitan Elementary Teachers Academy—better known as META—is a relatively new initiative that began in the spring of 1998 and was designed in close alignment with the COE's conceptual framework to meet current state and national standards for teacher preparation. A cohort program that leads to a master's degree in elementary education, one key aspect of META is that it places students in the field as soon as they enroll in the program, and they take courses that integrate content traditionally separated in teacher education courses (for example, reading and social studies methods courses). Because it is a cohort program, it provides unique opportunities for students to bond with one another and to develop as a community.

This section is based on an interview with two students, Janice and Susan, in their first year of teaching following graduation from this cohort program. The two major topics covered in the interview were the nature and significance of democratic learning communities within the META program and the impact of these communities on their work as teachers. During the interview, both Janice and Susan clearly articulated their belief that the relationships they formed with cohort members played a significant role in their development as teachers. They described the emergence of a learning community within their cohort that both enriched their learning as students and continues to impact their practice as teachers. One of the ways in which their experiences in META are most clearly reflected is in their use of morning meetings. Both teachers use these meetings to establish routines, social norms, and a sense of community and democratic participation within their classrooms—something that META itself strives for in its teacher education courses. As Susan noted, morning meetings are "a ritual. This is one thing that children need. They need routine in their lives. They need to know what's going on."

Although they come from different backgrounds (Janice lives in the northern suburbs of Chicago, while Susan lives on the South Side of Chicago), they share a common interest in working with inner-city children. In the fall of 2002, they were both assigned to second grade teaching positions at the Adams School, a small Chicago public school located on the South Side. I began the interview by asking them to consider their experiences in the META program and to discuss their perceptions of learning communities within their cohort. Janice responded first: "I think having a cohort . . . helped me personally to solidify my own teaching philosophy. We heard different viewpoints. . . . It helped me to grow. . . . It really solidified what I thought was important because I wasn't going to these classes in isolation." Susan agreed with Janice, adding, "There were so many different personalities but all of us felt free to express however we felt. I felt I could always express my feelings without feeling that I was going to be attacked, other than challenged in a good way."

When asked how these bonds had developed, Janice responded that even though the program had started in January, she felt that her cohort had already come together as a group by the end of February: "We got together in January and I think even by the time we left Dunbar that first time and that was only in February. I felt that we had already bonded and it was probably that [Dunbar] experience." I asked them to say more about their experiences at Dunbar, an inner-city public school on the South Side of Chicago where they spent five days during their first semester in the program. Susan observed, "It was a different environment than the majority of us had ever experienced. And I think that helped bring us together. You could see that some sort of transformation had occurred." Janice added that while they were at Dunbar "it was easy to move right into the discussion on it [Dunbar]. If you are not in the cohorts you go at different times, to different schools, and there is not a lot of common discussion."

Clearly, being a member of a cohort with whom one shares a variety of experiences over time contributes to the cultivation of democratic learning communities. On the one hand, this means the honest sharing of ideas and perceptions—even when they entail conflict. However, it also means the development of trust and seeing others as potential resources for learning. When asked about the effect of being a student in a cohort, Susan said, "I think it made me love school for the first time ever. I looked forward to class, to seeing everybody and to hearing about everyone's experiences." Janice added that she is "still getting strength" from relationships with cohort members because she knows that "there are people from my cohort who are going through the same thing that I'm going through." Janice also contrasted her experiences in META with other classes she has taken recently: "It [META] seemed to be more a part of my life than just taking another class. In other classes it is just a thing that I go to and I leave and it's over."

As students, Janice and Susan both felt a sense of democratic participation in META. They agreed that they were most aware of this at the beginning of each semester when there was a discussion and often revisions of META course syllabi based on student input. They also felt that during the semester, adjustments were made to course agendas based on student needs and interests. Susan observed, "I think it made me feel more powerful in that my opinions mattered and were valued, which I think was important for everybody, especially for people who are becoming teachers. . . . They should value what their students are thinking." Janice added, "It gave more meaning to what we were doing because I could see the point to it."

I asked Janice and Susan to reflect upon how their experiences in META have impacted their work as teachers—the ultimate goal of teacher education programs. Susan observed, "I think the cohort community that we established has made me want to establish that among my students because I've seen how much I learned when I felt such a part of the community." Janice added, "If I hadn't gone through META . . . I see myself being a much more traditional teacher, where it would be me in front of the class. . . . Because I experienced a difference in graduate school, I'm definitely trying those ideas with my kids."

Since both Janice and Susan mentioned their desire to establish learning communities within their classrooms, I asked them to describe how they were trying to do this. Susan responded, "I think where I started was trying to institute a morning meeting every day so that we would have something common to build on every day." Janice added that she also begins her day with a morning meeting and that she and Susan have worked together in planning and establishing protocols for these meetings. Janice felt that these morning meetings have played an important role in her class because they provide opportunities for discussing classroom rules and developing social norms such as turn taking, "so the kids understand and can share their opinions and they know they're valued and what they want to say matters." She added, "I do think that is very important. If you would go to my kids and ask them what they think, they would say, I have a voice in this classroom."

Both Janice and Susan have remained in close contact with their cohort. It was, in fact, a fellow cohort member who first encouraged them to apply for their positions at Adams. They agree that they are both still "getting strength" from their relationships with other cohort members who are also experiencing similar challenges as they begin careers in teaching. The ability of cohort programs to establish learning and support communities well beyond the duration of the program is one of the key benefits of this unique approach to teacher education. Another important benefit of the cohort model has been its capacity to foster a commitment to democratic participation while at the same time preparing META students to incorporate this principle into their practice as teachers.

DISCUSSION

The Roosevelt University teacher education "community" encompasses a diverse group of stakeholders—university-based teacher educators, school-based practitioners, teacher candidates, children, their parents, school and district administrators, representatives of state and national departments of education, and state legislators, to name a few. Our conceptual framework calls for nurturing and sustaining equitable dialogue among these constituencies for the generation and dissemination of knowledge that leads to actions for the ultimate benefit of children and their communities. These are the lessons that we have obtained from our writing of the above portraits of our conceptual framework in action.

Clearly, external incentives impact the development and sustenance of dialogical, democratic, learning communities. For example, since we know that professional development is a primary incentive for teachers in the field to work with our department, we can foresee in the future offering multiple possibilities for cooperating teachers and others in the field to enhance their skills and professional knowledge at the same time that they facilitate the development of our teacher candidates. We also might extend the offer of adjunct faculty status to those cooperating teachers who are clearly leaders in their field and who could contribute in more extensive ways to our teacher education programs. We already have models of this sort of collaborative arrangement with practicing teachers in some of our student teaching seminars and other aspects of our programs.

Paradoxically, time for open-ended conversation and in-depth collaborative inquiry also are vital to the achievement of democratic learning communities. Adding a laboratory section for the elementary science methods course, for example, would provide students an additional class each week in which to do direct scientific investigations and to talk more with one another about their ideas. This extension of time for collaborative inquiry would assist teacher candidates in experiencing the benefits of this kind of democratic science learning, further convincing them, we hope, of the importance of taking the time necessary to provide this science learning for their K–8 students. This added time could also give these future teachers more opportunities to attend to fundamental scientific concepts, which are the backbone of democracy, making efforts to achieve democracy authentic and viable.

Given the current shortage of qualified teachers and the growing number of teachers who leave the profession during their first three years of work, cohort programs also may be a valuable resource for the creation of democratic learning communities in urban schools. The early and extensive field-based experiences in META play an important role in the development of cohesive learning communities within cohorts. In turn, the emergence of these communities helps to enrich classroom learning, while at the same time providing a sense of connection and support among cohort members. It is important to note that this sense of connection and support has continued well beyond completion of the program, continuing to benefit cohort members as they begin their careers as teachers, and thereby contributing to teacher retention and teacher quality in urban schools.

These three insights and the time and effort that we have put into the construction of this essay remind us that the cultivation of democratic learning communities requires a good deal of energy, coordination, and creativity on the part of all participants. Integrating cohorts into traditional teacher education programs is not easy and poses numerous bureaucratic and structural obstacles. Correspondingly, involving cooperating teachers and other teachers in program development requires constant outreach, communication, and the acquisition of material resources to foster equity and collaboration. Even integrating labs and other opportunities for in-depth collaborative inquiry within method courses and teacher education programs requires that teacher educators play roles not normally conceived as integral to scholarly activity. Continued enactment of the kind of reciprocal, in-depth, and critical teaching and learning that we have highlighted here requires flexibility on the part of teachers and learners, and especially university administrators used to more individualistic approaches to teaching and learning, as well as approaches less driven by the needs of workplaces and civic communities.

CONCLUSION

As Joseph Harris (1989) has pointed out, the term "community" is often used to veil the stratifications and differences that characterize any given group of people or programs. Looking back at our portraits, we can see that we, too, have emphasized the positive and synergistic in our representation of our efforts to achieve our department's commitment to "democratic learning communities." As much as we would hope that unity and consensus exist among the various participants in our teacher education community, we must admit that we continually run up against several social tensions and barriers that undermine our best efforts. These tensions and barriers (suburban vs. urban, experienced vs. novice, university oriented vs. school oriented, etc.) limit students' capacity to benefit equally and universally from cohort structures. They limit the capacity of cooperating teachers to acquire internally persuasive insights, satisfactions, and rewards from orientations and other initiatives. They even limit science teacher candidates and teacher education faculty from finding agreement and perceiving the importance of questioning their assumptions about teaching and learning. One of the more pressing challenges that we face in our teacher education community is finding effective ways of breaking down race, gender, class, and ideological barriers to communication and learning such that all who participate in our community benefit in ways that are truly reciprocal and vision transforming.

Regardless of the challenges that we face, we share the historic commitment of our college and university to surmount these barriers and cultivate critical conversation and social action. As our portraiture writing demonstrates, and as the dialogue we have initiated with one another and our colleagues teaches, we have a long way to go in terms of achieving our vision. But we look forward to the journey and the opportunity to make the achievement of democracy and social justice a core characteristic of every educational setting in our nation.

REFERENCES

Dewey, J. (1916). *Democracy in education: An introduction to the philosophy of education.* New York: Macmillan.

Elbow, P. (1986). *Embracing contraries: Explorations in learning and teaching.* New York: Oxford University Press.

Freire, P. (1984). *Pedagogy of the oppressed.* New York: Continuum Publishing.

Frerichs, R. (Ed.). (1997). *The many roles of the cooperating teacher: An orientation program for new cooperating teachers.* Millersville, PA: Millersville University.

Ganser, T., & Wham, M. A. (1998). Voices of cooperating teachers: Professional contributions and personal satisfaction. *Teacher Education Quarterly, 25*(2), 43–52.

Giebelhaus, C. R., & Bowman, C. L. (2002). Teaching mentors: Is it worth the effort? *Journal of Educational Research, 95*(4), 246–254.

Hamlin, K. (1997). Partnerships that support the professional growth of supervising teachers. *Teacher Education Quarterly, 24*(1), 77–88.

Harris, J. (1989). The idea of community in the study of writing. *College Composition and Communication, 40*(1), 11–22.

Koerner, M. E. (1992). The cooperating teacher: An ambivalent participant in student teaching. *Journal of Teacher Education, 43*(1), 46–56.

Lawrence-Lightfoot, S., & Davis, J. (1997). *The art and science of portraiture.* San Francisco: Jossey-Bass.

McIntyre, E., Rosebery, A., & Gonzalez, N. (Eds.). (2001). *Classroom diversity.* Portsmouth, NH: Heinemann.

Roosevelt, E. (1945). Roosevelt College Founders Day Dinner Address. November 16, 1945.

Roosevelt University. (1999). Democratic participation in learning communities: An overview of the revised conceptual framework of the College of Education of Roosevelt University. Retrieved August 15, 2004, from http://www.roosevelt.edu/education/framework.htm

Whaley, C. R., & Wolfe, D. M. (1984). Creating incentives for cooperating teachers. *Journal of Teacher Education, 34*(4), 46–48.

7

Converging Voices: Teaching and Learning to Teach

Marguerite Sneed and Siri Voskuil
Alverno College

The use of reflection to guide continuing growth marks the field-based teacher preparation program at Alverno College. Reflection by faculty and by teacher candidates provides both the grounding and the impetus for ongoing improvement in courses and field experiences, thus allowing and inviting a condition that might best be termed "stability in motion." To create a rich portrait of the teacher preparation program at Alverno College, two sets of voices must be acknowledged—voices that represent different positions and perspectives yet reflect a common commitment to learner-centered teaching at the college and in the P–12 setting. As the voices of faculty and teacher candidates converge, a series of images takes shape, and soon one is presented with a true and complete picture of field-based teacher education at Alverno College. Within this portrait, the voice of the faculty is a communal one. It is portrayed as a single voice because it represents the collective work of the faculty in departmental meetings where considerations about program were undertaken in collaboration and where decisions were made through consensus. On the other hand, the candidate voices are individual and many, culled from teacher candidate self-assessments, written reflections, and presentations in courses and field seminars. Although names have been changed to preserve the privacy of the teacher candidates, these voices represent the actual commentary of Alverno teacher candidates who have shared their criticism as well as their affirmations, and thus have helped to shape and refine the program over time.

BACKDROP: ALVERNO'S EARLY REDESIGN

To fully appreciate the texture, the form, and the dimension of the teacher preparation program at Alverno College, one must first envision the "canvas" on which the portrait is painted. Since its founding in 1887, Alverno College, a small liberal arts college in Milwaukee, Wisconsin, has served women in its undergraduate program. In 1972, as was the case with many colleges in the United States at the time, Alverno College was at a crossroads (Alverno College, 1976). Faculty had to decide what needed to be accomplished in order for the college to survive and grow. Instead of choosing to redesign itself as a coeducational institution as most colleges had, the faculty decided instead to concentrate their efforts on redefining Alverno's baccalaureate degree in terms of eight abilities that women would need if they were to be successful in both their personal and their professional lives. Describing an ability as the integration of knowledge and skills, behaviors, values, attitudes, and self-perception, faculty in the various disciplines and professional programs then considered the abilities in relation to the candidates they were preparing to graduate. Communication, analysis, problem solving, valuing in decision making, social interaction, global perspective taking, effective citizenship, and aesthetic responsiveness composed the original eight abilities (Alverno College, 1976). Faculty agreed to direct their teaching toward and hold candidates accountable for these abilities (see "Appendix").

Faculty across the college in the 1970s believed that they must teach for the development of the Alverno abilities, not as a separate program or curriculum, but within the context of the academic disciplines and professional programs themselves. They believed that, in addition to acquiring knowledge, learning involved *doing*. Recognizing that candidates use knowledge as they think, make decisions, discover, interact, and create, faculty believed that learning would increase developmentally when candidates understood what they were supposed to learn. This intentionality on the part of faculty resulted in statements of explicit standards candidates were required to meet in relation to the designated abilities. These standards take the form of developmental criteria that define expected student performance at different levels. These criteria are applied consistently across disciplines and programs. For example, in the communication ability, criteria have been created that define effective writing, speaking, listening, and reading at four distinct levels. Because faculty also believed that the abilities could be made visible, they designed assessments to elicit behaviors from candidates that could demonstrate particular abilities. Learning was further strengthened through the feedback faculty gave on learners' strengths and needs and in candidates' own self-assessment of their performance (Alverno College, 1979).

The study and application of the Alverno abilities is an ever-evolving process (Mentkowski & Associates, 2000). Put into motion with the inception of the original abilities, this process is a deliberate commitment on the part of the college faculty to focus continuing and sustaining work on the abilities. When this work began and departments were seeking ways to develop curriculum and design assessments that would guide development in the abilities, faculty recognized the need to share ideas and understandings from their departmental work across the college. As a result, *ability departments* were created that were composed of faculty from various academic and professional departments and staff from various departments across the college, including the departments of academic affairs, research, and assessment (Alverno College, 1976). A coordinator for each ability group was selected to lead these meetings and to work with faculty in academic departments and professional programs. Friday afternoons were set aside as times for the ability groups to meet to discuss issues and plan further development of their respective ability. Changes to an ability or the descriptions of its developmental levels, clarification of the language of an ability, and planning for faculty development have been among the results of these ability groups' work.

Through these frequent meetings and continued attention across the college and within departments, the abilities have continued to *live* and affect the work of the college. From the original ability work, research led to faculty articulation of essential principles and performance assessment elements related to student learning (Loacker, Cromwell, & O'Brien, 1986). Emerging from this research was the understanding that if the learner is to benefit, self-assessment and feedback are critical components of performance assessment.

Developing the Education Abilities

As their work continued on the collegewide abilities, faculty began to realize the need to articulate the abilities as outcomes of each major. As a result, faculty in each department designed performance assessments in which students could demonstrate growth in the abilities within the context of the curriculum of that discipline. To begin this work in teacher preparation, an interdisciplinary study group, including faculty from the professional areas of education and nursing, was formed and were given the charge to investigate abilities that encompass the role of teacher. After several years of reading literature reviews on teacher *competencies*, separating the components of the teaching role from the competencies or abilities, they named, defined, and refined the abilities of teaching performance. Five professional teaching abilities were agreed upon to guide the program: conceptualization, diagnosis, coordination, communication, and integrative interaction (Diez, 1990). *Conceptualization* is the ability to integrate knowledge with education frameworks and a broadly based understanding of the liberal arts in order to plan and implement instruction. This ability is used as candidates plan lessons and units to meet current and future needs of students. *Diagnosis* is the ability to relate observed behaviors to relevant frameworks in order to determine and implement plans that will meet students' needs and lead them to the next level of development. It is the ability to analyze and solve problems, and it is used as candidates make judgments about student learning, evaluate student performance, and self-assess their own teaching performance. *Coordination* is the ability to manage resources effectively to support learning goals. This ability is used as the candidate identifies and allocates resources to answer the question "What is the best approach in this situation at this time?" *Communication* is the ability to use verbal, nonverbal, and media modes to establish the environment of the classroom and to structure and reinforce learning. Communication skills are a key factor in the abilities demonstrated by effective teachers. *Integrative interaction* is the ability to act with professional values as a situational decision maker, adapting to the changing needs in the environment in order to draw out students as learners. Integrative interaction is the ability in which we see all of the other abilities come together in action. Candidates use this complex ability when they direct learning by guiding student discussion, when they model learning by making explicit what they are doing, and when they encourage individual participation while effectively directing a group activity (Alverno College, 2003). These abilities continue to serve as the conceptual framework for the teacher preparation program at the college.

THE PORTRAIT: A PATTERN OF CONTINUOUS IMPROVEMENT

The education faculty of Alverno College is a diverse group of individuals who have come together with a shared vision and common goals. Committed to the development of an exemplary teacher preparation program, we knew that the identification of the teaching abilities was but a first stroke on our "canvas." We recognized the need to prioritize further work. In so doing, we determined that the first effort should be the redesign of the seminar component of the field experience. Based on the theoretical assumption that candidates learn best when knowledge and action are interrelated, field seminars were redesigned so that they were developmental in nature; for example, candidates in the first field experience seminars learned the "language" of the education abilities in relation to the collegewide abilities with which they already had experience. Logs were revised to make better use of their reflective nature through guiding candidates to *use* the abilities. Rather than merely asking candidates to describe an event in their field placement, they were directed to work with the abilities. For example, after a field visit, candidates might be asked to make connections between theory and application, thus demonstrating ability in conceptualization and diagnosis. Each field had at least 12 logs with each log focusing on one of the five abilities. Among the log foci were application of knowledge, appraisal of student attitudes, and reflection on teacher candidates' own participation in the field setting (Diez, 1990). Through reflection on their performance, skills, and attitudes, candidates learned to develop accurate self-assessment, recognizing strengths and needs themselves.

Building on the efforts of the early revisions made to the field seminar and accompanying logs, in the early 1990s we agreed that further improvements were needed to make both the seminar and the fieldwork more meaningful to teacher candidates, to provide further means of assessing candidates' development in the five education abilities, and to make the link between theoretical knowledge and practical application even stronger. To begin this effort, we discussed and agreed upon the expectations they had for candidate learning at each level of field experience; for example, teacher candidates in the first field experience were expected to plan two lessons and teach them to small groups of students, while in the fourth and final field experience, candidates planned and taught a minimum of eight lessons in whole-group settings. As our work progressed, we invited and encouraged candidates to share their perspectives and make recommendations for change.

> Diane: At first the logs were really helpful in getting me to think about what I was seeing in my field placements. The questions helped me focus on the teacher, the students, and my role as a field student. As I completed more of these logs, however, I began to wish there had been questions that made me "dig deeper." I was so happy when my field supervisor asked us in seminar to suggest the kinds of questions we think should be asked. As I became more of a "veteran" in responding to the log prompts, I wanted my voice to be heard and I felt that I had something to say.

A small group of faculty took the lead in redesigning the logs to reflect the changes in expectations we identified as well as candidate recommendations. Log revisions included the addition of readings and other support material to assist candidates in understanding particular areas of teaching and learning. Additionally, an area of emphasis was identified for each field experience to sustain and enhance the developmental and sequential nature of the program. For example, in the first field experience, the question "What is good teaching?" is investigated; in the second field experience, "How is literacy taught?" provides the focus of the course; the third field experience now concerns itself with questions of effective classroom management; and the final field experience requires candidates to put their prior learning into action as they teach integrated and cross-curricular lessons.

Rethinking Feedback

Another area of the field experience that has been addressed in recent years is the observation/feedback form used by the college supervisor to assess and give feedback to the candidates on their strengths and areas of need in an observed teaching performance. Previously, all four fields used the same feedback form. This form provided space for supervisors to describe candidate actions and provide comments along with a separate checklist based on the college's social interaction ability. Over time, it became evident that a "one-size-fits-all" mentality was not consistent with the developmental design of the field program.

Kristi: The feedback from my observation let me know that I did well. However, I needed to know more. The feedback from a previous semester also indicated that I had done well. What did this mean? How had I grown from one semester to the next? Had I grown at all? I needed more information.

Based on candidates' feedback and faculty discussion of expectations of candidate teaching performance at each level of field experience, a faculty group designed forms that reflected those expectations. While maintaining elements from the earlier social interaction instrument and space for supervisor observations and comments, the new forms also provide for feedback on actions, skills, and attitudes expected at that level of field experience.

Coming to Consensus on Lesson Planning

Lesson planning was another area that surfaced as a concern and demanded our attention. Frustration voiced by candidates and problems identified by faculty in our attempt to present a coherent and developmental approach to this vital teaching skill prompted a reconceptualization of this facet of the program as well.

Ebony: Just when I thought I had lesson planning "down," I would enroll in a class with a different professor and it seemed that I was starting all over again. I found myself having to relearn definitions and format so I could "march to the current drummer." It was frustrating because I never felt that I really learned the "right" way.

In response, we agreed that a common lesson plan format was necessary. We realized that even though fieldwork was developmental in nature, a lesson plan format could be universal. Currently, one lesson plan format is used in all courses and field experiences. Candidates are introduced to its components in the initial education course, and from there they develop their expertise in writing lesson plans as they progress through subsequent courses and fieldwork in which discrete components of the plan format are made the focus of course goals and objectives.

Considering Curricular Revisions

Once the abilities were defined and introduced to candidates as a way to guide their field experiences, and field experiences were reconceptualized to support candidate development, curriculum work began in earnest in the 1980s as we examined and redesigned courses in the program to provide systematic development of the knowledge, skills, and dispositions expected in the abilities. In addition to needing to continue the work begun by the interdisciplinary study group, another motivation arose for this program evaluation (Diez, 1990). In 1985, the Wisconsin Department of Public Instruction (DPI) made changes to the codes for teacher preparation and licensure. The INTASC Core Principles are used as the teacher standards in Wisconsin (Interstate New Teacher Assessment and Support Consortium, 1992). Major revisions included focus on knowledge, skills, and attitudes, the same aspects that the Alverno study group had identified.

In its continuing focus on the teacher preparation program, we began to investigate how well candidates were developing the abilities required of a beginning teacher through their education courses as well as field experiences. From that study, we learned that they needed additional means of assessing candidate development in the program and designed within-course and external assessments as means of designing more points at which candidates could develop abilities and through which we could track candidate development (Diez, 1990)

As with the field revisions, study of the entire educational program, courses, fieldwork, and assessments has continued. Most recently, again encouraged by Wisconsin DPI changes that included different licensure levels, we have made design changes. Among the common interests of DPI and Alverno's teacher preparation program, we have been investigating ways in which teacher candidates can exhibit dispositions of teaching and understand and show how their teaching impacts student learning

Defining the Initial Course

We have been researching and piloting various means for measuring evidence of teacher candidate quality. In their introduction to the teaching profession, all candidates in the program take an initial course that should help them to determine if teaching is for them. Through this initial course, candidates learn about the outcomes for the Education major—the five abilities upon which the Education Department's conceptual framework is built. With the adoption of state teacher standards, they also begin to consider teaching in terms of knowledge, performances, and dispositions. In redesigning this initial course, we agreed that knowledge as defined by the state standards has always been a strength of Alverno's education program, so we could now focus our efforts on candidates' teaching performance and its effects on student learning and the dispositions of teaching.

In the initial course, candidates participate in K–12 classrooms where they observe teachers and students in action and teach lessons themselves. Because this is the first formal experience in a classroom, candidates are introduced to lesson planning, including language and format as adopted by faculty for use in all fieldwork in the teacher preparation program. As a result, in the fieldwork component of the initial course, candidates are required to teach two lessons in which they are observed by the faculty supervisor. In the first teaching experience, the lesson plan emphasis is on procedures, as the candidates are asked to plan and direct an activity that engages a small group of students. The goal is to allow candidates to become comfortable in the classroom so they can begin to recognize their impact on student learning.

> Amanda: I was excited, instead of nervous, the first time that I was observed in my field this semester. I received the true teacher experience by coming up with the ideas to teach, creating my own lesson plan, carrying out the lesson. As I stood in front of the class, I felt comfortable and I knew that teaching was the right thing for me to do.

By the second lesson, candidates expand their work with lesson planning as they are required to plan instruction including teaching procedures, assessment, and consideration of alternative instructional planning for diverse learners. After every observation, candidates self-assess their planning, interactions, and intended outcomes to see how their performance should inform future practice.

> Tarita: I thought I could just walk into a classroom and teach. Despite what I had already learned at Alverno, I tried that and found it didn't work. I can see now why lesson planning is so important. Once I thought about what I was going to "do" in order to get my students to accomplish what I said they would "do," I began to write my lesson plans in a way that could make that happen.

Early in the course, candidates are introduced to the conceptual framework of the education department as well as the state teacher standards.

Both of these frameworks address knowledge, performances, and dispositions. Candidates become conversant with these abilities and standards separately and in relation to one another. Building on their own school experiences, candidates then share portraits of teachers who have had a positive impact on their learning and their lives. From these shared descriptions, candidates draw out those abilities that they agree are necessary for all teachers to possess. Finally, candidates are asked to link these identified abilities to the INTASC Core Principles.

In reflecting on their field experiences in this initial course, candidates demonstrate their growing understanding of all that is involved in teaching, especially their own teaching in relation to teacher dispositions. Examining teacher characteristics from the "inside out," candidates share insights with their peers and reflect candidly on their own professional growth as they construct beginning understandings of essential teaching dispositions.

The process includes a final project in which candidates defend their growth in essential teaching dispositions that they have identified for themselves. Through reflective logs written throughout the semester, a collage used to depict chosen dispositions, a written paper, and an oral presentation before their peers and a panel of education faculty, each candidate provides evidence of growth in the dispositions and defends his or her decision to pursue a career in teaching. While this process provides candidates with multiple opportunities to examine their own values and dispositions throughout the course, it also serves as a framework for ongoing reflection by candidates who continue in the program or as the impetus for others to choose a different career path.

> Susan: This assignment really forced me to sit down and dig deep within myself. I found it extremely hard to describe my thoughts and feelings at this point in my life. I guess the reason for this is because I was realizing things about myself and thinking about things that I had not taken the time to dwell on before. As a result of this course and this assignment, I have decided to discontinue my career as a college student for the time being. I am now embarking on a journey to discover who I really am and what my talents are. This does not mean that I cannot be a teacher. I am just not ready to make the decision at this time.
>
> Brenda: After the first day at my field this semester, I had this excited energy that lasted the rest of that day. I looked forward to going to my field

placement every week, which I perceived as a sign that I would not have to worry about loving what I do.

Autumn: Seeing how I affected the students and changed their levels of interest and knowledge is a reason that I like being in front of a class. Although I had planned to be a teacher before I took this class, going through this first field experience has solidified my desire to teach. Interacting with students, affecting their lives, and working with other teachers are reasons that I know I have made the right career choice.

Improving the Interview Assessment

In their next semester, in conjunction with their second field experience, all teacher candidates participate in an interview process in which they have an opportunity to discuss and reflect on their growth in relationship to the Wisconsin teacher standards and the education abilities. The interview previously asked candidates to share stories detailing their experience with children as a means of developing candidates' understanding of the five education abilities. With the adoption of state teacher standards—that is, INTASC Core Principles—we recognized the need to highlight the dimensions of knowledge, performance, and dispositions in the standards as well. As we conducted these interviews with the standards in mind, it became more and more obvious that, while candidates talked easily about knowledge and performance, they were less likely to discuss their attitudes and beliefs—dispositions. The interview protocol has now evolved to include prompts that lead candidates to reflect specifically on dispositions as evidence of their growth.

> Linda: It wasn't until my assessor asked me to talk about my work in relation to knowledge, performance, and dispositions that I began to understand that the lesson I had brought to share showed more about me as a teacher than simply my ability to plan a lesson. When I described how I had to change my plan to actually show students how to work together before they could continue with the assigned work, my assessor asked me, "What did that tell you about yourself as a teacher?" As we looked through the dispositions, I was able to identify those that addressed the ability of students to value and respect each other. Through this assessment, I realized how much more there was to teaching than just knowing the material.

Merging Fields and Methods

The third field experience builds upon the previous two in regard to lesson planning, ongoing reflection, and understanding the many roles of a teacher. As our portrait of an exemplary teacher education program was developing, we recognized the strength of a course in which pedagogy and field experience were combined. As a result, a conjoint course was developed that included both the middle school methods component and a middle-level field placement. Candidates taking this course learn about the middle school student, middle school structure, and middle school curriculum. Concurrently, they can compare what they are learning to the reality of the particular classroom to which they have been assigned.

In this field experience, candidates must teach three lessons as whole-group instruction. As we observed candidates teach and assisted them in assessing their performance, it became evident that classroom management needed to be a focus of the course.

> Martha: I was learning so much in my methods courses about curriculum, lesson planning, the organization and structure of schools, technology in the classroom, all about assessment (rubrics and criteria), yet I felt that there was one area that was never really a focus of our investigations and our studies. Everyone seemed to understand that discipline is effective when it is a central part of learning, but we always seemed to "skirt the issue" when the topic was introduced. I came to believe that discipline was just something that would "happen" or that it wouldn't be an issue if I were doing all of the other things correctly. Then I found myself in a middle school classroom as one of my field placements, and I soon realized that I could no longer "skirt the issue."

Candidates enrolled in this course are now introduced to classroom management theory and strategies that they can apply in practice. What emerged from this restructuring was the realization on the part of candidates that student learning was directly impacted by candidates' performances and dispositional behaviors; for example, creating a smoothly functioning learning community and taking responsibility for establishing a positive climate in the classroom. This realization is not serendipitous, but rather results from an intentional process where the candidates consider classroom management in planning lessons and then self-assess their teaching to identify both the instances of and opportunities for adjustments to improve the classroom environment. Faculty supervisors' feedback assists candidates in this process.

> Jesusita: When I read in the syllabus that I would have to videotape myself teaching a lesson with middle school students and focus on my classroom management, I knew I was in for a challenge. However, what an enlightening experience it was to be given an opportunity to see myself in action actually using strategies that I had learned. Even more sobering was being able to step back and see all of the places where I could have used discipline more effectively.

Re-examining the Portfolio Process

In addition to the field-based experiences, Alverno teacher candidates have multiple opportunities to experience various aspects of the role of a teacher; to refine their abilities in different subject areas, contexts, and modes of expression; and to reflect on their strengths and areas of development. One of these is a major out-of-class portfolio assessment preceding the student teaching semester. The purpose of the portfolio has historically been an opportunity for the candidate to demonstrate the five education abilities and to have a further experience of responding flexibly in an interview setting. With the adoption of the state teacher standards, we recognized a larger purpose for the portfolio. We understood the necessity to assist candidates in looking closely at the knowledge and performances and particularly at the dispositions required at this stage of their development. As we articulated stronger criteria reflecting both Alverno's education abilities and the state standards, dispositions were emphasized and expectations in all areas were made clearer to candidates.

Based on improved criteria and candidate and assessor feedback, we are now forced to rethink the interview component of the portfolio assessment process. Previously, the portfolio was reviewed by the candidate's college advisor before it was delivered to a K–12 practitioner who served as the candidate's primary assessor. The assessor then had an opportunity to review the portfolio material before meeting with the candidate to discuss its contents and the candidate's readiness for teaching. Based on the review and discussion, the assessor then made a recommendation as to whether the candidate should go on to student teaching. With the implementation of improved criteria, assessors now have more evidence on which to base their recommendation. However, we still note discrepancies in assessor judgment and feedback.

> Jodi: I was really sure my assessor didn't like me. She just tore apart my portfolio when we met, but then she recommended me for student teaching. Although I'm relieved that I will be able to student teach, I really would like to know what I did well that helped her make that recommendation.
>
> Toni: My assessor was really nice. He asked me to talk about my portfolio and my goals as a teacher. He recommended me, but I really didn't find out what he thought about my work or how he thought I could improve.
>
> Pua: I was nervous going into the portfolio interview because I had heard that my assessor was really tough. Sure enough, she had specific questions she had written out ahead of time. She asked me what I would do in particular classroom situations. Then she told me exactly what she saw as my strengths and also areas of need. That was so helpful to me.

To address issues of assessor judgment and feedback discrepancy, we plan to pilot a different interview format in which the candidate will be interviewed by a three-member panel consisting of a K–12 practitioner, a college faculty member representing the candidate's content teaching area, and an education faculty member other than the candidate's advisor. We believe that this will result in a more equitable and comprehensive assessment of the candidate's readiness for student teaching in terms of the abilities and the standards.

Looking Back to Move Ahead

Responding to the increased demands placed on us by state and national accreditation agencies, we recognized the need to hold preservice teachers as well as practicing teachers accountable for student gains. As a result, a project was developed through which candidates provided evidence of their effectiveness as beginning teachers. In this project, candidates were guided to plan for, teach, assess, give feedback to, evaluate lessons, and continue planning for students in their student teaching setting. In addition to these components, candidates were directed to provide examples of student work at least twice in each student teaching placement, reflecting in writing on each. Although we had designed the project as a means for candidates to identify learner outcomes, designate criteria to meet those outcomes, and use teacher feedback and candidate self-assessment as powerful tools for reflection, some candidates regarded this as "just one more thing to do." As a result, the benefit of the project was lost for them and candidate performance overall was sporadic.

Based upon candidate resistance and the unevenness of project performance, we reassessed our expectations. After several attempts to "fix" the problem by making adjustments to outcomes and clarifying directions, we realized that it was the process rather than the product that needed to be reconceptualized. We were well aware that Alverno's teacher candidates had been educated in a developmental program in which they had learned to define context setting, to recognize different candidate abilities, to plan lessons that meet the needs of students, and to identify and apply different instructional and assessment strategies, all requirements of this project. Therefore, we agreed that any adjustment to the expectations would have compromised the program. Instead, we concluded that candidates needed to have practice in accomplishing the individual components of the project before being asked to integrate them as a single project in their student teaching experience.

In looking for a logical way to provide candidates the needed practice, we began to look backward to the fourth and final field experience. In this field, candidates plan and teach eight lessons as whole-group instruction, applying all of the tenets of effective lesson planning and teaching that they have learned and practiced in previous courses and fieldwork. Since this is the only field placement that guarantees candidates the opportunity to teach and assess on a weekly basis, it was the perfect vehicle for giving them the prerequisite experience needed for the student teaching project. Now, rather than candidates tackling the whole project at once, they accomplish each component of the project in a discrete phase, and thus understand its developmental and sequential nature. The decision to introduce this project in the fourth field placement and in this manner was validated this past semester when faculty supervisors found that candidates who had had this final field experience reported being more comfortable and confident in completing the project as student teachers. Furthermore, we noted improvements in the quality of the completed projects and in the level of candidate reflection and self-assessment.

> Mary: Having had the practice of completing each phase of the project separately during my final field placement really prepared me for assessing my impact on learners in a formal way during student teaching. In the field seminar, we went through each part of the project and talked about its importance. That really set the tone for looking at the student—all the factors that affect student learning. It forced me to look at the whole picture. Completing the whole project during student teaching helped me to move beyond being a field student to think as the teacher.

Looking Ahead to Move Forward

We are now in the process of looking across the program to determine where and how continued work in the field-based teacher preparation program should be implemented, reinforced, or highlighted. As we continue to apply the defining strokes of our portrait of teacher preparation, new questions emerge from the convergence of voices, and these voices continue to be acknowledged and appreciated. How should dispositions be addressed across courses and fieldwork so candidates continue to develop dispositions that will support their teaching lives? How can classroom management be addressed more directly earlier in the program so candidates preparing to teach in middle school will have a firm grounding in classroom management and be more prepared for the unique issues they confront when working with young adolescents? These and other questions form the basis for further reflection on the part of both faculty and teacher candidates, and it is this reflection that insures the continual refinement of what is already a rich portrait of field-based teacher preparation at Alverno College.

> Melissa: As I reflect on what it means to be a teacher, I think about the kind of teacher I see myself becoming. The field experiences that I have had at Alverno have given me hands-on training with what teaching in a classroom setting entails. I have been able to identify and learn from mistakes made in planning and teaching lessons. If I had to identify the most powerful aspect about my teacher preparation program at Alverno, I would have to say it has been my field experiences—the way they are designed to support my

growth as a teacher, the variety of teachers and classrooms I observed, and especially the many teaching opportunities I was provided. What would I want to see changed? Let me think. . . .

APPENDIX

Communication

- Making connections that create meaning between oneself and one's audience.
- Learning to speak, read, write, and listen effectively, using graphics, electronic media, computers, and quantified data.

Analysis

- Thinking clearly and critically
- Integrating experience, reason, and learning into considered judgment

Problem Solving

- Defining, articulating, and taking effective action
- Using discipline-based problem-solving methods
- Collaborating with others

Valuing in Decision Making

- Recognizing different value systems, including one's own
- Recognizing the moral dimensions of one's decisions and accepting responsibility for consequences of one's actions

Social Interaction

- Getting things done in teams, committees, and task forces
- Collaborating to learn

Effective Citizenship

- Becoming involved and responsible in the community
- Acting with an informed awareness of contemporary issues

Global Perspective Taking

- Knowing how to think about and act on global concerns
- Analyzing, articulating, and understanding the interconnectedness of global and local concerns

Aesthetic Responsiveness

- Engaging various art forms in contexts from which they emerge
- Taking and defending positions regarding meaning and value of artistic expressions

REFERENCES

Alverno College. (1976, revised 1985, 1992). *Liberal learning at Alverno College*. Milwaukee, WI: Alverno College Institute.

Alverno College. (1979, revised 1985, 1994). *Student assessment-as-learning at Alverno College*. Milwaukee, WI: Alverno College Institute.

Alverno College. (2003). *Handbook for education students part II: Conceptual frameworks*. Milwaukee, WI: Alverno College Institute.

Diez, M. (1990). A thrust from within: Reconceptualizing teacher education at Alverno College. *Peabody Journal of Education, 65*(2), 4–18.

Interstate New Teacher Assessment and Support Consortium (INTASC). (1992). *Model standards for beginning teacher licensing and development: A resource for state dialogue*. Washington, DC: Council of Chief State School Officers.

Loacker, G., Cromwell, L., & O'Brien, K. (1986). Assessment in higher education: To serve the learners. In C. Adelman (Ed.), *Assessment in higher education: Issues and contexts* (Report No. OR86-301, pp. 47–62). Washington, DC: American Association of Colleges of Teacher Education.

Mentkowski, M., & Associates (2000). *Learning that lasts: Integrating learning development, and performance in college and beyond*. San Francisco: Jossey-Bass.

IV

LEARNING TO TEACH THROUGH SOCIAL CONSCIOUSNESS

> There is no true teaching preparation possible separated from a critical attitude that spurs ingenuous curiosity to become epistemological curiosity, together with a recognition of the value of emotions, sensibility, affectivity, and intuition. To know is not simply to intuit or to have a hunch, though there is an intimate connection between them. We must build on our intuitions and submit them to methodical and rigorous analysis so that our curiosity becomes epistemological.
>
> (Freire, 1998, p. 48)

The sense one has of being a "self" is partly one's sense of who one is in relation to others. This is one's identity relationship to the world within which one lives and works. Teacher preparation is, in part, identity formation as a teacher. To become a teacher, one must become self-aware, must recognize the "self." To become a teacher also requires that one develop a social consciousness, an awareness of the lives of those around her or him and how the conditions of those lives affect the individual and the larger society as a whole.

Teachers who fist enter the classroom are confronted with the cultural patterns of the school, imprinted with the dominant ideologies, unbalanced by the asymmetrical nature of power and knowledge, and challenged by the issues of difference, equity, and social justice. Teachers who first enter the classroom need to know, as Cochran-Smith (1991) suggests, "that they have a responsibility to reform, not just replicate, standard school practices" (p. 280). Teacher educators, in working to foster a social consciousness, must recognize that learning to teach "occurs within a particular historical and social moment and is embedded within nested layers of context, including social and academic structures of the classroom; the history and norms of teaching and learning at the school; and the attitudes, values, beliefs, and language uses of the community and its web of historical, political, and social relationships to the school" (Cochran-Smith, 1995, p. 504).

Teaching for social consciousness, equipping oneself as a socially conscious teacher, requires a recognition that to talk of respect for students, we must take into "consideration the conditions in which they are living and the importance of all the knowledge derived from life experience, which they bring with them to school" (Freire, 1998, p. 62), never underestimating this knowledge. As teachers, we must be "constantly 'reading' the world inhabited by [children] . . . that world that is their immediate context and the wider world of which they are a part" (Freire, 1998, p. 76).

Teacher preparation works to shape the individual's identity as a teacher, and it works to enable the individual to discover that one's own authentic voice is linked with the discovery and articulation of one's own identity (Taylor, 1991), the development of a sense of efficacy, of personal dignity and worth. In practical terms, this means that learning to teach occurs through the development of social consciousness and involves the provision of multiple opportunities for students of the teaching profession to practice that which it is hoped they will learn, and the encouragement and support, on the part of teacher educators, necessary for future teachers to direct their own learning and growth.

Learning to teach through social consciousness means understanding the importance of fostering a means of critical analysis of situationality, of what Freire (1973) refers to as *conscientização*:

> People, as beings "in a situation," find themselves rooted in temporal-spatial conditions which mark them and which they also mark. They will tend to reflect on their own "situationality" to the extent they are challenged to act upon it. Human beings *are* because they *are* in a situation. And they *will be more* the more they not only critically reflect upon their existence but critically act upon it. (p. 90, emphasis in original)

This *conscientizacão*, critical social consciousness, is the deepening attitude of awareness in which one acquires the ability to intervene because of one's historical awareness. It is through reflection and historical awareness that reality is unveiled. One's self-awareness is only one dimension of learning to teach; one must also embrace a social consciousness that is motivated by a critical concern for the conditions of "others." One's situatedness shapes one's identity, just as "others'" situatedness shapes the identity of "others." Understanding the situatedness of "others" is critical to understanding the conditions in which "others" find themselves, and equally important to understanding how such conditions shape the identity of "others."

The authors in this part share portraits of teacher preparation concerned with the pluralistic nature of society and the rapidly shifting demographic profile of society. Learning to teach in a changing America demands that teachers understand and "work both *within* and *around* the culture of teaching and the politics of schooling" in diverse settings (Cochran-Smith, 1991, p. 284). Teaching through social consciousness speaks to the concern for all children and the importance of being culturally responsive to cultural diversity while also being sensitive to social adversity—seeing teaching as a fundamental social project to help students develop a deep and abiding belief in the future possibilities, and overcome economic, political, and social injustices.

REFERENCES

Cochran-Smith, M. (1991). Learning to teach against the grain. *Harvard Education Review*, *61*(3), 279–310.

Cochran-Smith, M. (1995). Color blindness and basket making are not the answers: Confronting the dilemmas of race, culture, and language diversity in teacher education. *American Educational Research Journal*, *32*(3), 493–522.

Freire, P. (1973). *Pedagogy of the oppressed*. New York: Seabury Press.

Freire, P. (1998). *Pedagogy of freedom: Ethics, democracy, and civic courage*. Lanham, MD: Rowman & Littlefield.

Taylor, C. (1991). *Sources of self*. Cambridge, MA: Harvard University Press.

8

A Portrait in Time and Context: The TE Collaborative 20% Internship Program

*Nancy Lourié Markowitz, Patricia Swanson,
Andrea Whittaker, and Morva McDonald
San José State University*

The purpose of this chapter is to describe the evolution of the Teacher Education (TE) Collaborative 20% Internship Program, a field-based, K–8, multiple-subject teacher preparation program in California. In this unique two-year program, candidates completed carefully sequenced graduate coursework while participating in a 20% internship their first year, and a full internship with credit toward tenure their second year. This is a story of an alternative program born of inspiration when extramural money was available, which responded to external influences from an ever-changing regional and state context and survived even when the funding did not.

Our portrait provides a picture of a program defined and renegotiated in relation to a rapidly changing political and economic context. Three essential themes shape this story—collaboration, commitment to equity, and resiliency. The program's development demonstrates the power of collaboration between school districts and the university—an illustration of how mutually shared goals and trust led to innovative and powerful teacher preparation and sustained change. It is a story of a school/university partnership's evolving commitment to equity as manifested first by program design and later through course content. Finally, it is a portrait of resiliency, a description of a program conceived in the context of economic surplus and sustained amid political and economic turmoil. We use these organizing themes—collaboration, equity, and resiliency—to tell the story of the TE Collaborative.

1996–1997: PROGRAM DEVELOPMENT: THE POWER OF COLLABORATION

In the fall of 1996, the state implemented a plan for class-size reduction in kindergarten through third grade, resulting in a statewide teacher shortage. As school districts scrambled to find space for classrooms and competent teachers to work with students, universities worked to develop new programs to put well-qualified teachers into classrooms quickly. For the district and university partners that would form the TE Collaborative, the emphasis would be on "highly qualified" rather than "quickly."

The state was also concerned with teacher preparation and offered a round of grants, known as the Comprehensive Teacher Education Institute Grants. These grants were designed to strengthen the tenuous links between university preservice education and district induction programs through university/district partnerships. In California, credential candidates completed a year of coursework and field experience beyond the baccalaureate degree in order to earn a teaching credential. Often, links between coursework and field experience were weak and communication between the districts and universities tenuous. Universities had no formal role in the induction of newly hired teachers, and in most cases, districts had little voice in preservice coursework. The Comprehensive Teacher Education Institute Grants were designed to address this situation.

In 1995, San José State University joined in partnership with two metropolitan school districts, Oak Grove and Campbell Union, and was awarded one of the state's Comprehensive Teacher Education Institute Grants. Oak Grove School District, situated in south San José, included sixteen elementary schools and three middle schools with a student population of 31 percent White, 36 percent Hispanic, 18 percent Asian, and 6 percent African American. Campbell Union, west of San José, included eight elementary schools and three middle schools, with a population of 44 percent White, 34 percent Hispanic, 13 percent Asian, and 5 percent African American students. These two districts faced the challenges of educating the culturally and linguistically diverse student population characteristic of schools in California today.

A small cadre of district and university leaders began a series of meetings around the grant director's kitchen table. These conversations, informal and unpaid, laid the philosophical groundwork for the university/district partnership. At the core of our belief system was the concept that the university and the districts could do a better job preparing and supporting new teachers by working together than they could by working apart. It was an amazingly energizing idea to consider what our ideal teacher preparation program might look like and to design it. So energizing was this notion that six representatives from the two participating districts (two district assistant superintendents and four teachers) and six faculty from the Department of Elementary Education at San José State University met twice a month from November 1996 through March 1997. The compensation provided was a free dinner and the opportunity to discuss issues of teacher education and professional development with other respected professionals.

Our conversation began with districts' needs. In the midst of a teacher shortage, the districts needed an ongoing pipeline of highly qualified beginning teachers. In addition, because the districts were hiring so many new teachers (approximately 90 to 100 each year), they needed a large cadre of new teacher support providers to coach these first- and second-year professionals. This coaching was mandated through the state's Beginning Teacher Support Program (BTSA). BTSA support providers were expected to observe beginning teachers once each week, provide them with feedback, and conduct formal coaching cycles. The districts were in a quandary because they could not fund enough full-time support providers, nor did they want to release classroom teachers part time, as this undoubtedly compromised the quality of that teacher's instructional program. Finally, the districts let the university faculty know that they were not happy with the preparation of candidates in the area of literacy instruction. They wanted to establish greater consistency between reading and language arts courses and what the new teachers were expected to do in their district classrooms.

Those of us from the university knew our district colleagues would keep us grounded in the realities of classroom teaching. We respected the expertise around the table and we knew that our candidates often complained they were unable to use the strategies we taught in their classrooms. Furthermore, we wanted to strengthen the connection between preservice coursework and the first years of teaching. From these kitchen table conversations, the Teacher Education Collaborative and the 20% Internship were born.

We discussed our assumptions about best practices in teacher preparation. First, we believed that the university and districts could prepare and support beginning teachers by working together better than by working apart. Each partner would have a voice in the selection of interns and the classroom teachers with whom they were placed. Inspired by recent work on the importance of teacher education (Darling-Hammond, 2000; Darling Hammond & McLaughlin, 1999), we believed lengthening the preparation period and carefully aligning coursework and field experiences would make our candidates better prepared and more likely to stay in the profession. We also agreed that, unlike traditional programs in California that required two student teaching placements at different grade levels, we wanted our partial interns to work in one classroom with a highly skilled teacher throughout the first year. They would see the complete school year—from classroom setup through the last day of school—and watch children develop over time. Further, we agreed that we needed to create alignment between our preservice assessment practices and those used by the districts with beginning teachers. We believed that this would decrease the amount of stress experienced by the first-year teachers. Finally, we agreed that maintaining individual relationships was key to our partnership. Providing explicit ways to foster and support human relationships within the Collaborative was essential. Individuals participating in this difficult and time-consuming work were not interchangeable parts.

The TE Collaborative hoped to effect change in the culture of both the districts and the university. In this program, interns, participating teachers, administrators, and faculty would act as a community of learners, each engaged in inquiry into practice, development of teacher leadership skills, and always focused on increasing student achievement. From these broad goals, the 20% Internship program emerged.

Unlike most internship programs in which beginning teachers have the responsibility for full-time teaching in addition to university coursework, we wanted a gradual induction "partial internship" model. Throughout their first year in the program, our candidates would complete coursework while working part time in the classroom of a highly skilled teacher. Their second year, they would become full-time teachers and continue to receive classroom support through *both* the district and the university, while completing their remaining university coursework. This would lengthen the teacher preparation period and allow beginning teachers time to reflect deeply upon practice. Coursework and field experience would be ongoing and closely linked. Finally, we at the university could support our candidates during their first full-time year of teaching.

A DESCRIPTION OF THE 20% PARTIAL INTERNSHIP PROGRAM

The two-year partial internship program that we conceived required new roles and greatly enhanced communication between the districts and the university. The first role created was that of the faculty associate. We wanted to increase the professional stature of teachers who mentored the partial interns throughout their first year in the program. We made the selection process for becoming a faculty associate rigorous and collaborative to heighten the status of the position. Interested teachers completed a questionnaire and self-assessed themselves using rubrics developed by the Santa Cruz New Teacher Project for their Beginning Teacher Support and Assessment Program (University of California, Santa Cruz, 1997). Site administrators rated the teacher applicants using the same rubric and were asked to supply a letter of support. The applicants then participated in an interview that included both district and university personnel.

Faculty associates shared evaluative power with university supervisors and provided continuous input into the program content and structure. While the intern taught solo one full day each week, the faculty associate mentored one to two beginning teachers (depending on the agreement the district made with the teacher unions) or engaged in other teacher leadership activities. Faculty associates worked with the interns from the week before school began to the end of the school year. It was in a sense a brief, but intense, marriage. Faculty associates were paid an enhanced yearly stipend of between $1,500 and $2,500, again depending on district policy. The stipends were externally funded by the Comprehensive Teacher Education Institute Grant.

Faculty associates were supported in their work with the interns through coaching seminars. Initially these seminars were conducted within each district, but after two years, biweekly seminars were held for all participating faculty associates together. The faculty associate seminars were two hours long and included lunch. Interns covered the classes for the duration of the seminars. University and district personnel teams taught both the intern field seminar and the faculty associate seminar in order to ensure strong field/university communication.

As part of our ongoing inquiry into practice, faculty associates completed end-of-year surveys reflecting on their role. Their responses gave testimony to the importance of the faculty associate role in our partnership. Faculty associates valued working with beginning teachers as a means of examining their own practice and developing teacher leadership skills. They valued working in a community of learners with other faculty associates to broaden their knowledge base of best practices. And finally, they valued access to additional resources (e.g., workshops, training) that being part of the partnership provided. A personal account from one faculty associate highlighted many of these issues:

> As a faculty associate and new teacher support provider I feel a huge responsibility. In the past student teachers have come and gone. . . . I felt that the ultimate success of student teachers was the responsibility of the university faculty who evaluated them and taught their classes. . . . [The TE Collaborative] has changed all that. To begin with, their classes are taught by a combination of university and district personnel, just one way in which the lines begin to blur. I am critically involved in the evaluation process and in this way share with the university and district instructors a view of what needs to be taught and what skills need to be [demonstrated] to successfully complete the program. . . . While I am empowered by this new model of collaboration, I am also held more accountable, and I think that this is where much of the intensity of this program comes from. Beyond what I can define with words is a visceral feeling on the part of all the faculty associates I have spoken to that something important is happening here . . . in the way we are seen and treated, something different in the way interns are learning about teaching and something different in the quality of instruction students get because of the interplay of teacher and intern teacher.

In addition to the faculty associate position, we created the role of district liaison and hired a teacher leader from each district full time (grant supported) to serve in the position. The district liaisons served as boundary spanners between the university and the districts, recruiting new faculty associates, coteaching the intern field seminars and faculty associate coaching seminars, and representing the districts at university faculty meetings.

With these new roles established, the structure of our program took shape. The interns spent two years in the program, one year as a 20% intern, and the second year as a full-time teacher in the same district. During the first "20%" year, the interns worked three days each week in a classroom of their faculty associate and attended university courses the other two days. Starting in October, one of the three days in the classroom the intern taught the class independently while their faculty associate was released to work with one or more other beginning teachers as designated by their district. For this one day of teaching, the intern was paid a 20% teaching salary. This day-long teaching time was separate from the two to three hours when the intern covered the classroom while his or her faculty associate attended the afternoon coaching seminars (interns were not paid at these times).

Assuming they performed well in Year I, the TE Collaborative candidates were hired by the district Year II as full-time, fully paid interns working in their own classrooms, while continuing to attend the remaining university seminars. Given the teacher shortage, the districts could almost guarantee job placements for all interns in Year II. A successful second year counted toward tenure in the district and culminated in a full professional teaching credential.

Table 8.1 shows the two-year course/fieldwork sequence and illustrates the continuous blend of university theory and field practice.

Unit modifications in three courses taught in the general program supported the goal of a sustained university/field connection. First, the literacy course was divided into a two-semester course (3 units each semester) instead of the normal one-semester 6-unit course (as taught in the regular university program). The interns could then practice literacy strategies while inquiring into their practice in the university seminar over the entire first year of the program. We divided the units in the two field experience courses (originally 2 units and 10 units, respectively) such that the program could sustain a field seminar with the interns over the entire two years (3 units each semester).

University and district personnel agreed that instruction in literacy and classroom management were essential beginning courses in the program. We wanted coursework to support the classroom as well as the candidates' growth in teaching skills, habits of mind, and pedagogical knowledge base. For example, the Reading/Language Arts instructor taught the interns how to do reading assessments at the beginning of the year both to support the

Table 8.1. Iteration 1: A Gradual Induction Model

Year 1: 20% Intern

Summer Prior to Year 1	Fall Semester	Spring Semester
August Two-Day Orientation	EDEL 108A Language and literacy	
	EDEL 143A Field experience / seminar	EDEL 108A Language and literacy
	EDEL 102 Psychological foundations of education	EDEL 143A Field experience / seminar
	EDTE 246 Creating effective learning environments	EDEL 108C Social studies methods

Year 2: Full-Time Intern

Summer Prior to Year 2	Fall Semester	Spring Semester
	EDEL 143B Field experience / seminar	
EDEL 162 Language development for second language learners	EDEL 108D Math methods	EDEL 143B Field experience / seminar
EDEL 103 Multicultural foundations of education	EDEL 108B Science methods	EDEL 102 Psychological foundations of education
EDSE 192 Mainstreaming the exceptional child		
EDTE 190 Health education		

needs of the faculty associates doing assessments at this time and to provide the interns with authentic classroom assessment experience. In the course, Creating an Effective Learning Environment, interns did a case study on an at-risk student, honing their inquiry skills while providing helpful information to the faculty associate.

Supporting Communication and Inquiry

We purposely put in place structures to build community for both the interns and faculty associates. These structures were designed to provide ongoing support, enhance lines of university/district communication, and facilitate professional growth.

The support began at the start of the program when interns, faculty associates, and university faculty met for a two-day August orientation. The purpose of this orientation was to begin the process of building a learning community across the school districts and between the interns and their faculty associates, discuss program goals and course expectations, and clarify individual roles and responsibilities.

To support the interns, we admitted them to the program as a cohort group. They proceeded through the two-year program with this cohort taking a specific sequence of courses. This differed from the traditional university program in which students could start fall or spring semester and proceed through coursework in whatever sequence they chose. We wanted to build a learning community among the interns that would support them not only in the program, but through their first year of teaching. Data indicate that the support we put in place was effective. As one intern described it,

> From the beginning . . . I learned that this program was going to be about support. . . . As I began my experience in the classroom with setting up the classroom arrangement, I immediately received the support of my faculty associate who guided me through the process as well as introduced me to the staff members who later became key to my support as a first year teacher. The critical part in receiving the support came from others viewing (me) as a professional. My identity as a professional did not just remain within my classroom experience as an intern teacher, however. The professors made it quite clear that they viewed the interns as professionals as well. In the first year of my internship it was a struggle to manage the demands of the classroom and the university coursework. At times, I was overwhelmed with the work. . . . The professors actually worked together to formulate their class syllabi and for each semester, we were given a master schedule and calendar of assignments. . . . The connection between the classroom experience and the university coursework was constantly reinforced. . . . Now I am seven months into my first year of teaching, and while I do not have the luxury of another extremely well-experienced teacher to share my class with, I have close to the same level of support that I had in my first year of the internship.

We also needed to ensure effective communication across institutions. To do so, we formed the TE Collaborative Advisory Board. This board initially met monthly during the first several years. We now meet three times annually. Two representatives from each district attend—one faculty associate and one district administrator—as well as the program co-coordinators and two university faculty.

By academic year 2000, we had established an innovative teacher preparation program that had doubled in the size and expanded to an additional district. It was still heavily dependent on external funding. Districts had an 80 percent retention rate for our graduates over a three-year period, and administrators commented that the interns' first-year performance rivaled that of skilled second-year teachers. We were established. The regional context in which we worked now began to exert a profound influence on the direction of our program. We would move beyond innovative structure to struggle with an essential issue: equity within the classroom.

1999–2002: THE SECOND ITERATION: A FOCUS ON EQUITY

As the program entered its third successful year, educational reform movements were sweeping California. The state was enjoying tax revenues from a rapidly growing economy. The metropolitan region in which our partnership was nested was earning its name as "the Silicon Valley," the home of high-tech industry. Businesses were eager to support school reform and charitable foundations were flush with money. As local industries clamored for well-trained and highly educated employees, business leaders and regional foundations began strategically giving grants in support of local educational reform efforts. The Bay Area School Reform Collaborative (BASRC), established with Annenberg funding, represented one of the most prominent efforts. Our collaborative applied and was accepted as one of seven California Bay Area School/University Partnerships (BASRC-SUP), funded for three years. The focus of this regional school/university consortium was on issues of equity in our schools and how to close the achievement gap.

As members of BASRC, we were able to support eight to ten of our collaborative's district and university faculty members to attend off-site retreats three to four times each year. At these retreats, we worked with representatives from the six other regional school/university partnerships. Each year we would designate a different team composed of representative faculty associates, principals, interns, district administrators, and university faculty. By rotating team members each year and having membership from each of our role groups, our collaborative kept a range of individuals involved in this reform effort. At BASRC events, we discussed readings from authors such Lisa Delpit, James Banks, and Marilyn Cochran-Smith and used these articles to reflect on our own practice. Prominent scholars in the area of equity and racism such as Claude Steele and Guadalupe Valdes were invited to speak and interact with the group. Perhaps most powerful, structured opportunities were provided for cross-partnership discussions about personal and professional experiences related to equity and racism. Our work with BASRC had a profound impact on the direction of the TE Collaborative. It forced us to look inward at program content and to make explicit our commitment to equity.

In addition to our work with BASRC at this time, the TE Collaborative Coordinator was chosen as a Carnegie Scholar. For her Carnegie project, she began the TE Collaborative Faculty Inquiry Group (Markowitz, 2001). The group's work paralleled, at the university level, the opportunities for inquiry already available to interns and faculty associates. Each month, university faculty met to discuss issues of equity embedded in their own classroom practice. Different faculty members agreed to facilitate meetings on a rotating basis. These structured opportunities to engage in the hard discussions of how to apply an equity lens to teacher preparation led our group of professors to want to commit time to re-examine the intern program.

Finally, in addition to our focus on equity, we knew that two other curricular issues needed to be addressed: the move in California to encourage teachers to apply for National Board Certification and the need to embed new state technology standards into our coursework. It was clear that each of these issues needed time for closer examination and decision making. As the local economy was still thriving and grants were abundant, we obtained funding for curriculum revision from the Noyce Foundation.

Our subsequent curriculum revision focused on three major areas: (1) how to thread a focus on equity throughout the program; (2) how to align the program with the National Board Certification process; and (3) how to embed the new state technology standards within the program. We wanted to ensure consistent focus and coherence within and across courses, and between the field experiences and the coursework.

Our curriculum revision group was composed of 12 educators: one district liaison, one faculty associate, and 10 faculty members. We met for a series of full-day retreats over one year. We decided to use both "inside" and "outside" expertise to accomplish our tasks. Rather than relying solely on the substantial wisdom of those within our collaborative, we sought outside knowledge by working with individuals with expertise in areas we were looking to embed more deeply in our program. For example, we met with a Bay Area equity researcher, Edmundo Norte, to discuss ways in which we might better infuse discussions of equity and racism in our curriculum. An expert working in the area of National Board Certification at Stanford University came to summarize both the content and process of certification. Finally, two technology educators, one from our faculty and one from the field, talked about the new California state standards and ways of embedding technology into our curriculum.

Additionally, on the advice of our funding partner, we asked a colleague from another teacher education institution in the Bay Area known for its work on issues of equity to serve as our "critical friend." In this capacity, she spent a day visiting one of our schools and attended one of our intern seminars and a faculty associate seminar. She also reviewed our written syllabi and assignments. She then met with our faculty for a morning to give us her assessment of our program, particularly related to its work on issues of equity. It was a very useful part of the revision process. While we thought we had embedded equity in every course, she reflected back to us after reading our syllabi that the focus on equity was not explicit.

We read and discussed current articles by leading teacher educators and experts on educational equity such as Sharon Fieman-Nemser, Sonia Nieto, Gloria Ladson-Billings, and Linda Darling-Hammond and juxtaposed what we read with what we were currently doing. We also relied substantially on our "inside" expertise—the knowledge base of our own faculty group. We each shared what we were currently teaching in our courses and the extent to which we embedded issues of equity and technology in our readings and assignments. As part of this sharing, each of us faced those aspects of our courses with which we were not satisfied. In retrospect, it was the opinion of the faculty members that this sharing and the level of group problem solving that resulted from it that was the most powerful part of our curriculum revision work. It not only allowed us to move forward in building greater program coherence, but it also cemented a level of trust that had begun in the TE Faculty Inquiry group.

Looking at the course sequence through an equity lens, we realized that certain courses needed to be at particular points in the program while others could be more flexibly placed. Interestingly, while in the first program iteration, our only rationale for course sequence was what we thought interns needed when they first walked into the classroom (which was everything!), we now had a different perspective. The Multicultural Foundations course needed to be one of their first courses. It challenged the interns' beliefs and assumptions about children, parents, and communities with which they were often unfamiliar—those who were poor and those of color. We knew that our candidates' beliefs and assumptions about the children and the community would guide the instructional decisions they made and the expectations they held. Before we could talk about curriculum planning, they needed a heightened awareness about students and the contexts from which they came.

Table 8.2 shows our revised course sequence. We moved the curriculum methods courses based on two factors: when the interns would most need them and when the interns would have the most opportunity to use them. Based on these two factors, we placed math and literacy in the first year of the program and moved science and social studies to the second year of the program. Given that California schools were focusing heavily on literacy instruction and giving less attention to social studies and science, our first-year 20% interns were often having difficulty finding time to implement social studies and science units required by their university professors. By placing the courses in the second year of the program, we avoided this conflict. The interns were teaching their own classes and were free to do as they needed.

We decided to connect to the National Board Certification process by preparing our interns to think about their practice using the three kinds of writing expected on the board exams—descriptive, analytical, and reflective. These forms of writing provided a structure for their inquiry into practice. They provided a powerful thread that wove throughout all our courses and served as another source of program coherence.

As for the technology strand, each instructor learned about the state expectations and examined how to embed authentic technology use into the program. Some faculty began using a web page to support their class.

Table 8.2. Iteration 2: A Focus on Equity

Year 1: 20% Intern

Summer Prior to Year 1	Fall Semester	Spring Semester
August Two-Day Orientation	EDEL 108A Language and literacy	
	EDEL 143A Field experience / seminar	EDEL 108A Language and literacy
	EDEL 103 Multicultural foundations of education	EDEL 143A Field experience / seminar
	EDEL 108D Math methods	EDEL 102 Psychological foundations of education
		EDTE 246 Creating effective learning environments

Year 2: Full-Time Intern

Summer Prior to Year 2	Fall Semester	Spring Semester
	EDEL 143B Field experience / seminar	EDEL 143B Field experience / seminar
EDEL 162 Language development for second language learners	EDEL 108C Social studies methods	EDEL 108B Science methods
EDTE 190 Health education		
EDSE 192 Mainstreaming the exceptional child		

Others made greater use of e-mail and student-to-student online communication. Video documentation was also used extensively to bring the classroom to university courses. Further, certain courses had designated responsibility to meet particular technology standards as required by the California Commission on Teacher Credentialing. Finally, as part of the curriculum revision process, each instructor crafted a portfolio assignment for his or her course reflecting key concepts in a performance-based assessment. These "signature assignments" were included by the interns as part of their final second-year portfolio.

Our second program iteration resulted from a period of looking inward, a time in which we moved from a focus on program structure to its essential content. This period resulted not just in a conceptually stronger course sequence, but courses characterized by parallel themes: a focus on equity and making instruction accessible to diverse learners, high-quality analytic writing paving the way to National Board Certification, and finally the effective use of technology to enhance our teaching and our student's learning. We had also identified inquiry as the process by which our interns engaged in the study of their teaching. As we made our teacher educator practice public through the inquiry group, we developed stronger collegial relationships and deeper mutual trust. Looking forward, this mutual trust would provide a professional shelter to maintain our resiliency and the ability to respond to ever-changing and an often demoralizing external context.

2003–2004: THE THIRD ITERATION—A TEST OF RESILIENCY

We experienced one year of relative calm with a revised program structure and content before the economy put our two-year internship program in jeopardy. The Silicon Valley and California began to experience a sharp loss of jobs and a significant drop in tax revenues. Facing devastating budget cuts, some districts considered rolling back class-size reductions. While just a year before, schools could not find enough teachers to fill their classrooms, our district administrators were suddenly not sure they could provide jobs for our second-year interns. Where districts had counted on our program as a pipeline to highly effective beginning teachers, now they faced not having enough positions to keep all of their experienced credentialed teachers. Interns were desperate to obtain their credentials and a job in the most expeditious way possible.

At the same time, Senate Bill 2042, originally proposed in 1998, took effect. This legislation was written when California was suffering from a serious teacher shortage with about 25 percent of the classroom teachers working on emergency credential. It was intended to increase the quality of teachers placed in California classrooms. However, this legislation took effect when there was an overload of teachers. In Senate Bill 2042, the state mandated a new credentialing system in which the university recommended only the preliminary credential. Districts were responsible for providing a two-year induction program and recommending candidates to the state for a clear credential. The state's new program supported the same belief as the TE Collaborative—that teachers require gradual induction into the teaching profession. Ironically, by instituting its own change in credentialing, the state made it all but impossible for an alternative program that supported the same goal to continue. In essence, the new state credentialing requirements made it necessary for the district to take over the second year of the internship. What had been a joint effort by the district and the university in the original TE Collaborative no longer seemed possible.

In January 2003, the TE Collaborative Advisory Board met off-site to discuss options. Participants included 18 individuals from both the university and the school districts. That district personnel attended in the midst of their own district budget crises spoke to their commitment to retain the program. Two major issues threatened to completely derail the program. First, as previously mentioned, participating districts were no longer able to guarantee our interns a full-time position for the second year of the program. Second, after three years, our BASRC grant had ended and the state budget crisis summarily eliminated the possibility of further grant funding.

Our two-year program structure was no longer viable. Because the university could award only a preliminary credential, we could not ask candidates to take two years to earn it. That would have lengthened the time needed to obtain a clear credential from three to four years. After much soul searching, the faculty and district personnel agreed yet another program iteration was needed.

First, we addressed the issues of our two-year internship program. Not only did we need to shorten the length of the two-year internship, we needed to reduce the cost of the 20% salary for the districts. Districts had previously been able to pay for this salary through various grants. With the downturn in the economy, most of this funding had disappeared.

The response to this first challenge was relatively easy. Rather than placing interns on part-time salary, districts paid candidates as substitutes (not 20% salary, which included benefits). This change provided the districts with an approximately 40 percent salary savings. However, the option still allowed the districts to benefit from the interns soloing each week while their faculty associates left to support other beginning teachers. The quality of the classroom teaching stayed consistent, and the interns still obtained solo teaching practice within a carefully supported environment.

An alternative option chosen by two participating districts that did not need interns to substitute weekly was to place them in the classroom two days each week, leaving them the third day to substitute in the district of their choice. In some ways, this option had the potential to provide greater flexibility for candidates who were not as ready for the intensity of the 20% intern aspect of the program.

The second challenge of the internship program, compressing the program into one year, was wrenching. We were deeply concerned that by shortening the length of the program we would compromise its fundamental integrity. However, state mandates had forced us to consider a one-year model. The interns would begin with an intensive three-week summer session where two professors team-taught two courses: Multicultural Foundations of Education and Language Development for Second Language Learners. These courses had some assignments in common, focused on challenging the candidates' beliefs and assumptions about students, and providing the necessary foundation on issues of equity and racism necessary to inform the rest of our program work. The two methods courses in social studies and science that had been offered during the second year were moved back to the first year. Of utmost concern was whether the workload would overwhelm the interns. We could not be sure until we tried. Table 8.3 shows the course sequence for the one-year model.

We are currently in our first year of implementation of the one-year model. We continue the faculty associate seminars and the TE Faculty Inquiry group meetings and maintain the level of communication and inquiry into practice that have been hallmarks of our program. The revised content of our courses reflects our commitment to equity. The link between coursework and field experience remains strong, and district and university communication continues to shape the program. We watch, wait, and continue to assess to see whether this year's cohort will be as well-prepared as those that preceded it. If not, it is likely we will return to the drawing board and reinvent ourselves yet again.

A WORD ABOUT SOME ADDITIONAL CHALLENGES

The TE Collaborative illustrates what can happen when a program remains resilient in response to external contextual shifts. While external political and economic challenges have played an important role in precipitating the

Table 8.3.   Iteration 3: Resiliency

	Course Sequence for One-Year Model	
Summer Prior to Program	Fall Year 1	Spring Year 1
	EDEL 108A Language and literacy	
August Two-Day Orientation	EDEL 143A Field experience / seminar	EDEL 108A Language and literacy
EDEL 103 Multicultural foundations of education	EDEL 108D Math methods	EDEL 143B Field experience / seminar
EDEL 162 Language development for second language learners	EDTE 246 Creating effective learning environments	EDEL 102 Psychological foundations of education
	EDEL 108B Science methods	EDEL 108C Social studies methods

need for new program iterations, we have also struggled with other challenges worth mentioning.

First, while a major program focus is equity, we have had difficulty over the years recruiting a substantial number of candidates of color. In large part this is because, at the height of the teacher shortage, candidates of color were drawn to the full intern program on our campus where they could begin earning a full salary immediately. Although now approximately 15 percent of our candidates come from minority groups, we would like to increase that number.

Second, as anyone who has worked in a collaborative knows, the time commitment required to maintain the individual relationships can be staggering. Certainly, it requires a passion for the work, a commitment to the program, and mutual respect among those involved. However, the time is worthwhile as all who participate—from assistant superintendents and classroom teachers to university faculty—have experienced the TE Collaborative as a source of their own professional growth. As one faculty member put it,

> The discussions in this group . . . provide a common language for discussing not only our practice, but program issues in general. . . . This format has en-

abled me to engage with colleagues in the kind of dialogue we so rarely have time for.

While the rewards are great, the time commitment is substantial.

Third, we have learned much about the need for clear guidelines related to governance when schools and universities collaborate. When we started in 1997, most work was agreed upon with a handshake because of the nature of the relationships among those involved. As district leadership changed and funding evaporated, agreements were no longer clear. Leaders had new and different agendas. While the university was clear about the need to expand the program to other districts, participating districts were fearful of losing diminishing resources if we continued to grow. We needed to be clear about the decision-making process and the roles and responsibilities of partnership institutions. In essence, we needed to formalize our governance structure. Now, participating districts and the university sign a Memorandum of Understanding, outlining the roles and specific responsibilities of each institution.

IN SUM

By sharing our portrait, we have provided a window into the process of developing, implementing, and sustaining an alternative teacher preparation program embedded within a large state university that must contend with a highly complex and constantly changing regional, state, and national context. Our hope is that our story may inform and give courage to other educational institutions. The TE Collaborative, as one teacher educator put it, represents "the best of what preservice teacher education can be." Perhaps that is why university faculty, district teachers, and administrators won't let go, in spite of turbulent and uncertain times.

REFERENCES

Darling-Hammond, L. (2000). *Studies of excellence in teacher education*. New York: National Commission on Teaching & America's Future.

Darling-Hammond, L., & McLaughlin, M. (1999). Investing in teaching as a learning profession. In L. Darling-Hammond & G. Sykes (Eds.), *Teaching as the learning profession: Handbook of policy and practice* (pp. 376–411). San Francisco: Jossey-Bass.

Markowitz, N. (2001, April). *Collaboration and change in teacher preparation: In search of a brave new world.* Paper presented at the American Educational Research Association Conference, Seattle, WA.

University of California, Santa Cruz New Teacher Project. (1997). *A developmental continuum of teacher abilities.* Santa Cruz, CA: Santa Cruz County Office of Education.

9

Adapting to Meet the Needs of a Growing, Urban School District

Jeffrey C. Shih, Lori J. Olafson, and Lori A. Navarrete
University of Nevada, Las Vegas

This chapter focuses on how the College of Education at the University of Nevada, Las Vegas, continues to meet the needs of the Clark County School District, the sixth-largest school district in the country. By creating field-based programs that target specific needs of the community, including in-service teachers in collaborative efforts, and encouraging reflection and communication among teachers, faculty members, and teacher candidates, the UNLV College of Education has taken the initiative in educational reform to address the challenges of a growing, urban school district.

Teacher education program revision can be initiated by an idea, a small group of people, a department or college, or by the accreditation process. Whatever the catalyst, two things are apparent: the current standards-based environment of teacher education will influence whatever shape revisions do take, and it will not be a simple task. Creating innovative learning environments within diverse contexts that incorporate technology and practical experience, developing performance assessment rubrics, and collecting multiple forms of evidence that demonstrate candidates' knowledge, skills, and dispositions are all part of changing the teacher education landscape.

In spite of these calls for reform, in many teacher education programs, candidates still experience learning to teach as "learning about teaching" through discrete three-hour credit courses. In traditional programs, these courses consist mainly of lectures, readings, and peer teaching in contrived settings. It is no surprise, then, that teacher candidates today undervalue their college coursework (Knowles, Cole, & Presswood, 1994) as they have in the past (Lortie, 1975), believing that experience in classrooms is more beneficial to the development of their teacher identities. Teacher educators can assume an important role in revising these kinds of programs. In fact, Fullan (1993) insists that teacher educators must take some initiative themselves in educational reform. Specifically, he maintains that faculty should

- commit to continuous improvement through program innovation and evaluation
- engage in constant inquiry
- model and develop collaboration among staff and students
- form partnerships with schools

As Loughran (2002) notes, one outcome of teacher educators examining their own practice is that they commonly design and implement new approaches. The following portraits offer glimpses of how departments in our college of education designed new approaches by taking seriously Fullan's call for initiative from teacher educators. One common goal between the programs is that they each address concerns regarding the content and delivery of the traditional programs. In other words, we questioned the efficacy of what Clandinin (1995) calls the "sacred" theory-practice story in which the role of teacher educators is to fill their students with theory that they can then apply in practice. The increasing diversity in rapidly growing urban centers like Las Vegas animates the need for "new ways of thinking," in particular as teacher educators and teacher practitioners strive to meet the challenges of societal needs.

UNLV: DYNAMIC AND GROWING RAPIDLY

In its brief 46-year history, UNLV has evolved from a small regional institution with 41 students, three faculty, and one building to the state's largest comprehensive doctoral-degree granting institution with 25,000 students, more than 2,300 employees, including 800 faculty members, and over 70 buildings on a 337-acre campus in a cosmopolitan setting. Fifteen colleges and schools, 51 academic departments, 31 centers, eight institutes, and a CSUN Preschool support more than 180 undergraduate and graduate programs offered at UNLV.

As a premier metropolitan research university, UNLV demonstrates how the traditional values of higher education can be adapted to rapidly changing conditions and needs of individuals and communities in the 21st century. UNLV concentrates its resources on instructional and research programs that are student centered, demonstrably excellent, and responsive to the needs of local, regional, national, and international communities.

Context of the College of Education

The College of Education (COE) is a dynamic and productive unit within UNLV. One hundred and one full-time faculty, 19 staff, 1,900 undergraduate students, and 1,200 graduate students interact to respond to the challenge of preparing educational personnel within the fastest-growing metropolitan area in the United States. The COE is evolving within a landscape of political, economic, and cultural conditions created by a constantly changing and increasingly diverse environment, and by the pressures incurred as a result of the university's commitment to becoming a research-extensive institution. The challenges inherent in this dynamic setting provide the opportunity for faculty to work in collaborative ways with a wide range of stakeholders, the Nevada Department of Education, the local school district and other school districts across the state, private organizations, community groups, and institutions of higher education at state, national, and international levels.

In 1997, COE programs at both the undergraduate and graduate levels were recognized by NCATE as being derived from a coherent knowledge base. The underlying strength of COE programs continues to be reflected in the large number of teacher education candidates (70 percent) who go on to full-time employment as teachers. This is outstanding in comparison with the national average of 36 percent.

Clark County School District: Unparalleled Growth and Change

For the past decade, Clark County has experienced unparalleled growth and change. From 1990 to 2000, the population grew by 68 percent to 1,375,000 (U.S. Department of Commerce, 2003). For many, Las Vegas is synonymous with Clark County. It is not only unique in its rapid growth and rapid ethnic and racial change but also in its social and economic contrasts. Enormous amounts of money are made every day. There is extraordinary local wealth, especially when the incomes of entertainers and sports figures are included; and there are many multimillion-dollar guard-gated communities throughout the valley. At the same time, several of the lowest-income census tracts in the state are located in Las Vegas, and the numbers of limited English-speaking and working poor increase annually as the inmigration of low-income people to minimum-wage service-sector jobs continues. And, while Nevada has a relatively high per capita income, it ranks 44th among the 50 states in annual per-pupil expenditure ($1,650 below the national average) (Nevada Department of Education, 2003).

Clark County also has one of the lowest ratios of high school diplomas per capita of any equivalent county and one of the highest dropout rates nationally, especially among Hispanics. Moreover, Clark County ranks 196th out of 216 metropolitan areas nationwide in the percentage of residents holding at least a BA degree. While many dropouts end up in low-income jobs or the legal system, some find casino-based employment, offering annual incomes in excess of $40,000—so the lure of money over education is there.

CCSD's K–12 population has also diversified dramatically. From fall 1998 to spring 2002, minority enrollment in CCSD increased from 45.9 percent to over 54.3 percent. Minority enrollment for the two districts now totals 139,000—more than the enrollment in many school districts. Higher education institutions are also experiencing high growth rates overall and in minority student populations.

Currently, the bulk of the federal funds awarded to CCSD, the nation's sixth-largest district, support the literacy development of at-risk students, especially English language learners (ELL). Literacy is crucial to school and life success for these students. At the same time, learning mathematics, science, and technology may be even more important. At-risk students who achieve beyond expectations in these subjects are more likely to stay in school, pass the Nevada High School Proficiency Exam and earn a high school diploma, enter higher education and major in mathematics or science, and enter teaching or other higher-paying professions.

The rapid growth also requires CCSD to build new schools—100 over the next 10 years—and to hire new teachers—1,800 for this year alone. The sheer number of new teachers required each year to keep up with the population growth, combined with turnover (retirement, relocation, and career changes), poses another challenge.

The College of Education, in addition to its traditional undergraduate teacher education programs, has developed three new teacher education initiatives: (1) the professional development degree in science and education; (2) the secondary education minor; and (3) the graduate licensure program. Despite these initiatives, the College of Education graduated 641 licensed teachers in June 2001. For the 2001–2002 school year alone, the CCSD needed to hire more than 1,800 new teachers.

In response to CCSD's need for teachers, the UNLV College of Education has been creative and diligent in its effort so provide a quality teacher pool. One early step was to dramatically increase the number of new teachers prepared at UNLV, which has increased from 183 in 1991 to 638 in 2001. This increase has been accomplished in part by the creation of a unique array of alternative teacher education programs. They include a number of intensive field-based programs, two of which are discussed in this chapter: an elementary school in which an integrated curriculum is being piloted and the Special Education Cohort Program. Brief descriptions of the projects follow below:

- During the spring 2002 semester, a pilot program in elementary teacher education began at Ullom Elementary School, a CCSD Title I elementary school located approximately eight miles from the UNLV campus. The Block program consists of two to three methods courses along with instruction in technology, children's literature, classroom management, and effective teaching strategies. Candidates receive content knowledge in classes on the UNLV campus, then put this knowledge into practice by spending two to three days a week in K–5 classrooms at the Ullom school site. The goal of this field-based program is for students to have two semesters of integrated method course content with practical experience at a local elementary school. We hoped that integrating method course content along with practical experience in a Title I school would be a more authentic approach to prepare teachers for urban contexts. The coursework is completely integrated with a team of three to four instructors who work together to plan instruction, teach content, and evaluate students. Candidates

will finish their teacher education program by student teaching at another school in the Clark County School District.
- After 12 months of intensive coursework, the Special Education Cohort Program provides an opportunity for students to finish their undergraduate teaching degree while working as support staff in the local district. The Cohort is a nontraditional route to teacher certification for individuals that are interested both in teaching students with disabilities and in working as support staff. After 12 months of intensive coursework, participants earn their bachelor of science degree in education with a special education generalist endorsement for the state of Nevada that allows them to teach students with disabilities in a resource room.

BLOCK PROGRAM PORTRAIT

In this portrait, we describe our experiences implementing a pilot program for elementary education that grew out of our frustrations with the traditional program of study. As newly arrived teacher educators at a large metropolitan university we inherited a traditional format for the content and delivery of the elementary teacher preparation program. We found ourselves in a program in which the "sacred" theory-practice story (Clandinin, 1995) seemed to be the dominant story line. In this story, the role of teacher educators is to fill their students with theory that they can then apply in practice at a much later date. Developing and implementing the pilot program was our attempt to respond to our frustrations in a productive manner while also meeting the needs of a growing, urban school district.

We were surprised to discover that candidates shared our frustrations with the traditional program. For the first weekly reflection, occurring during week one of the semester, candidates were asked to respond to the question, "Why did you choose to become a part of this Cohort?" Their responses indicated a deep dissatisfaction with the traditional program that mirrored the frustrations of the instructors. Of the 28 comments made by the candidates, 12 responses indicated that being immersed in an elementary school setting in order to experience the realities of teaching in a hands-on manner was an important factor. Teri noted, "I chose to join the Cohort project because it is a great opportunity to see the 'real world' of teaching. In a university classroom, you are limited to only the stories instructors tell through lectures" (1/26/02). In this example, Teri seemed to recognize the fallacy of the "sacred" theory-practice story. Instead of listening to instructor's stories, Teri wanted to construct her own stories of teaching.

Candidates also rejected the traditional approach to teaching: "I wanted to get away from the normal class experience of boring lectures, random note taking, and tests and quizzes" (Joy, 1/26/02). The opportunity to have earlier entry into the classroom in order to work with elementary school children was seen as a benefit by the majority of our candidates: "I like the thought of having the hands-on experiences with the children in a classroom setting as opposed to sitting in a classroom without any children learning how to work with them without actually seeing how well you work with the children themselves" (Ann, 1/26/02). The voices of these preservice teachers indicated dissatisfaction with the traditional program, and also clearly articulated beliefs about learning to teach that captured a more reform-minded vision of teacher education.

Defining Qualities

In this section of the portrait, the defining qualities of the pilot program are described. Contextual information is included in the descriptions of these relevant dimensions, and the voices of the candidates are interspersed to provide evidence for our claims.

Integrated, Field-Based Curriculum

The goal of the pilot project, the Spring Block, was to provide a program that more closely connected theory with practice. To assist candidates with this transition in thought, the content of the courses was taught through a field-based approach with the goal of helping preservice teachers recognize the multiple dimensions of elementary classrooms, to become increasingly aware of ways to assist K–5 students' literacy development in an urban setting, and to have practical experience with the ways that technology can assist teachers in their practice.

The Spring Block integrated four required courses along with the first practicum. During the fall semester prior to the spring 2002 implementation, we developed a one-semester, 15-hour block consisting of Computers in the Elementary School, Children's Literature, Effective Teaching Strategies, and Reading and Writing Methods. By developing a matrix that outlined what teacher candidates should know and be able to do by the end of the semester, and as a result of experiencing the integrated curriculum, we were able to identify and eliminate redundancies that occurred between the four required courses.

Next, we selected a school site that was committed to the idea of field-based teacher education. We felt that it was important to choose a Title I school so that our candidates could experience firsthand the realities of teaching in a low-income school where over 60 percent of the students are Hispanic and ELL learners. After obtaining the principal's support, we met with the entire staff to solicit volunteers to act as mentors for our candidates. Teachers who were interested in having a pair of candidates working in their classroom met with the principal, who made the final decision on classroom teachers. Nine mentor teachers were selected by the principal.

After selecting a school site, the integrated curriculum was further refined and developed in collaboration with teachers and the principal. For example, during one curriculum development meeting, we asked teachers if a case-study assignment was a worthwhile undertaking for our candidates. In the case-study assignment, candidates worked closely with one student throughout the semester, assessing the student's performance in language arts and providing one-on-one tutoring. Teachers overwhelmingly responded that their lower-ability students and English Language Learners would certainly benefit from receiving individual instruction from our candidates. Additionally, we visited classrooms to discover the kinds of instructional materials being utilized. Eight of nine classrooms utilized *Words Their Way* (Bear, Ivernizzi, Templeton, & Johnson, 2000), and so we decided to incorporate this word study program into the Spring Block curriculum. *Words Their Way* became a required textbook for our candidates. These actions and decisions ensured that the curriculum would be consistent with the philosophy and instructional programs at this particular school site.

Weekly planning meetings were held throughout the semester because implementing the Spring Block demanded a high degree of collaboration for both content and delivery. For example, developing a single syllabus that combined critical learnings for each of the four courses required us to think carefully about the content of the integrated curriculum. We considered what experiences were most worthwhile for our candidates, and some of our taken-for-granted assumptions about teacher education were challenged. Striking the appropriate balance between teaching structured "techniques," course content, and candidates' experience in the classroom was an ongoing conversation. We had to think about the meaning of "experience" in the classroom, and whether or not this was a valuable place for candidates to begin to talk about methods and techniques of teaching in addition to thinking about the meaning of their experience.

Initially, we followed the content of the traditional courses. However, within the first two weeks, it became apparent that candidates were gaining firsthand knowledge about literacy instruction, technology, and general teaching strategies. The university instruction had to be revised to support the on-site learning and experiences of the candidates rather than adhering to a prescribed content. The candidates still gained the knowledge and skills needed to teach; however, this was accomplished through practical situations contextualized in an urban setting, coupled with professional readings, class discussions, and assignments.

A key theme emerging from our reflections was the realization that the boundaries created by traditional courses and traditional delivery are indeed artificial. The complexities of teaching are masked by traditional courses. Integrating the content of preservice teacher education courses more closely matches the multiple dimensions of teaching found in the field. It was possible, then, to discuss how teachers met the needs of English Language Learners within this school.

Community

The development of a community of learners as a result of participation in the Spring Block was a recurring theme in our data from the perspectives of both candidates and instructors. Not surprisingly, candidates indicated that the opportunity to develop relationships with faculty, peers, and K–5 classroom teachers was an important aspect of the Cohort experience. Within our institution's large traditional program, candidates find they have few opportunities to develop relationships with peers and instructors, as one candidate noted: "In the past I have felt like the education department was so large that I never really connected with anyone" (Ray, 1/26/02). Within the Spring

Block however, candidates recognized the importance of community: "The Cohort has created a very strong and tightly woven community among the participants and the instructors. The program is more personalized and I feel like I am an important part to an intricate puzzle" (Teri, 3/18/02).

Candidates also felt that they were able to experience community within K–5 classrooms. In the Spring Block, candidates spent more time in the classroom than candidates typically spend in the traditional, six-hours-per-week practicum. Because they spent more time at the school, they believed they were able to develop stronger bonds with their students. Misty, a candidate, described this phenomenon by saying, "With most practicum students, they come in and they leave, but they don't get to experience the classroom dynamics, the actual community that's there day in and day out. They can't form a strong bond with them" (12/08/02). Knowing that the students had an impact on instruction was noted by another: "It's easier to teach when you know the kids, especially their special needs. With our ELL students, we've learned how to adapt our instruction" (Chrissy, 5/8/02). Thus, we've learned that placing candidates in diverse settings can play a role in developing their sense of efficacy for teaching diverse learners.

In addition to the relationships developed between participants, K–5 students, and instructors, candidates also identified supportive relationships with their partners in the K–5 classrooms as an important aspect within the theme of community building. "It has been helpful having Casey as a partner as we have discussed many concerns together, and given each other feedback on classroom events. It has been great to have someone to talk to who is experiencing the same classroom situation" (Sally, 3/18/02). In addition to being supported personally, candidates supported one another professionally as they continued to grow as teachers: "We bounce ideas off each other and say 'Did I see this right? Did you know this?'" (Misty, 5/8/02). We learned from our candidates and from ourselves that the sense of community that arose from participation in the Cohort was a crucial factor in the success of the pilot project.

Reflectivity

According to Hertz (1997), to be reflexive is "to have an ongoing conversation about experience by simultaneously living in the moment" (p. viii). As Calderhead (1991) suggests, candidates' reflection on their own learning enhances understanding of the learning process and provides them with opportunities to explore their own beliefs about teaching and learning. We invited the candidates to join an ongoing conversation as they were experiencing the Spring Block. They had weekly opportunities for reflection within their required reflective response letters. The purpose of the letters, as described in the syllabus, was for candidates to better understand their ongoing thinking, learning, and reflecting about topics, issues, and questions that arose from the assigned readings, class sessions, and elementary classroom experiences. Initially, we encouraged students to select their own focus for the response. Many candidates, such as Joy, experienced difficulty with the open-ended responses, saying, "The reflective response letters are what I hate about this class. I find it very difficult to tie everything I did in the week together" (Joy, 3/18/02). We responded by providing additional guidelines that candidates could utilize if they chose. (For example, "This week, reflect on how an author study promotes literacy in the classroom. Think about the activities you have done over the two-week period in relation to reading and writing. Consider how technology plays a role.")

As we progressed through the semester and provided clearer expectations and examples of reflection, our students began to see the value of reflection. Ray (3/18/02) noted that the weekly reflection provided her with a space to make connections between theory and practice:

> I do think reflecting is important. Finding the connection between what we talked about in class and actually seeing it in the elementary classroom has been most important to me. For example, we learned about the "Think-Pair-Share" strategy and then I used it with a small group and it worked. I thought, "Wow, I'm really teaching." This might not seem that exciting but it gave me quite a thrill.

In addition to connecting theory and practice, the weekly reflections provided candidates with the opportunity to consider how what they were learning and experiencing might impact their practice when they were teachers in their own classrooms. Mona, another candidate, described how the reflections enhanced her ability to make connections between the present and the future:

> So often while I am going to school I will go to each class, do the work, take the tests and then leave, having never made any connections between the

class, my life and my future as a teacher and these letters have helped me to make those connections. (Mona, 3/18/02)

We remain convinced of the value of candidates completing weekly reflections. Primarily, we see them as a way for candidates to connect course content from various disciplines to what they are observing and doing in the elementary classroom. The weekly reflections allowed candidates to have ongoing conversations about experience while simultaneously living in the moment (Hertz, 1997). What we have learned from this experience is that asking candidates to reflect on their experience without being clear about what we mean by "reflecting" does not result in meaningful reflection.

Communication

Clear and timely communication was the biggest challenge faced by instructors, mentors, and candidates. In our traditional program, instructors are responsible for communication within their discrete classes, and there is no direct communication with mentor teachers in the field. Communication in the Spring Block was not as straightforward and simple. The creation of a community of learners across two sites (the university and the elementary school) and involving four instructors, 18 candidates, and nine teacher mentors meant that the dissemination of information was more complex, especially at the beginning of the semester as Merry (5/8/02)noted, "It was kind of chaotic at first." Instances of miscommunication that occurred at the school site were difficult to correct on days when instructors were at the university. During the school day, it was nearly impossible to talk to an elementary school teacher by telephone. We responded to these kinds of communication challenges in two ways: creating a lead mentor position at the school site and implementing a common, electronic platform to assist with communication.

We felt that it was important to have a person at the school on a daily basis that could facilitate communication between our mentor teachers. The teachers at the site agreed, and one of the participating teachers volunteered to act as lead mentor for the school site. The role of the lead mentor in Spring Block 2003 was to participate in the program meetings, inform teachers about the content and requirements of the program, assist with placement of candidates, and provide professional development on mentoring preservice teachers. When questions arose about when candidates needed to teach lessons or how midterm conferences could be scheduled, the lead mentor was able to provide the needed information in a timely manner.

In order to further address the communication issues, we applied for and received a Reinventing Education 3 (RE3) Teacher Education grant from the IBM corporation. The grant program is intended to design and implement changes in teacher preparation using innovative applications of IBM Learning Village technology. Learning Village technology provided a common electronic platform for candidates, mentor teachers, and university faculty. Previously, electronic communication involved two uncompatible systems: university instructors and candidates used WebCT and mentor teachers used InterAct. We plan to use Learning Village applications that include the Instructional Planner (candidates can create and share lesson plans that are viewed and evaluated by mentor teachers and university faculty), Private Conferences (between candidates and mentors), Home Page Designer (candidates, mentors, and faculty create home pages), and Events at School (calendars for the school site and university classroom). As part of the grant, all mentor teachers, candidates, and instructors will receive a laptop computer. We are hopeful that the use of a common electronic platform and the capability to communicate any time, any place will increase the level of communication between instructors, candidates, and mentor teachers.

SPECIAL EDUCATION COHORT PROGRAM

The Special Education Cohort is designed for individuals who are already working in the school district as support staff and who have a desire to teach in the area of special education. Thus, in this portrait we describe a program that provides an opportunity for staff and paraprofessionals to extend their career ladder and earn a teaching degree. The students in this program work for CCSD and have completed approximately 60 core credits toward a bachelor's degree. The students take the same courses as their peers in the traditional undergraduate special education program, including practicum experiences and student teaching. The Cohort students, however, are grouped as a cohort, attend school full time, and complete two years of professional teaching courses in one year instead of two years. They earn a Bachelor of Science degree in education with a special education generalist endorsement. The participants do not work during this 12-month period; CCSD pays their regular salary, giving them the opportunity to concentrate on the program requirements and coursework. In the state of Nevada, a generalist endorsement allows teachers to work in resource rooms with students who have mild disabilities or to teach provisionally in a self-contained classroom with students whose disabilities are more severe.

Evolution of the Special Education Cohort Program

The Special Education Cohort Program grew out of a need to increase the number of special education teachers in CCSD. The conversations between key individuals in the CCSD human resources department and the UNLV Department of Special Education faculty started in 1992. The catalyst for these conversations was the fast-growing, diverse student population in CCSD and the need to recruit and retain highly qualified, fully certified special education teachers. The need continues today. In 2000–2001, 10 percent of the CCSD student population were identified as having a disability (Nevada Department of Education, 2001). There were 195 special education personnel in CCSD teaching without the specific endorsement required for their assignment in 2000–2001. Given that there were 344 special education personnel vacancies in the state of Nevada from 1996 to 2001, the aforementioned number of teachers in special education classrooms with limited or temporary endorsements is not surprising (Nevada Department of Education, 2001). The Special Education Cohort was and has continued to be an effective solution to meeting the teacher shortage demands in a large and fast-growing urban school district.

The majority of the individuals who apply to the Cohort are working as educational assistants or paraprofessionals, in either general or special education settings in CCSD. Others who apply work in support staff positions such as clerical staff or bus drivers. The educational assistants and support staff are targeted for the Cohort for several reasons: (1) They are halfway through completing a bachelor's degree when they apply so they do not have to start their degree at a freshman level. (2) Most of them already have skills in working with students who have disabilities because they are currently working in special and general education classrooms when they apply. (3) Many educational assistants and support staff have aspirations to become teachers; however, due to family obligations and financial constraints, they have not been able to complete their degree. (4) Educational assistants and support staff are typically native or individuals who have established themselves in the community; therefore, they are less likely to leave the community. A by-product of targeting educational assistants and support staff is that a disproportionately high number of them are from culturally or linguistically diverse backgrounds and/or are male. The CCSD population has grown by more than 13,000 students over the past decade, especially among Hispanic students. The trend reflects a need to train, recruit, and retain diverse teachers, especially Spanish-speaking teachers.

The first group of graduates in the Cohort started teaching in the classroom during the fall semester of 1993. Since then, the program has produced six more groups of special education teachers, approximately 120 teachers over the last 10 years. The collaboration between CCSD and the UNLV Department of Special Education has strengthened and become more dynamic as a result of their efforts toward developing and implementing this innovative teacher preparation. Together, the partners have collaborated on curriculum development, teacher evaluations, field experiences, teaching faculty, and licensing logistics, to name a few. As stated earlier, CCSD made a commitment to pay the Cohort students' salaries for the duration of the program as long as they maintain the grade requirements and responsibilities required of them. While the students are not obligated to pay the school district back time or money, there is an expectation that they will teach a minimum of three years in the district. Most have gone back to teach in CCSD and have remained there or gone on for advanced degrees since completing the program.

Nontraditional Route to Licensure for Paraprofessionals

Various models of nontraditional and alternative routes to certification programs for educators have been developed since the 1980s to meet teacher shortages in general and specialized areas. A nontraditional program is one in which the curriculum remains the same as in a traditional teacher training program, but the courses are delivered in extended sessions, often on weekends, and in fewer semesters. On the other hand, the curriculum in an alternative program is modified to include licensure-only courses. These courses might be combined or shortened and delivered at atypical times over fewer semesters than in a traditional model. Some of the high-demand areas in which programs have been developed include: rural teacher recruitment (Cegelka & Alvarado, 2000), Title I programs (LeTendre, 1998), urban schools (Clewell & Villegas, 1999; Perkins et al., 2001; Schoon & Sandoval, 2000), African American male recruitment (Okezie et al., 2002), and special education (Pierce et al., 2001). Some programs target only paraprofessionals and teaching assistants with the goal of extending their careers in order to meet teacher shortage demands (Dandy, 1998; Harper, 1994; Rintell & Pierce, 2002; Sealander et al., 2001). Similar to those listed above, the Special Education Cohort at UNLV is designed for paraprofessionals, educational assistants, and support staff.

Paraeducators have the potential to become excellent teachers. They expand the pool of potential teachers from underrepresented groups. They know their students and communities well; therefore, they are able to bridge the gap that often exists between home and school culture. In many cases, they are native speakers of the students' language and provide a sorely needed language resource. Paraprofessionals as a group, however, may face unique challenges due to several factors, including limited educational background, age, family demands, and possible language barriers. The literature identifies four potential impediments they may face as a result of these factors when completing a degree program: financial barriers, limited social support networks, academic challenges, and employment demands (Genzuk, 1998). We have worked hard to prevent these potential obstacles. The financial burden of tuition and books is paid for by the school district, thus relieving the students of the financial constraints that come with going to college. Members are required to attend a weekly study hall/support seminar during the first semester of the program. Students receive academic support such as editing and study skill strategies, as well as formal and informal counseling to alleviate social and emotional stress that accompany group-learning dynamics and academic overload.

Qualifications

In order to apply to the Cohort, students must meet the following requirements:

- six months of service with the Clark County School District
- a minimum of 60 college hours in general studies
- three satisfactory evaluations from the school district
- three letters of recommendation
- a minimum grade point average consistent with university requirements
- a passing grade on the Pre-Professional Skills Test (PPST) or California Basic Educational Skills Test (CBEST)

There are approximately 20 students in each Cohort. They take all coursework together, with the exception of their field experiences in the second semester. Cohort members continue to receive their salary from their last assigned position while attending school full time. This gives them the opportunity to concentrate on the program requirements and coursework for the duration of the year. Students are responsible for paying for their own tuition and books; many apply and receive financial aid or grant funding to defray these costs. Once graduated, Cohort members are eligible to apply for contracted teaching positions in the CCSD.

Curriculum

Students enter the Cohort program with 60 college hours in general studies. Once accepted, they complete two years of coursework, 76 credits, in one year. In their fall semester, students take 15 courses that provide a foundation for working with special needs students. A sampling of courses fall include Introduction to Students with Disabilities; Characteristics of Learning Disabilities, Mental Retardation, and Emotional Disturbance; Oral and Written Language Instruction; Behavior Management Techniques for Students with Disabilities; Collaborative Consultation in Special Education; Legal Aspects of Special Education; and Strategies for Students with Disabilities. In the spring semester, students take six courses, including field experiences. The courses in the spring include Pre-Student Teaching, Instruction and Assessment in Reading and Writing, and Diagnostic and Prescriptive Strategies for Students with Disabilities. In their summer semester, students complete their student teaching requirements full time in the school district.

In all, 124 credits are required for graduation. The aforementioned teacher education curriculum is the same curriculum required of traditional undergraduate majors earning a bachelor's in education with a generalist endorsement. Cohort members take their coursework during the day, 8:00 a.m. to 4:00 p.m., five days a week. Each 3-credit course is one week long. The 40 hours they spend each week per class is equivalent to the number of hours their typical counterparts spend in a 16-week semester.

Faculty who teach in the Cohort express satisfaction with the model and find it creatively challenging to teach a 16-week, 3-credit course in one week. It "challenges me to build in active learning activities, use technology more, and prepare differently," one faculty member stated. "Faculty who teach these classes become better teachers," according to Dr. Tom Pierce, chair of the UNLV Department of Special Education. "They have learned to cover their course material in a different fashion. They express satisfaction in teaching a nontraditional group of undergraduate students who have worked in the schools and who have experience with students who have disabilities." Also, faculty members have the opportunity to earn extra money by teaching a Cohort class as part of their load or extra compensation overload.

Ten years after its inception, the Cohort program has evolved into an exemplary model nationally. The program's unique features are what makes this model work. Individuals who are already working in schools as paraprofessionals or support staff are targeted. The participants earn their regular salary for this one year while they are completing coursework. Their coursework is the same as that of any student completing a teaching degree in the last two years of their undergraduate coursework. The courses maintain the same integrity and rigor as in the traditional program. The difference is in the intensive blocks in which the content is delivered. The Cohort program continues to be a popular option for CCSD paraprofessionals and educational assistances. Every year, several individuals apply to the program. Cohort graduates have been observed using effective strategies once they graduate. Also, many have taken on leadership roles in schools and continue to participate in ongoing professional development activities. An extensive research study examining the effects of the program on the graduate's teaching effectiveness is being conducted currently. Several graduates have enrolled and have graduated with advanced degrees following their participation in the program.

Acceleration and Financial Support

Universities need to be more responsive to the economic, social, and familial demands of their students. The Cohort offers the opportunity for students to finish a degree, maintain their health benefits, not work for one year, and keep their family intact. When asked, "Why did you choose to participate in the Cohort program versus the traditional program?" the response from candidates included

> "I was able to commit all my time to school and I didn't have to work. . . . I am so ready to teach, thus teaching a year earlier was very appealing."
>
> "It was a timing thing. I'm not getting any younger. It was such a wonderful financial opportunity."
>
> "I was a single mom in the beginning, going to school at night. The Cohort offered the option to 'survive' and finish college."

Community of Learners

We have observed a camaraderie that evolves among the students during the year they are in the program. They spend eight hours a day together, five days a week, for 16 weeks. They grow to know one another quickly, build trust and tolerance, and support one another. Faculty members have commented that the students' behaviors and conversations in and out of class reflect characteristics of a learning community. The classroom has become a place where students can be themselves and where their ways of knowing, thinking, and expressing are valued. There is a lot of learning that goes on as students process new knowledge and problem-solve new concepts with one another. Over the years, there have been significant events that have occurred in the lives of one or more of the Cohort members. True-to-life events from the past include the death of a family member, a spouse leaving for overseas war duty, a home that burned down, and babies that were born. We have seen the group rally around one another in support when such circumstances have occurred. In these instances, Cohort members have assisted with homework completion, offered rides, and even spoken to instructors on behalf of the person who is experiencing difficulty.

Collaboration

Both the university and the school district benefit from the collaboration that occurs as a result of the Special Education Cohort. The university benefits because student FTE increases significantly. This is due to students taking so many credits in a concentrated area. The school district benefits because teacher shortage gaps are filled with highly qualified teachers in a short time for minimal expense. The university and school district must work cooperatively in order for the aforementioned benefits to be realized. From an operational standpoint, the university and school district's administration must be responsive and flexible. The infrastructure to address the challenges that surface in a nontraditional teacher preparation model must be present. In each institution, the human resources department, the financial aid office, the bursar's office, and the registrar's office all have to work together in a cooperative fashion for the program to be successful. It is important to note, as a result of the ongoing collaboration between the UNLV Department of Special Education and CCSD relative to the Cohort program, additional collaborative programs have been developed in the areas of autism and early childhood special education, in particular.

In sum, the Special Education Cohort program provides an opportunity for paraprofessionals, educational assistants, and staff assistants to extend their career ladder and to earn a teaching degree in a relatively short time. The model condenses two years of professional teaching courses into one year. Cohort participants maintain their regular income while they attend school full-time over three semesters. Students graduate with a Bachelor of Science degree in education with a special education generalist endorsement. They complete the exact same coursework as their peers in the traditional undergraduate program. Students express numerous benefits from participating in the Cohort. One student said,

> I certainly would recommend the Cohort program to others interested in teaching in special education. This isn't just a job for me—it is a dream of a lifetime! I'm still in a "pinch me" mode over how fortunate I feel being in this program.

These are individuals who previously worked as paraprofessionals in the school district but are now working as teachers. As teachers, they have substantially higher wages, better benefits, and they are now in positions of authority (Pierce et al., 2001). The model works in this large urban setting where special education teacher shortages are at an all-time high and highly qualified teachers are a priority.

CONCLUSION

Moving against the grain in teacher education as a response to the growth and needs of the school district is very challenging without support from colleagues and a group of teacher education candidates willing to try new ways of doing things. Working together promotes risk taking and creative problem solving, two approaches viewed as resourceful in rapidly changing contexts. These programs help make the school district seem smaller and more manageable to our teacher education candidates.

The present and pending need for large numbers of quality teachers has provided the impetus for designing alternative programs to help meet this need; however, little has been done to change the ways teacher educators interact with one another and with teachers in the field to facilitate the process. For the most part, teacher educators teach in isolation, write in isolation, and provide service to the profession on a drive-in basis. This needs to change. Teacher education institutions must continue to evaluate and reform programs to meet societal needs so that professors, graduate assistants, classroom teachers, and teacher education candidates can work together to create a community of learners in a university setting. The goal of these programs is to help teacher candidates become reflective educators who act upon their reflections while responding to changing demographic contexts.

REFERENCES

Bear, D., Ivernizzi, M., Templeton, S., & Johnston, F. (2000). *Words their way: Word study for phonics, vocabulary, and spelling instruction*. Upper Saddle River, NJ: Merrill.

Calderhead, J. (1991). The nature and growth of knowledge in student teaching. *Teaching and Teacher Education, 7*, 531–535.

Cegelka, P., & Alvarado, J. L. (2000). A best practices model for preparation of rural special education teachers. *Rural Special Education Quarterly, 19*(3), 15–29.

Clandinin, J. (1995). Still learning to teach. In T. Russell & F. Korthagen (Eds.), *Teachers who teach teachers: Reflections on teacher education* (pp. 25–31). London: Falmer Press.

Clewell, B. C., & Villegas, A. M. (1999). Creating a nontraditional pipeline for urban teachers: The pathways to teaching careers model. *Journal of Negro Education, 68*(3), 306–317.

Dandy, E. B. (1998). Increasing the number of minority teachers: Tapping the paraprofessional pool. *Education and Urban Society, 31*(1), 89–103.

Fullan, M.G. (1993). Why teachers must become change agents. *Educational Leadership, 50*(6), 12–17.

Genzuk, M. (1998). *Diversifying the teaching force: Preparing paraeducators as teachers.* Washington, DC: Office of Educational Research and Improvement. (ERIC Document Reproduction Service No. ED406362)

Harper, V. (1994). Multicultural perspectives in the classroom: Professional preparation for educational paraprofessionals. *Action in Teacher Education, 16*(3), 66–78.

Hertz, R. (1997). *Reflexivity and voice.* Thousand Oaks, CA: Sage.

Knowles, J. G., Coles, A., & Presswood, C. (1994). *Through preservice teachers' eyes: Exploring field experiences through narrative inquiry.* New York: Macmillan.

LeTendre, M. J. (1998). *Paraprofesssionals: A resource for tomorrow's teachers.* Washington, DC: Office of Elementary and Secondary Education. (ERIC Document Reproduction Service No. ED427001)

Lortie, D. (1975). *Schoolteacher: A sociological study.* Chicago: University of Chicago Press.

Loughran, J. (2002). Understanding self-study of teacher education practices. In J. Loughran & T. Russell (Eds.), *Improving teacher education practices through self-study* (pp. 239–248). London: RoutledgeFalmer.

Nevada Department of Education (NDE). (2001). *Improving methods, procedures, and results for Nevada: OSEP continuous improvement monitoring process.* Reno, NV: Author.

Nevada Department of Education (NDE). (2003). *Nevada education quickstats: A pocjet guide to statistical and graphical information about Nevada's public education system.* Reno, NV: Author.

Okezie, C. E., McClanaghan, M. E., McFedries, G., & Graves, E. H. (2002). Using a non-traditional scheduled program to meet a community need for African

American male school teachers. *Metropolitan Universities: An International Forum, 13*(1), 70–76.

Perkins, P. G., Odell, S. J., McKiney, M., & Miller, S. P. (2001). Collaboration in preparing urban teachers. *Action in Teacher Education, 23*(1), 64–71.

Pierce, T., Kennedy, K., Higgins, K., & Terpstra, J. (2001). *A comparison of teacher education programs in the Clark County School District.* Unpublished raw data.

Rintell, E. M., & Pierce, M. (2002). Becoming maestra: Latina paraprofessionals as teacher candidates in bilingual education. *Journal of Hispanic Higher Education 2*(1), 5–16.

Schoon K. J., & Sandoval, P. A. (2000). Attracting, preparing and keeping great urban teachers: The urban teacher education program, Option II. *Urban Education, 35*(4), 418–441.

Sealander, K., Eigenberger, M., Peterson, P., Shellady, S., & Prater, G. (2001). Challenges facing teacher educators in rural, remote, and isolated areas: Using what we know and what we have learned. *Rural Special Education Quarterly, 20*(1), 13–21.

U.S. Department of Commerce, Bureau of the Census. (2003). Retrieved September 15, 2003, from http://www.census.gov

10

Teacher Education for Our Schools and Our Community

Beth Berghoff and Jacqueline Blackwell
Indiana University School of Education at Indianapolis

Suzanne asks whether we have a minute. She has been observing and coaching one of our student teachers in a nearby public school, and she is agitated and not quite sure how to think about the situation.

"I am just sick about what I am seeing in the classrooms. I was observing a student teacher today in Sholanda's room, and I just wanted to cry. Sholanda is a great second grade teacher, but this morning it was impossible to teach in her classroom. The children were so needy the student teacher could not keep them focused. One child kept sliding out of his chair and crawling on the floor. Another child was throwing pieces of a chewed up pencil every time the student teacher turned her back. A third child, who was sitting in a "time out" chair, kept erupting, shouting that he was not going to behave. The school counselor came in, and I thought help had arrived, but he called out two girls who had been fighting on the bus. They were exchanging slaps as they went out the door. Some of the children could not find their work folders in their desks, and others were simply ignoring the instruction. I have never seen anything like it in my 30 years of teaching. And it was not because the student teacher was unprepared. She was doing all the right things. It was just an impossible situation.

"I talked to Sholanda—who is very discouraged. This is her fourth year of teaching and her second year at this school. She transferred to this school because she heard it was a good school, and she liked the philosophy of the principal, but the problems are overwhelming to her. She has several children who qualify for special education services, but the special education teacher is a limited license teacher who has no experience with changing children's behaviors or working with families. Sholanda is especially struggling with the children who suffer from emotional disturbances and continually disrupt the class. She told me that she is doing everything she can to support her student teacher, but even when she teaches the class herself, she can't maintain an atmosphere that is conducive to productive learning. She says this is probably going to be her last year of teaching."

As colleagues, we listen carefully to Suzanne's report. We know Sholanda and her school well, and we have seen what Suzanne is describing firsthand. We too are worried about what seems to be an impossible situation. Sholanda and the principal at this school are two of the most professional educators anyone could ever hope to have working with new teachers, but they work in an institutional setting that puts everyone at risk because no one has the resources needed to solve the overwhelming problems and challenges that walk in the door of this school that serves a high-need population.

As we listen to Suzanne, we realize that Sholanda's problem is also our problem and the problem of all our teacher education colleagues at the Indiana University School of Education in Indianapolis because we have made a commitment to work in the Indianapolis Public Schools (IPS). We have taken on the challenge of figuring out how to help these urban schools better serve the children who attend them and better serve the community that develops through them. This commitment, once implicit in our work, has become far more explicit in the last five years. We work on an urban campus, and we have authentic and important work to do to improve the quality of life in our city. Our work starts with the important responsibility of preparing the best urban teachers possible, and that has been a major focus for us. But we cannot ignore the fact that we are sending our new teachers into schools that have to find ways to leverage the support they need to succeed. We have institutional bureaucracy and social justice issues to help solve in our community because classrooms like this one can be a life sentence to young learners and the last straw for a tired, frazzled, or exhausted teacher.

Suzanne finishes her report by saying that this particular student teacher wants to stay in Sholanda's classroom. The student teacher feels like she is contributing in meaningful ways—that she is making a difference for the children. Suzanne acknowledges her appreciation for this attitude, but wonders aloud whether we should stop assigning student teachers to this difficult school. We remind her that this school is one of the better IPS schools we have worked in. "I guess I know that," she sighs with understanding. "I just wish it didn't have to be so hard."

CHANGING OUR MODEL

The Indianapolis Public Schools (IPS) serve approximately 42,000 students in kindergarten through 12th grade. Seventy percent of these children qualify for free or reduced lunch, and 19 percent come from families with incomes below the poverty line. Fifty-five percent live in single-parent households, and 41 percent of the parents have less than a high school education. There are approximately 90 schools in the district, and in 33 of these schools, less than 40 percent of the students pass the Indiana competency tests. The district has a 67 percent minority enrollment with 16.4 percent of the population designated to receive special education services. And like many other urban districts, IPS is dealing with an explosion of students who speak English as a second language (IDOE, 2003). The Indianapolis Public School district lies in the center of Marion County, and it is surrounded by a ring of township school districts that are smaller but similarly challenged by the problems of low-income and marginalized families and the achievement gap between African American and other minority students and their White counterparts. Our campus, Indiana University Purdue University Indianapolis (IUPUI), is situated in the middle of Marion County, just on the west edge of downtown Indianapolis, and these public school districts surround us. They also hire many of our graduates, and we are in the perfect position to make a difference—even though most of our students come from outside the beltway and do not see themselves as potential IPS or urban teachers and question why they must have their field experiences in IPS.

IUPUI advertises for students using the slogan "Why Not Both?" because the campus is home to both Indiana University and Purdue University programs, and our teacher education program belongs to the Indiana University "Core-Campus" School of Education—a three-campus entity with separate faculties at Indianapolis, Columbus (40 miles to the southeast), and Bloomington, Indiana (60 miles to the south). Both IUPUI and IU Columbus have primarily commuter students who take undergraduate and master's-level classes. IU Bloomington, on the other hand, is a residential campus, and the School of Education has multiple doctoral programs, research institutes, and policy centers. The School of Education faculty at IUPUI is about a fifth the size of the faculty at Bloomington, so we have very different pragmatic concerns, but we enjoy the benefits of being part of an active, intellectual, research-oriented community.

In 1992, when the Indiana legislature passed a law creating the Indiana Professional Standards Board and state committees started the extensive work of developing professional standards for beginning teachers, the education professors in Bloomington circulated a white paper about the evils of standards. They saw the *INTASC Standards for Beginning Teachers* (1991) as a violation of their academic freedom, but we were struggling at IUPUI with quality issues in our teacher education program and felt like the INTASC standards gave us a reasonable framework from which to work. IUPUI was in the midst of making a transition from being a sleepy little community college where education classes were mostly taught at night to becoming a viable option for full-time, four-year degree students. In 1994, when the Indiana Professional Standards Board set forth new licensing frameworks and requirements for accreditation designed to usher standards into the teaching profession in Indiana, our teacher education program consisted of mostly night classes, taken in any sequence. Often, the students were expected to find their own daytime field experiences in schools and received little supervision in the schools until they were student teaching. As a result, we saw student teachers coming out of our program "who could have done what they were doing if they just walked in off the street"—as Michael Cohen, the chair of teacher education at that time, used to lament.

Along with standards for the teaching profession came research evidence of the effectiveness of professional development schools (PDS). Professional development schools, first described by the Holmes Group in the 1980s, were shown to positively affect all the stakeholders involved (Teitel, 1994). As Darling-Hammond (1994) explains in the introduction to a book of PDS case studies,

> Virtually all these PDSs [in this book] have introduced or strengthened existing arrangements for team teaching at the school sites and frequently, for

teacher education courses as well. Teacher educators learn more about teaching as they teach collaboratively with veteran teachers. . . . Teachers comment at the extent to which they find themselves learning from the interns or student teachers as well as from each other and from their experiences as mentors. (p. 12)

We were easily convinced we needed to develop PDS relationships. We decided that we needed to ease into this new world cautiously, so in 1995 we created one elementary cohort and one secondary cohort and started the work of developing PDS relationships. Education reformers (Beane, 1991; Fogarty, 1991; Zemelman, Harvey, & Hyde, 1993) also suggested that teacher education programs should reform their curricula, making it more "interdisciplinary, integrated, problem oriented, socially constructed, and student centered" (Ishler, Edens, & Berry, 1996). Toward this end, we started having meetings every other Friday to work our way through standards alignment and assessment development. As a result, our teacher education group grew more cohesive as a faculty community. We discovered that we shared many common beliefs and goals and that most of us tried to teach the students everything we thought they should know in our particular 3-credit course. This meant that we were all frustrated because none of us could get it done in our little part of the curriculum. We began to realize that we had to work together as a team to create a program. We had to agree on the critical understandings and standards we wanted our students to develop and to distribute the learning of those concepts and skills over time and courses. We also began to see that our urban context was a defining feature of our program. As a faculty, we shared a commitment to preparing teachers for the IPS and township schools. Thus many of our curriculum discussions centered on the question of what we needed to teach our students if they were going to be successful urban teachers.

Through our dialogues and deliberations, we identified three key strands of curriculum that needed to be woven from beginning to end of our program. These included:

1. Multiculturalism/Diversity: New teachers, especially urban teachers, need to develop an intercultural competence that enables them to work with diverse groups of learners (Ladsen-Billings, 1995; Nieto, 1994; Zimpher & Ashburn, 1992). The local urban schools where we

were taking our students were studies of diversity, presenting our students with differences in race, ethnicity, social class, and language (Zeichner & Hoeft, 1996) as well as children with differing academic, physical, social, and emotional needs (Ellis & Larsen, 1995).
2. Constructivism: New teachers need to understand the difference between teaching and learning as the transmission of information versus the social construction of knowledge (Good & Brophy, 1994) and make the paradigm shift to "teaching for understanding" (Darling-Hammond, 1993). This conceptualization of teaching recognizes the importance of building on students' prior experiences and knowledge and requires the teacher to become a facilitator or co-constructor of knowledge with the learners. The constructivist perspective also suggests that teachers need to foster collaborative learning communities where learners are supported in taking risks or making mistakes and sustaining serious efforts at learning (Short, Harste, & Burke, 1996).
3. Child Development and Multiple Ways of Knowing: New teachers also need an expansive understanding of children's learning and development in multiple ways of knowing—cultural ways of knowing (Heath, 1983; Sacks, 1995; Wertsch, 1995), literacy in multiple sign systems (Eisner, 1998; Gallas, 1994; Gardner, 1983), multiple disciplinary perspectives (Coble & Koballa, 1996; Lampert, 1990; McEwan & Bull, 1991), and theories of motivation and pedagogy (Bruner, 1986; Piaget, 1969; Vygotsky, 1978).

We also began to invite colleagues from the arts and sciences departments at our university to discuss teacher education with us because our curriculum discussions helped us to understand that we were building on their teaching. Our teacher candidates could be only as prepared as the whole of the university curriculum enabled them to be, and we started understanding in new ways that the development of teachers happens through the collaborative efforts of the entire campus.

Implementation of Standards-Based Teacher Education

In the 2002–2003 school year, almost 10 years after our first discussions about the role professional standards should play in teacher preparation, the Indiana University School of Education at Indianapolis went to full-scale implementation of our standards-based teacher education program with 210 elementary education majors and 90 secondary education majors. Students in this new program spend four semesters in a coherent curriculum woven carefully with school-based experiences that develop the concepts underlying the professional standards for teaching (Smagorinsky, Cook, & Johnson, 2003). They travel through the program in cohort groups and take their education courses in blocks that allow for team teaching, integration, immersion, and field experience. Children's learning is central to the program, and students complete performance assessments that show they can assess what a child or adolescent understands about a concept and can document that the children they teach are learning.

As we have worked with cohorts of students in urban partnership schools, we have learned a number of important lessons: Principal buy-in and support is critical; relationships take years to develop and nurture; professional development of mentor teachers has to be continuous and ongoing; everyone involved in the relationship has to be valued and supported; and tension and conflict are inevitable. Of all the strands of work to be accomplished, the work with the schools is the most challenging because it so diffuses our energies.

Prior to the reform of our teacher education program, we let our students tell us where they wanted to go to do their student teaching. We were placing student teachers anywhere within a radius of 30 miles from our campus, and many of our students were opting to go back to their suburban, small-town, or rural settings to student teach. In redesigning the program, we decided that we wanted to work systematically with a small, fixed number of schools for the long term. To accomplish this, our elementary teacher education program sends a cohort of 25 to 30 interns to what we call an "anchor school" for two years. An anchor school is an urban school where the teachers and principal want a partnership with the IU School of Education, and the school has a classroom that they can make available to us. We teach our college classes at the anchor schools. During the first year of the program, the "interns" (our education students) have field experiences in the classrooms of the anchor school, and during the second year, they student teach in the classrooms. Because many of the classrooms are complex places to teach, we place two interns together for their first student teaching assignment and let them practice coteaching as if they were working with a resource teacher or paraprofessional.

Finding the schools where we are wanted and getting the faculty out of the university and into these schools is an unfinished project—one that makes our work as teacher education professors far more complex. We have to meet and work out solutions to our school problems together. We have to operate as a program, not as individuals, so Friday morning meetings are a common occurrence in the Education Commons.

A Day in the Life of Teacher Education Reform

On a Friday in October 2003, the teacher education faculty members assemble around a group of tables. It is hard to predict how many faculty members will attend this meeting. Maybe 15. Maybe 25. Too many to fit into a quiet conference room, so we hope there will not be too many fussy babies or loud groups of students in the adjacent waiting area this morning. It can be hard to maintain our focus when there are major distractions.

Block 1 Schools: Option 1 Report

Our first discussion is about Block I schools. Our program is growing, and we have to have places for 90 more teacher education students in 2003 than we did in 2001, so we are bringing new schools onboard. Block I is a 14-credit-hour block of courses that meets two days a week. On Tuesdays, two instructors teach early literacy in language and mathematics. On Thursdays, the students meet with two instructors teaming to teach multicultural, educational psychology, and special education frameworks. All of this starts on campus at the beginning of the semester and then moves out into the schools. After the first four weeks of the semester, Block I students actually attend their college classes on-site at elementary schools where a variety of field experiences are woven into the fabric of the instruction.

We start with a report from the teaching team for Option 1. Their anchor school is the Center for Inquiry. This is a longtime partner school that has been on the cutting edge of pioneering new teacher education possibilities with us. We consider this school to truly be a professional development school. Lenore, a member of Option 1 team, reports that the interns are complaining because we are asking them to spend time in a nearby public school that is not as innovative as the Center for Inquiry. The interns do not know that this is not a new practice. We have always given the interns at the Center for Inquiry a parallel experience at another school. We are not surprised to hear that they believe they will learn more from seeing innovative practice than from being in more typical urban classrooms. Neither are we surprised to learn that they have asked the faculty to rework their field experience plans. We encourage our interns to make their needs known to us. But Dave, the special education professor working with the block, cautions that the instructional team should not change the arrangements. He feels certain the interns are making their requests on the basis of their stereotypes of urban schools, and he argues that they do not yet know what they will learn by being in the second school. Lisa, another team member, adds that the students in Option 1 are doing something none of the other Block I cohorts are doing. They are teaching "Adventure Clubs" every Tuesday at the Center for Inquiry, in addition to spending time in classrooms. Adventure Clubs have been a dynamic part of IUPUI's involvement with its elementary professional development schools, and many of the faculty around the table smile because they know how much interns learn by teaching Adventure Clubs in their first semester. They do not discount the interns' frustration, but know that it will ease up as the interns grow and gain more informed perspectives.

Block I Schools: Option 2 Report

We move on. Option 2 is also taking interns to two urban elementary schools. One is a township school, and the other an Indianapolis public school. It has been easy to negotiate placements in the township school because it has been a partner school for a long time, but the new school declined to meet with us until after all the ISTEP tests, our state standardized exams, were given. The teaching team for this block is all new, so they have needed a lot of help with the logistics of scheduling meetings and arranging field experiences with teachers. They were first assigned to a classroom with primary-sized furniture and windows that would not open. After a sweltering day (only a handful of IPS schools are air conditioned), they had to ask the principal to find them a different classroom. They were lucky because this school has more than one empty room, and now they have full-size desks and adequate ventilation. Sonia, a member of Option 2 team, shares that one of the teachers at the school offered to teach a demonstration math lesson for the interns, and it was a good lesson. This is a positive beginning.

Block 1 Schools: Option 3 Report

Cohort 3 is at the Key Learning Community, a school that operates on Howard Gardner's theories of multiple intelligences (1983). We have been working with this school for more than 10 years. Unfortunately, their principal passed away recently, and they are regrouping. And our liaison professor, who has had a long-term relationship with the school, has also just retired. In addition, the school has added a grade level each year for the past four years to become a K–12 school, and there is no longer room for us to meet at the school. So the cohort of interns will have experiences divided between two schools in this option as well. When we divide the interns between two schools, we pair schools that are close in proximity but unique in character. We have learned from 10 years of action research with our school partners that cohorts of interns benefit from staying together in a school or pair of schools for their full program. In four semesters, the interns develop an understanding of the community surrounding the schools, the culture of the schools themselves, and how students and faculty learn in those contexts over time.

Block I Schools: Option 4 Report

The last Elementary Block I report is about two new schools on the east side. John is the new liaison to one of the schools, and he is missing from the meeting. Lisa helped us find the mentor teachers we would work with at the second school. She was drafted at the last minute when our Block I coordinator quit on the second day of the semester. Because we offer all of our teacher education classes during the day when we can be out in the schools, finding and keeping high-quality instructors is a constant struggle. We cannot use teachers as adjuncts. Neither do we have an education doctoral program on our campus to supply graduate students who can serve as teachers. What we have done with some success is hire experienced master teachers as full-time clinical faculty. These individuals teach in three options (90 students) with different teaching partners and work with teachers in up to six different schools. We know that the complexity of working in so many different contexts is burning them out. Being out in the schools is hard for them because they change schools every semester and have to haul their teaching materials from building to building.

Nonetheless, these instructors spend hours and hours preparing for their classes, coaching the interns during field experiences, responding to the interns' reflections, and grading the interns' projects and academic work. Instructors are truly the most committed of educators; we could not run our program without them.

Making Sense as a Community of Educators

The Friday morning meeting continues. We hear about the rest of the elementary cohorts and discuss whether the fine arts instructors can offer their classes on campus instead of out in the schools. The instructors want to meet where they have access to instruments and art supplies. Another faculty member wants to stop taking interns out to the schools because she believes our interns are learning all the wrong things by being in classrooms with teachers who teach rote knowledge and have low expectations for the children's learning. "We would be better off to keep our students on campus and show them videotapes of good teachers than to take them out to schools where they see bad examples. How can they learn to do teaching of a new quality if they never see it in practice? They think what they see in the schools is good practice, and that we don't know what we are talking about." These comments leave us tense and uncertain about what we are trying to do. At the same time, some of our colleagues remind us that we do see best practices in many classrooms and support for our university students. Often, these experiences convince our students to consider IPS as an option when they begin their job searching.

Meanwhile, one of the secondary cohorts has lost its spot in the media center at the middle school where they were meeting for class two afternoons a week. There was a misunderstanding with the principal about how many classes the cohort would have on-site at the school. The professors have regrouped and changed the field experience plans, and they are happy to report that the middle school's monthlong test preparation period has ended, and the interns are finally seeing some better demonstrations of teaching. The physical education teachers have stopped using their time to proctor prompted writing, and the art teachers can teach art instead of practicing math test items with the students.

We yo-yo from the bright side to the gloomy, from our successes to our failures, and try to make sense of what we are doing as a community of educators. Friday meetings ground us in important ways because otherwise, we are in constant motion. As teacher educators, we move from course to course, team to team, and cohort to cohort, and from university to public school, school to school, principal to principal, classroom to classroom, teacher to teacher, intern to intern, and child to child. Many of us add full agendas of research and service or administrative responsibilities to our teaching responsibilities, and the result is the sort of complexity that makes it hard to remember what day it is or what we are supposed to be doing at any given time. It helps to touch base, to tell our stories, and to get other perspectives on the work. It is not hard to understand why some School of Education faculty have opted out of teacher education and now teach only graduate classes that meet in the evenings. If an individual does not have a passion for the work of educating future urban teachers, it is impossible to sustain this kind of effort.

ASSESSING OUR STUDENTS' LEARNING

While it seems that the problem solving never ends, we also have many successes to our credit. We are graduating students who want to be urban public school teachers and who understand and teach in accordance with the new standards set for the children and the teaching profession in our state and at the national level. This is critical to the success of the schools in our community because it is clear that the quality of the teacher in each classroom has a major impact on children's learning. We know that we are meeting this goal because we are tracking the data. We get information from the Indiana Professional Standards Board that shows that 34 percent of our graduates took jobs in the local urban schools in 2002–2003. The rest of our students went back to their suburban or rural school districts, where their knowledge, skills, and dispositions will be equally valuable. In 2001–2002, we also started to survey the principals who hire our graduates and asked for their impressions about the quality of our graduates' preparation. Of the principals responding the first year, 66 percent indicated that our graduates were in the top 25 percent of all the new teachers they had hired. Another 31 percent rated our graduates in the top 50 percent. These percentages provide a snapshot of the situation as we transition from the old program to the new and will give us an interesting point of comparison in the coming years.

We also know that we are making progress toward preparing outstanding teachers because we have been piloting and implementing a performance-based assessment system to check our candidates' achievement of the standards. We believe that we need multiple measures of the interns' readiness to begin teaching, so we have a series of four benchmark assessments built into our new teacher education program. Benchmark I is a rubric that assesses whether or not the interns are making sense of and beginning to operate in accordance with the *Principles of Teacher Education* (School of Education at IUIP, 2003–2004). These six principles are a distillation of all the different standards these new teachers have to meet (INTASC, Indiana K–12 Standards, Indiana Professional Standards Board Standards for Beginning Teachers in Developmental Levels and Content Areas, national-level professional organization standards) and serve as a framework of goals and assessment criteria for the program. The Benchmark I rubric is used to structure an evaluative conversation among the multiple professors who have taught a given intern in the first 7 to 14 credit hours (Block I) of the teacher education program. At the end of each semester, Block I faculty members discuss each intern's (1) conceptual understanding of core knowledge including the ability to communicate in oral and written language; (2) ability to analyze and critique experiences and teaching episodes from multiple perspectives, including the ability to accurately self-assess; and (3) developing professionalism as demonstrated by a positive attitude, flexibility, organization, and ability to give and receive constructive feedback. If the professors see a problem in any of these areas, they call the intern in for a conversation and discuss both the concerns and ways the intern might improve performance. Sometimes interns make a commitment to use the campus writing center for support with their writing or decide to find less-demanding jobs or work fewer hours so they can give the energy they need to the teacher education program. Often interns with content deficits sign up for extra courses to fill those gaps. And some interns, who just do not see the value in the high expectations, decide to leave the program on their own.

When our faculty asked themselves what essential teaching skill they could expect to see and assess midway through the program, they began a long discussion that ended in the creation of the Benchmark II performance task. This task requires the interns to assess the prior knowledge of a learner. Each intern gets paired with an age-appropriate learner and then plans an interview or activity to do with the learner that will allow the intern to assess what the learner knows relative to a specific concept or standard typically taught in the school curriculum at that grade level. As it turns out, the Benchmark II assessment has been a fascinating program assessment tool because the first sets of interviews and analyses we collected from the Block II interns made it clear that the interns were not being well prepared by our program to succeed on this task. We saw major conceptual gaps and unsubstantiated analysis statements in the work of the interns. After we got over the initial shock of the poor quality of their performance, we realized we could not blame the interns. Rather, we had to ask what we needed to do differently in the program. We ended up adding a second mathematics methods course to the elementary sequence of courses and more work in the secondary program with the K–12 standards and assessment. Now the secondary content methods professors assign the Benchmark II task and support the interns in preparing their submissions. These content experts and other arts and sciences faculty then help us to score these tasks using a rubric. If multiple indicators, such as the Benchmark I, course grades, alerts, and Benchmark II, show us that an intern is not meeting the standards, we counsel that individual out of the program at this time.

The interns complete Benchmark III during the first of their two eight-week student teaching experiences, and it requires them to submit a written lesson plan, a videotape of the lesson being taught, documentation and analysis of the students' learning during the lesson, and a critique of their teaching. Benchmark IV is a rubric developed from the INTASC standards filled out by the mentor teacher and university coach in the final student teaching experience. It assesses how well the interns are planning for instruction, orchestrating instruction, meeting the needs of the individual students in the classroom, assessing student learning, and contributing professionally to the school community.

Again, the development and pilot data from these assessments have impacted the quality of the program. The first videos of our interns' teaching gave us pause, and when we showed videos of a couple of our secondary student teachers (with the students' permission) to the arts and science representatives on our Committee for Teacher Education, we started an excellent dialogue about the importance of the pedagogy of the professors in arts and sciences. In the videos, our students were standing in front of the class lecturing, in spite of all our efforts in teacher education to provide them with other models for engaging learners. Time will tell whether we can work as partners to send out teachers who know better and do more to support the learning of the children in their classrooms and schools, but we are seeing growth in that direction, and as we continue to assess the preparation of our interns, we will know the answer to that question.

SUMMING UP

We believe that quality counts when it comes to preparing teachers; we are out in the community schools and working with our colleagues at the university because we believe that the work of educating teachers takes many partnerships. But we also see the complexity of the conditions that make it difficult to teach in urban schools like the high numbers of impoverished and immigrant families who struggle with basics needs and have few resources to offer in support of their children's success in school, the achievement gap predicated on cultural differences and systems of power and dominance, and the high number of children with emotional, cognitive, and physical disabilities who are included in classrooms alongside second language learners. The best teachers in the world—with all the right knowledge, skills, and dispositions—cannot be successful when too many variables are working against them. This, in the long run, is the bigger challenge, because teachers cannot stay sane and competent when they are continually overwhelmed. They either have to leave the profession or lower their standards and perpetuate the cycle of underachieving schools and children. Now that we are partners with the schools, this is our problem and challenge too. And it is it not clear at this time how we are going to make a difference, but if our efforts to prepare quality teachers are going to be of any value, we have to find the ways.

REFERENCES

Beane, J. (1991). The middle school: Natural home of integrated curriculum. *Educational Leadership*, *49*(2), 9–13.

Bruner, J. (1986). *Actual minds, possible worlds*. Cambridge, MA: Harvard University Press.

Coble, C., & Koballa, T. (1996). Science education. In J. Sikula (Ed.), *Handbook of research on teacher edcuation* (pp. 459–484). New York: Macmillan Library Reference USA.

Darling-Hammond, L. (1993). Reframing the school reform agenda. *Phi Delta Kappan, 74*(10), 753–761.

Darling-Hammond, L. (Ed.). (1994). *Professional development schools: Schools for a developing profession*. New York: Teachers College Press.

Eisner, E. (1998). *The kind of schools we need: Personal essays*. Portsmouth, NH: Heinemann.

Ellis, E., & Larsen, M. (1995). The challenge of preparing teachers for multiple ability classrooms. *Canadian Journal of Special Education, 10*, 1–2.

Fogarty, R. (1991). *The mindful school: How to integrate the curricula*. Glen Elyn, IL: Skylight.

Gallas, K. (1994). *The languages of learning: How children talk, write, dance, draw, and sing their understanding of the world*. New York: Teachers College Press.

Gardner, H. (1983). *Frames of mind: The theory of multiple intelligences*. New York: Basic Books.

Good, T., & Brophy, J. (1994). *Looking in classrooms*. New York: Harper Collins.

Heath, S. B. (1983). *Ways with words: Language, life, and work in communities and classrooms*. New York: Cambridge University Press.

IDOE (Indiana Department of Education). (2003). *K–12 School Data*. Retrieved August 10, 2003, from http://www.doe.state.in.us

INTASC (Interstate New Teacher Assessment and Support Consortium). (1991). *Model standards for beginning teacher licensing, assessment, and development: A resource for state dialogue*. Washington, DC: Council of Chief State School Officers.

Ishler, R., Edens, K., & Berry, B. (1996). Elementary education. In J. Sikula (Ed.), *Handbook of research on teacher education* (pp. 348–377). New York: Macmillan Library Reference USA.

Ladsen-Billings, G. (1995). *The dreamkeepers: Successful teachers of African American children*. San Francisco: Jossey-Bass.

Lampert, M. (1990). When the problem is not the question and the solution is not the answer: Mathematical knowing and teaching. *American Educational Research Journal, 27*(1), 29–64.

McEwan, H., & Bull, B. (1991). The pedagogic nature of subject matter knowledge. *American Educational Research Journal, 28*, 316–334.

Nieto, S. (1994). Affirmation, solidarity, and critique: Moving beyond tolerance in multicultural education. *Multicultural Education*, *1*(4), 9–12.

Piaget, J. (1969). *The language and thought of the child*. New York: Meridian Books.

Sacks, O. (1995). *An anthropologist on Mars*. Toronto: Knopf.

School of Education at IUIP. (2003–2004). *School of Education PRAC Report*. Retrieved September 7, 2004, from http://www.planning.iupui.edu/prac/03-04schoolreports/Education/education.htm

Short, K. G., Harste, J. C., & Burke, C. L. (1996). *Creating classrooms for authors and inquirers* (2nd ed.). Portsmouth, NH: Heinemann.

Smagorinsky, P., Cook, L., & Johnson, T. (2003). *The twisting path of concept development in leaning to teach*. Albany, NY: National Research Center on English Learning and Achievement. Report Series 16002.

Teitel, L. (1994). Can school-university partnerships lead to the simultaneous renewal of schools and teacher education? *Journal of Teacher Education*, *45*(4), 245–525.

Vygotsky, L. (1978). *Mind and society: The development of higher psychological processes*. Cambridge, MA: Harvard University Press.

Wertsch, J. (1995). *Sociocultural studies of the mind*. New York: Cambridge University Press.

Zeichner, K., & Hoeft, K. (1996). Teacher socialization for cultural diversity. In J. Sikula (Ed.), *Handbook of research on teacher education* (pp. 525–547). New York: Macmillan Library Reference USA.

Zemelman, S., Harvey, D., & Hyde, A. (1993). *Best practice: New standards for teaching and learning in America's schools*. Portsmouth, NH: Heinemann.

Zimpher, N., & Ashburn, E. (1992). Countering parochialism among teacher candidates. In M. Dillworth (Ed.), *Diversity in teacher education* (pp. 40–62). San Francisco: Jossey-Bass.

V

RE-CREATING TEACHER EDUCATION: IMAGINING POSSIBILITIES

> If the painter presents us with a field or a vase of flowers, his paintings are windows which are open on the whole world. We follow the red path which is buried among the wheat much farther than van Gogh painted it, among other wheat fields, under other clouds, to the river which empties into the sea, and we extend to infinity, to the other end of the world, the deep finality which supports the existence of the field and the earth. So that, through the various objects which it produces . . . the act aims at a total renewal of the world.
>
> (Sartre, 1949, p. 57)

Teacher education at its best represents a response to questions and issues posed by the tensions and contradictions of public education situated in a changing society. Teacher education at its best attempts to understand and intervene in specific problems that emanate from the social contexts and realities of everyday life in classrooms and schools (Giroux, 2001). Teacher education, like the arts, is both a cultural and intellectual voice, interpreting the conditions and needs of society and its educational systems.

Teacher educators, much like artists, serve a critical role of public intellectual. As public intellectuals, teacher educators work to continuously create and re-create preparation programs in response to societal issues and problems, while at the same time, and somewhat paradoxically, preparing future teachers to enter classrooms and schools being narrowly redefined by federal policy and standards and accountability agendas, as well as becoming increasingly more diverse—culturally, ethnically, economically, and linguistically.

Re-creating teacher education today challenges teacher educators with creating programs that offer alternative, imaginative possibilities to the more traditional and often problematic programs that work to culturally reproduce rather than transform existing educational systems. In this sense, the work of teacher educators must be animated by concerns with social justice and the democratic process, and, as public intellectuals, teacher educators must ask driving—that is to say, deeply substantive and political—questions in public, and in doing so stimulate the public debate and advance the discourse on education in relation to creating a just, equitable, and democratic society.

Teacher educators, in working to re-create teacher education, must embrace, as Dewey (1931) did, a belief in the power of human intelligence to deal with the deepest and most crucial social and educational problems that inevitably arise in a world of change. He believed that social intelligence was best utilized in the open climate of a democratic society. Teacher educators must also embrace a belief, as Dewey (1934) did, in imaginative experience, which "exemplifies more fully than any other kind of experience what experience itself is in its very movement and structure" (p. 282). As did Dewey, teacher educators in re-creating teacher education must understand that there is an aesthetic quality inherent in *an experience* carried by the flow of movement toward an integrated consummation. Such an aesthetic aspect brings the drama of life into fulfillment and makes transformation possible. Learning to teach as a form of imaginative experience must be developed by an intensified engagement of the individual's self in the world, and an interactive relation between doing and undergoing the dynamic combination of thinking and feeling (Greene, 2000). In re-creating teacher education, we must understand the relationship of "overt conflict and the impact of harsh conditions" that are hallmarks of life in a classroom, while valuing the aesthetic quality of an experience, recognizing that teaching "is the fusion in one experience of the pressure upon the self of necessary conditions and the spontaneity and novelty of individuality" (Dewey, 1934, p. 281).

Re-creating teacher education requires of teacher educators a concern for the aesthetic qualities of experiences that guide learning to teach, a concern for cultivating imagination—the source of human freedom and possibilities—in education. Through imagination, teachers, and in concert children, can be helped to understand that things have not always been as they are and that in the future they can be changed (Greene, 2000). Teacher educators' efforts, in re-creating preparation programs, necessarily must "go to create an imaginative body of experience and a state of consciousness the richness and diversity of which make real and celebrate the freedom and community of men and women" (Inglis, 1975, p. 39).

Teacher education as an aesthetic experience has its own rhythm, tone, resonance and drama. To follow Dewey's (1934) notion of *an experience* in its inception, development, and fulfillment, an aesthetic way of teaching needs to start with the wonder about life, evolve with an absorbed engagement with the world, and reach consummation in transformative moments. The beauty, the wonder, and the power of the world in both its minute details and its vastness can only be captured by sensitive eyes and appreciated by an open heart. To cultivate this sensitivity and openness is both an aesthetic and intellectual responsibility of teacher education.

Teacher educators must be able to see teaching and learning as an aesthetic whole, and in so doing realize that to teach is portraiture in motion, both authentic and evocative, to speak from the head and heart (Lawrence-Lightfoot, 1997). The authors in this closing part bring an understanding of the aesthetic whole shared through the portraits of teacher preparation presented in this book and offer a sense of imaginative possibility for teacher education.

REFERENCES

Dewey, J. (1931). *Philosophy and civilization*. New York: Minton, Balch.

Dewey, J. (1934). *Art as experience*. New York: Berkley Publishing Group.

Giroux, H. (2001). Public intellectuals and the challenge of children's culture: Youth and the politics of innocence. *The Review of Education/Psychology/Cultural Studies, 21*(3), 193–225.

Greene, M. (2000). Imagining the future: The public school and possibility. *Journal of Curriculum Studies, 32*(2), 267–280.

Inglis, F. (1975). *Ideology and the imagination*. New York: Cambridge University Press.

Lawrence-Lightfoot, S. (1997). Illumination: Shaping the story. In S. Lawrence-Lightfoot & J. H. Davis (Eds.), *The art and science of portraiture* (pp. 243–260). San Francisco: Jossey-Bass.

Sartre, J.-P. (1949). *Literature and existentialism* (R. Frechtman, Trans.). Secaucus, NJ: Citadel Press.

11

Reflective and Aesthetic Inquiry: Seeing the Whole

Karen Embry Jenlink
Stephen F. Austin State University

The portraits of learning to teach presented in this book reflect a new order in urban teacher preparation, an order that extends a transformative cultural agency role for colleges and schools of education, a role purposed with preparing teachers through their reflective pedagogy and practice, to challenge society's existing order so as to develop and advance democratic imperatives in a changing America. These portraits present a complex array of sociocultural and pedagogical considerations for responding to demographic and societal change and political tensions within urban centers across the country. In this chapter, the portraits are explored holistically through reflective and aesthetic inquiry, identifying common themes and characteristic elements that present to the reader a composite portrait of the defining characteristics in urban colleges and schools of teacher preparation today.

This composite portrait offers an illuminating look into the evolving identity of teacher preparation in the urban setting whose programs are defined through inquiry and collaboration within urban public schools and communities. Examined collectively, the portraits also offer the reader an honest and candid look at the process of the identity formation of colleges and schools for teacher preparation and informed by empirical research on professional development schools and school-university partnerships (Abda-Haqq, 1998; Darling-Hammond, 1994, 1997; Petrie, 1995) and shaped within the context of an unflinching political agenda of raised teacher accountability measures and alternate routes to licensure and certification though high-stakes testing and classroom performance. Through inquiry into these portraits, teacher educators and their partners in teacher preparation are provided an opportunity to better understand how teacher preparation programs may consciously and purposefully guide their evolution, reconceptualizing educator preparation to design new programs that foster socially conscious citizens who are prepared to participate as democratic citizens in a changing America and world.

THE URBAN/SUBURBAN SETTING: A CONTEXT FOR INQUIRY AND COLLABORATION

Establishing the Context for Inquiry

From Boston to Los Angeles, Milwaukee to Indianapolis, whether in urban colleges or suburban schools of education, the reconceptualization of teacher preparation in every college and school of education originated with focused, deliberate, and purposeful inquiry and collaboration. These two elements, inquiry and collaboration, serve as two primary attributes for defining the portraits. In some colleges of education, the nature of this inquiry was critical, beginning with a dialogical nature that examined questions such as "How does this program honor its commitment to teacher preparation as integrated, whole, occurring over time in social contexts?" (Center X at University of California, Los Angeles); "What does it mean to be a transformative social justice educator in a metropolitan environment in which economic opportunity and access to higher education are largely taken for granted but economics and social stratification remain enduring characteristics?" (Roosevelt University); and "How shall a teacher foster the conditions in her classroom such that students want to be there?" (Ohio University). For other schools, the inquiry was more reflective in nature: "Looking back to move ahead" (Alverno College) or imaginative: "To move us toward what is not yet" (Long Island University) to create, transform, and enact social change.

In two of the schools and colleges of education, the context for inquiry was borne out of response to shifting demographics or regional economic change. Within Clark County School District, the sixth-largest public school district in the United States, the University of Nevada, Las Vegas (UNLV) faced questions of how to meet the needs of the growing teacher shortage in schools whose diverse student populations swelled with increasing diversity from a rapid and constant influx of new students. Inquiry at San José State University began in response to external, federally funded educational reform initiatives and continued through the challenges of sustaining programs in a rapidly changing economic context as wealth from the technology boom in the Silicon Valley dwindled.

Political mandates provided an early impetus for inquiry as education faculty at Indiana University Perdue University at Indianapolis (IUPUI) explored ways to adopt a standards-based curriculum within a constructivist teacher preparation program that recognized alternative pedagogies and multiple ways of learning. At IUPUI, the Center for Inquiry was conceived from responses to this inquiry. Finally, at Boston College, the Lynch School of Education reconceptualized its more traditional teacher preparation program through an alternative lens of "inquiry as a stance for teaching and learning." Clearly, these portraits of learning to teach in a changing America share a common, connecting thread of continual inquiry, initiating transformative change by a re-engagement and rethinking of their design, their purpose, and their value in teacher preparation within constantly changing sociocultural and environmental contexts.

Realizing Inquiry Through Collaboration

The second primary attribute that appears predominantly and characterizes these portraits is the collaboration that guided the identity shaping of the programs. Members of the colleges and schools of education portrayed in these chapters engaged in critical conversations and collaboration with public schools and the larger educational community to raise questions about local educational needs and to problem solve together. The differences in the nature of their collaboration occurred in the design and purpose of the collaborative activity. Some schools were concerned with providing critical voice to underrepresented populations in order to bring in perspectives of difference, while others engaged in collaborative inquiry in the formation of university/school partnerships. This central aspect of collaborative inquiry served as both a medium of exchange and a shaping element for the radical changes in curriculum and pedagogy that are boldly displayed in the individual portraits.

SOCIOCULTURAL PATTERNS IN PEDAGOGICAL CHANGE

Rethinking Role and Stance for Teacher Preparation in Urban Settings

The collaborative and dialogical inquiry shared among the portraits reveals a rethinking of role and stance for teacher preparation. Consistently, the portraits display a cohesive philosophical and programmatic shift from a traditional training model of teacher preparation to a fluid, evolving, socially active role for urban teacher education programs that seek to prepare teachers to be cultural agents for social change within innovative, contextual, field-based programs.

For example, at the Lynch School of Education at Boston College, a cross-disciplinary team of faculty negotiated policies and practices for the design of an integrated field-based teacher education program. This element of collaborative inquiry is ongoing and integral to the program, providing collaborative feedback for the continual evolution of coursework. Likewise, San José State University established collaborative networks across school and university partnerships through collaborative discussion to address issues of equity and marginalization of students. With the aid of comprehensive state funding, the regional Bay Area School Reform Collaborative (BASRC) was organized to address authentic, equitable ways to close achievement gaps in student populations. Today the BASRC continues to examine curriculum revision in teacher preparation through a social justice lens.

Creating Space for Critical Conversations: Cultivating Relationships and Voice

Honoring voice among all members of the learning communities appeared consistently in many of the conversations featured in the portraits presented in this text. At Alverno College this meant acknowledging two sets of voices, the college faculty and the students whose voices offered valuable input, from two perspectives of experience within the program. The cohort design at Roosevelt University was intended "to seek out the expertise of insiders" fostering a more democratic dialogue. This critical feedback was important to continually adapt and evolve the two programs. Honoring voice animated the philosophical stance of cultivating democracy within socially just environments at Alverno College and Roosevelt University.

Constructing Alternative Pedagogies for Urban Populations

Critical dialogue was also utilized to question and critically examine existing structures and practices and to challenge standing normativities within existing teacher preparation programs, so as to meet the changing needs of students and teachers in diverse communities and teacher preparation programs within urban and suburban school settings. Inside these conversations, several patterns emerge across the portraits. In addition to the sociocultural patterns of rethinking role and stance and cultivating voice, commonalities emerge from the discourse that focus upon the rethinking of individual programs' philosophical ideals and subsequent changes in pedagogy and practice. These pedagogical changes have included field-based delivery of instruction, constructivist approaches to teaching and learning, apprenticeships, and socially just learning environments.

By situating the social environment of learning to teach within authentic, field-based learning communities, the teachers and students utilize reflective inquiry to co-construct new and alternative pedagogies, pedagogies that honor difference, and view diversity as an asset, embedding the integration of theory and practice within experiences in contextualized, authentic apprenticeships in urban and suburban settings. Extending a sociocultural learning perspective, these new pedagogies focus on constructivist approaches to teaching and learning, seeking to foster social democracy within a practical setting. Reflection, action research, and performance-based assessment stand as distinguishing hallmarks of the alternative pedagogies of difference and social justice described in the portraits.

Constructing Pedagogies of Difference and Social Democracy

Valuing Diversity

Honoring difference and valuing diversity consistently appear within the portraits of urban teacher preparation. At Center X at UCLA, faculty adopted a "view of teaching which moves us outside traditional frames of classrooms into larger examinations of societal inequity and conditions of schooling." Seeking to provide authentic apprenticeships for equipping well-prepared teachers to practice within the urban setting, Center X formed its partnerships in the hardest-to-staff schools within low-income neighborhoods, primarily working with students of color. Center X also conveyed a valuing of diversity when it flattened the existing hierarchal system within the teacher education program and set up a collaborative governance structure by committee for the new programs. This act of restructuring addressed inequities in the previous power structures in decision making, provided more equitable representation of the community partners, and allowed for a wider variation in perspectives on the redesign of curriculum and pedagogical practice in the school community. Center X went even further to examine the lack of representative diversity among the teacher education faculty and actively set about recruiting faculty that would provide racial, ethnic, and sociocultural symmetry to the population of students served in the local schools.

Indiana University Perdue University at Indianapolis (IUPUI) and Long Island University echoed perspectives similar to those at Center X, recognizing and valuing diversity as a strengths, not a deficit, model: "The local schools where we were taking our students were studies of diversity" (Indiana University), and "strengthening a commitment to educate teachers of color for the public schools" (Long Island University). Like Center X, Long Island University examined the racial and ethnic makeup of its faculty and discovered a need to diversify the faculty to reflect the community of learners.

Fostering Democratic Practices

For several programs, necessary pedagogical change was defined through reflective inquiry borne out of frustration for the lack of integration of theory and practice. For Ohio University, Roosevelt University, and Long Island University, the frustration that led to inquiry explored ways to more closely connect the faculty's commitment to democratic philosophy and principles with the field-based learning experiences of their students. Within each of these schools, faculty designed participatory learning experiences to allow students to explore the epistemologies of educational theories pertaining to democracy and at the same time foster democratic practices and democratic culture within the urban community.

At Ohio University, the CARE (creating active, reflective educators) program was designed to connect the program's democratic philosophy and theoretical ideals with actual practice. Faculty in the CARE program at Ohio University applied a Deweyan perspective of social democracy to create "pedagogy of associative living" within the local school community. This "pedagogy of associative living" utilized collaborative research into social issues and service-learning experiences within the community, serving as the primary context for students to engage in reflective inquiry on what democratic education means and to explore the meaning of democratic culture through experiences in the schools.

Also, Roosevelt University faculty sought to foster "democratic participation within the learning community" by adopting a cohort design and setting aside a common time for students and teachers to engage in participatory dialogue. Likewise, Long Island University created "democratic open spaces" for more democratic participation among its teachers and students. As the portraits illustrate, alternative and new pedagogies were forged within a sociocultural perspective of learning that valued equity in diversity through social democracy. At Center X, IUPUI, Long Island University, Ohio University, and Roosevelt University, the design of alternative and contextual learning experiences situated in urban schools and communities evolved through collaborative and reflective critical inquiry.

Adopting Constructivist Approaches to Teaching and Learning

Examining the epistemological nature of change within the portraits, another connecting pattern of pedagogical transformation emerges. The portraits each convey a constructivist philosophy for teaching and learning as applied to preparing teachers in urban and suburban schools. Defining elements of constructivist pedagogy characterized within the different portraits include the use of reflection, action research, and performance-based assessment in the teacher education curriculum.

Reflection

The use of reflection in relation to inquiry and fostered through the use of reflective writing experiences in logs and authentic letters was noted in several portraits. At the Lynch School of Education at Boston College, reflection was described as integral and embedded within an inquiry stance "reflecting on and documenting relationships among the learning of teachers, students, and professional practice." Self-inquiry, another form of reflection, was portrayed by the faculty at Long Island University as a means of seeing and examining themselves in relation to their practices and beliefs. At Alverno College, students were explicitly taught the art of reflection and recorded their impressions and experiences in reflective logs. These logs were considered to benefit the student and provide direct and honest feedback for program renewal. Students at UNLV engaged in similar experiences with reflection as noted with the use of "reflective response letters."

Action Research

A second distinguishing element of constructivist learning and pedagogy commonly displayed in the portraits was the utilization of action research in the classroom. Like the use of reflective inquiry, action research was implemented to conjoin theory and practice by situating the *how* and *why* of learning to teach—the theoretical framework of the programs—within the *what*, actual practice in the urban center. Both the CARE program (Ohio University) and Center X (UCLA) fostered community research projects where the intersection of theory and practice could occur within the social interactions of teachers and learners in the urban schools and the neighborhoods of the local community. In addition, the "inquiry as stance" perspective of the Lynch School of Education at Boston College naturally lent itself to a research orientation for the reflexive, problem-posing experiences as students participated in teacher research in field-based classrooms.

Performance-Based Assessment

The third and final distinguishing element of constructivist pedagogy that appeared consistently in the urban portraits was the use of performance-based assessment, in particular, portfolio assessment. Viewing teacher development as an iterative process informed through self-knowing, representation, and self-reflection, Center X, Alverno College, IUPUI, and the University of Nevada, Las Vegas, each described the use of portfolio assessment as an integral and important part of the process of learning to teach.

Some of the portfolios were used to provide indicators of curriculum benchmark assessments as a requirement for NCATE-accredited institutions, while others were realigned with changes in state curriculum frameworks to provide documentation of compliance with state standards. However, the overarching purpose for incorporating portfolio assessment, action research, and reflection within the design and implementation of new pedagogies in the urban teacher preparation programs seemed to emanate from the programs' constructivist philosophical orientations and the motivation to construct alternate pedagogies to honor difference and foster social democracy among teachers and students.

FINAL REFLECTIONS: SEEING THE WHOLE

Clearly, the portraits featured within this text capture and provide actual and real glimpses into how learning to teach is evolving in major urban centers across America. The narrative portraits of these colleges and schools of education present ways in which a professional development model for teacher preparation was implemented and evolved in the urban teacher preparation programs in response to rapidly changing social and political contexts. Through these descriptions, the reader is able to clearly visualize and explore how programs changed from a traditional delivery system of teacher preparation to implement field-based models involving the formation of collaborative partnerships, situating teacher preparation in the context of urban public schools, and utilizing research in the practical setting to inform and shape the programs' social and pedagogical practice.

As a visitor in an art museum steps back to observe elements within a particular painting that are not readily perceived from a close stance, so, too, is the reader able to view the starkly defining elements of social democracy, renewal, and resiliency when looking across the portraits collectively through holistic inquiry. Embedded within the composite portrait is the element of collaboration through critical, reflective dialogue and conversation among the participants and the creation of a social culture of democratic participation to improve the existing order within the teacher preparation programs, the educational community, and the larger society.

Social Democracy

The commitment to creating a public sphere—or open space—for listening and speaking as described in these portraits demonstrates an important structural element in which preservice teachers are encouraged develop their critical voices, to challenge standing ideologies about teaching and learning, and to challenge practices within public schools that suppress difference, marginalize students and teachers, and silence groups who find themselves perhaps, in the majority number, but outside of the dominant culture. The element of cultivating voice through democratic participation as seen in the portraits illuminates an emerging role of teacher preparation as a cultural agency for change in the existing social order of urban schools and a significant return to democratic imperatives to develop and advance democracy in schools.

Self-Renewal

Another striking element that appears in the composite portrait is self-renewal. Seeking to transform practice, change in urban teacher preparation originated from an organic commitment to improve existing structures and student achievement in K–12 schools and was realized through reflective inquiry and collaboration. The nature of this reflective and collaborative inquiry spontaneously fostered self-renewal within the programs of teacher preparation as they implemented new programs and responded to and experienced rapid social, cultural, political, economic, and demographic changes. The portraitists did not convey perspectives of the urban setting as a threat to their existence but instead viewed the changing urban context as an opportunity for continual self-growth and improvement as members reconceptualized their purpose, mission, program content, and delivery. In essence, education faculty engaged in inquiry and adapted to changes in the social environment as a means for self-renewal and the conscious self-guided evolution of their programs.

Resiliency

In the face of rapidly changing social, political, and economic conditions, each of the programs demonstrated remarkable resiliency in response to change. In order to sustain their programs and continue to evolve, flexibility and, subsequently, resiliency was paramount to success. The element of resiliency was prominently displayed in the identity shaping that occurred through legislated educational reforms in public schools and colleges of education. For several decades, the implementation of standards-based curriculum and standardized testing for accountability and certification in teacher preparation was accompanied in the public schools by similar legislated changes. The effects of the mandated changes radically altered school practices and influenced the nature of field experiences, yet the nature of change within the pedagogy and social practice of the urban teacher preparation programs was not shown to be compromised by political mandates.

Instead, the programs of urban teacher preparation utilized the same approaches of reflective inquiry and collaboration to attain alignment and meet the regulations for program compliance as required by their respective state and federal mandates. None of the portraitists described selling out their philosophical and theoretical beliefs to meet changing federal and state guidelines. Essentially, the approaches of reflection, collaboration, and democratic participation that inherently characterized the social culture of these portraits provided an important medium for response to mandated change and allowed the programs to respond reflexively and inclusively from within, thereby mediating possibly adverse outcomes from external mandates.

Another external situation that fostered resiliency was the changing economy of the urban centers as many of the teacher preparation programs faced the residual effects of industry downturns. Loss of state funding created, in turn, losses in the operating budgets of the programs and posed potential harm to the programs' sustainability. Yet the response to economic change was similar to the previously described response to political change. Across the portraits, resiliency through adversity prevailed. The mutual trust formed in the relationships among the faculty, public schools, and the community also fostered this defining element of resiliency, as summed up by Center X: "We were fueled by our own commitment."

Final Thoughts

As of this writing, political pressure to change remains high in teacher preparation in America. Shifts in the funding of educational programs toward decontextualized perspectives of learning, standardized measures of assessment, and the awarding of federal research dollars to quantitative studies has effectively diminished the use of qualitative indicators of defining program success and identity. Many teacher preparation programs find their identity and solvency challenged through federal acts such as the No Child Left Behind Act of 2001 (2002) that is effectively dismantling the profession through legislated deregulation, thereby opening a market economy for other avenues of alternative teacher certification. On the other hand, legislation advances the notion of enhanced certification through a national teaching certificate based upon the National Board for Professional Teaching Standards (1989, 2003).

Amid political turmoil and conflicting legislative pressures, a viable and resilient identity of teacher preparation in the urban centers clearly emerges. This emerging identity as holistically explored within these portraits represents a culturally significant agency for preparing teachers to meet the needs of students in a changing America. Collectively, the portraits portray a strong focus on the moral, imperative, and sociocultural considerations of preparing teachers to serve as cultural agents with the necessary knowledge and skills to address social inequities in diverse settings and respond with social justice to build a more democratic society. The ability to flexibly and reflexively respond to changing social, cultural, economic, and political conditions portrays the necessary element of resiliency as these schools and colleges of teacher preparation continually inquire, adapt, and redefine their identity in relation to the rapidly changing social contexts of the schools they serve.

REFERENCES

Abda-Haqq, I. (1998). *Professional development schools: Weighing the evidence*. Thousand Oaks, CA: Corwin Press.

Darling-Hammond, L. (Ed.). (1994). *Professional development schools: Schools for developing a profession*. New York: Teachers College Press.

Darling-Hammond, L. (1997). *Doing what matters most: Investing in quality teachers*. New York: National Commission on Teaching and America's Future.

National Board for Professional Teaching Standards. (1989). *Toward high and rigorous standards for the teaching profession: Initial policies and perspectives of the National Board for Professional Teaching Standards*. Detroit: Author.

National Board for Professional Teaching Standards. (2003). *Standards and National Board certification*. Retrieved August 10, 2004, from http://www.nbpts.org/candidates/ckc.cfm

No Child Left Behind Act of 2001, H.R. 1 (S.R. 1), 107th Congress, 147 Cong. Rec. 1425 (2002). Retrieved August 15, 2004, from http://www.ed.gov/legislation/ESEA02/107-110.pdf

Petrie, H. G. (Ed.). (1995). *Professionalization, partnership, and power: Building professional development schools*. Albany: State University of New York Press.

12

Coda: A Portrait of Teacher Education: Imagining Alternative Possibilities

Patrick M. Jenlink
Stephen F. Austin State University

> Reality is life and life is society and the imagination and reality; that is to say, the imagination and society are inseparable.
>
> (Stevens, 1951, p. 28)

We are at a crossroads in teacher education where we must engage imaginatively in examining alternative possibilities for preparing future generations of teachers, while simultaneously attending the work of providing professional learning experiences for the teachers who currently populate the classrooms of our schools. Teacher educators must necessarily take on the mantle of responsibility for reimagining what it means to *learn to teach* against a backdrop of a changing America. This will necessarily require, almost paradoxically, that we re-create ourselves anew as teacher educators while simultaneously working to re-create the social, cultural, political, economic, and intellectual structures that currently animate teacher education. In part, we must learn to create extensions in space for educators that are "equivalent to the breaking down of those barriers of class, race, and national territory, which kept them from perceiving the full import of their activity" (Dewey, 1916, p. 87).

At the same crossroads, teacher education, as a cultural-transformative agency of society, must decide how to best realize its potential efficacy in relation to preparing teachers "with a moral and political vision of what it means to educate students to govern, lead a humane life, and address the social welfare of those less fortunate than themselves" (Giroux, 1994, p. 45).

Equally important is the need for teacher education to foster a renewed commitment for the role of education in a democratic society, a society whose identity is rapidly changing against a backdrop of growing diversity, global politics, technological advancements, capitalist-driven economy, and ideological struggles for dominance.

Dewey (1916), in analyzing the potential of education as a transformative agency for realizing a democratic ideal in our society, recognized the work ahead for educators when he wrote

> We are doubtless far from realizing the potential efficacy of education as a constructive agency of improving society, from realizing that it represents not only a development of children and youth but also of the future society of which they will be the constituents. (p. 85)

Realizing the potential efficacy of education as a transformative agency requires us to understand the function of education in a democracy, and more specifically to understand the transformative function of teacher education in a democratic society.

Meeting the challenges of a changing America is only part of the larger responsibility of teacher education. Importantly, teacher education, and therein teacher educators and the future generations of teachers that matriculate through the programs and institutions, are faced with a challenge to conjoin in fostering a deep and radical democracy within and across the schools, communities, and cultures that articulate America as a society. Such work is transformative in nature and requires individuals who possess the dispositions and understandings concerned with justice, equality, and democracy as well as an awareness of and capacity for addressing the implications of a growing diversity amidst America's evolving role and responsibility in a global society.

Necessarily, the role of education set forth by Dewey (1916, 1927) must be envisioned as the work of teacher preparation programs within our schools and colleges of education. Transforming public education must begin with transforming teacher preparation programs, rethinking curriculum wherein learning to teach is inseparable from a critical attitude that engenders "ingenuous curiosity to become epistemological curiosity, together with a recognition of the value of emotions, sensibility, affectivity, and intuition" (Freire, 1998, p. 48). Teacher preparation must enable the student of teaching with the methodological exactitudes necessary to authentic engagement in the cultural-political work of teaching. Teachers' political, ethical, and professional responsibility must figure largely in the rethinking of teacher preparation, with teacher educators conjoining with students of teaching, sharing jointly in the obligation to prepare and enable themselves before engaging in their teaching practice, an obligation equally shared in college classrooms as well as classrooms in the public school.

In order to learn to teach in a society that is increasingly culturally, linguistically, ethnically, and racially diverse, as Cochran-Smith (1995) argues,

> prospective teachers, as well as experienced teachers and teacher educators, need opportunities to examine much of what is usually unexamined in the tightly braided relationships of language, culture, and power in schools and schooling. This kind of examination inevitably begins with our own histories as human beings and as educators; our own experiences as members of particular races, classes, and genders; and as children, parents, and teachers in the world. (p. 500)

At risk here is whether schools and colleges of education are to serve and reproduce the existing society or to adopt the more critical role of preparing " teachers, and others as engaged and transformative intellectuals who engage rather than retreat from the problems of democratic life and culture" (Giroux, 1994, p. 36). As cultural workers, teacher educators and public school teachers, through a pedagogy of social justice, would "address the social, political, and economic conditions that undermine both the possibilities of democratic forms of schooling and a democratic society" (Giroux, 1994, p. 36).

Standing at the crossroads, teacher education, as a transformative agency, is purposed with preparing teachers who, through their pedagogy and practice, are engaged in challenging society's existing social order so as to develop and advance its democratic imperatives. At issue is developing a rationale for defining teacher education programs in political terms that make explicit a particular view of the relationship between teacher preparation and the future of our democratic society. The portrait of teacher education in America is being created each day as students are admitted to preparation programs, become candidates for teaching, and graduate to enter classrooms and schools across the country. Teacher educators as portraitists are challenged to ensure that the portrait being created for America is one that reflects the fundamental values and beliefs of a democratic society.

REFERENCES

Cochran-Smith, M. (1995). Color blindness and basket making are not the answers: Confronting the dilemmas of race, culture, and language diversity in teacher education. *American Educational Research Journal*, *32*(3), 493–522.

Dewey, J. (1916). *Democracy in education: An introduction to the philosophy of education*. New York: Macmillan.

Dewey, J. (1927). *The public and its problems*. New York: Henry Holt.

Freire, P. (1998). *Pedagogy of freedom: Ethics, democracy and civic courage*. (P. Clarke, Trans.). Lanham, MD: Rowman & Littlefield.

Giroux, H. A. (1994). Educational leadership and school administration: Rethinking the meaning of democratic public cultures. In T.A. Mulkeen, N. H. Cambron-McCabe, & B. J. Anderson (Eds.), *Democratic leadership: The changing context of administrative preparation* (pp. 31–47). Norwood, NJ: Ablex.

Stevens, W. (1951). *The necessary angel: Essays on reality and the imagination*. New York: Vintage Books.

Index

Alverno College, xiii, 133–34, 136, 137, 148, 222, 224, 225, 228; early redesign, 134–35
assessing students' learning, 210

backdrop: against a, 13–14; preparing a, 1–2
BASRC. *See* Bay Area School Reform Collaborative
BASRC-SUP. *See* California Bay Area School/University Partnerships
Bay Area School Reform Collaborative (BASRC), 164–65, 224
block program, 180–81; defining qualities, 181–87
Boston College, xiii, 54–55, 56, 57, 58, 61, 63, 70, 223, 224, 227, 228
Brighton High School, 53, 54, 57–58, 59, 60, 61, 62, 63, 71

California Bay Area School/University Partnerships (BASRC-SUP), 164
California SB 2042, 48, 169

CARE program, 99–100; elements of, 101–4; pedagogy for students, 100–1
Center X, 33–50, 222, 225, 226, 227, 228, 231. *See also* teacher preparation, at UCLA
changing America, 6–8
characteristics. *See* teacher education
child development and multiple ways of knowing, 204
Clark County School District, 175, 177–78, 180, 191, 222
collaboration, 56–64; realizing inquiry through, 223; structure of, 75. *See also* Teacher Education (TE) Collaborative
collaborative: faculty/student inquiry, 69–78; fellows, 61–64
communication, 186–87
community, 128–29, 183–84; of learners, 193–94; partnership, 41; perspective, 44
conscientizacão, 152–53
constructivism, 34, 53, 54, 55, 68, 204

239

constructivist approaches, 225, 227–29
context for inquiry and collaboration, 222–23
continuous improvement: coming to consensus, 139; curricular revisions, 139–40; defining the initial course, 140–43; merging fields and methods, 144–45; re-examining the folio process, 145–46; rethinking feedback, 138–39
critical social consciousness. *See* conscientizacão
curriculum, 191–93; field-based, 181–83

democracy, 17–19, 105–6; and learning to teach, 21–22; multiculturalism and, 17–19
democratic: ideal and education, 19–21; learning communities, 115–17, 120, 130; society, 102
Descriptive Review of the Child, 83, 85–87
Dewey, John, 5, 14, 18–20, 21, 23, 82, 95, 103, 105, 115, 218–19, 235–36
difference: as asset and strength, 77–80; constructions of, 76–77; facing, 88–91

education abilities, developing, 135–36
Ellison, Ralph, 20
equity, x, xi, 6, 7, 8, 10, 38, 67, 79, 97, 101, 102, 106, 129, 151, 155, 164–69, 171, 172, 224, 227

field-based curriculum. *See* curriculum
Follett, Mary Parker, 105
Freire, Paulo, 2, 5, 37, 42, 89, 90, 96, 115, 119, 151–52, 236

Greene, Maxine, 15, 18, 22–23, 29, 73, 77, 82, 95–96

high-stakes testing. *See* standardization
Holmes, 56, 202

Indiana University School of Education, 199, 200, 204
Indianapolis Pubic Schools (IPS), 200, 201
inquiry, 64–70; undergraduate, 67–69; stance, 65, 85–88; through collaboration, 223
INTASC. *See* Interstate New Teacher Assessment and Support Consortium
Interstate New Teacher Assessment and Support Consortium (INTASC): collaborative, 76; core principles, 140, 142, 143; descriptive, 75; establishing a context, 222–23; graduate seminar, 65–67; process, 66; standards for beginning teachers, 202
IPS. *See* Indiana Public Schools

Jones College Preparatory High School, 118

keeper of the flame, 99, 104, 112
knowledge-of-practice, 83

learning to teach: for social justice, 29–31; in a changing America, 13–14; in a democracy, 95–97; through social consciousness, 151–53
Long Island University (LIU), Brooklyn, xii, xiii, 73–75, 222, 226, 227, 228

Lynch School of Education, 53–71, 223, 224, 227, 228. *See also* collaboration; inquiry

Massachusetts Coalition for Teacher Quality and Student Achievement (MassCoalition), 57
META. *See* Metropolitan Elementary Teachers Academy
Metropolitan Elementary Teachers Academy (META), 124–25
multiculturalism, 17–19; and diversity, 203–4; infusing, 7

National Board Certification, 165, 166, 167, 169
National Council for Accreditation of Teacher Education (NCATE), 56, 114
NCATE. *See* National Council for Accreditation of Teacher Education
NCLB. *See* No Child Left Behind (NCLB) Act
New York State Department of Education (NYSDOE), 74
No Child Left Behind (NCLB) Act, 8, 13, 47, 114, 232
NYSDOE. *See* New York State Department of Education

Ohio University, xii, 99, 100, 222, 227, 228

paraprofessionals, nontraditional route to licensure, 189–90
Parker, Walter, 21, 106–7, 112
partnership: Boston College/Brighton High School, 54, 57

PDS. *See* professional development school
pedagogies: and social democracy, 226–27; constructing alternative, 225; of difference, 225–26
pluralism, 8, 77, 79, 106
policy tensions, 48–49
portrait: a pattern of continuous improvement, 137–38; concept of, 2; of cooperating teacher orientation, 117–20; of field issues, 83–85; of field-based preparation, 124; of multiple perspectives, *see* teacher dispositions; *see also* block program
portraitist, 1–2, 8, 9, 10, 11, 230, 231, 238
portraiture, 8–10, 115. *See also* teacher preparation
Principles of Teacher Education, 211
professional development school (PDS), 202–3, 206–7

reflectivity, 184–86
re-imagining, 80
resiliency, 155, 169, 172, 229, 230, 231, 232
role of school, 102
Roosevelt University, xii, 113–14, 115, 116, 117, 118, 128, 222, 224, 225, 226

San José State University, xii, 155–57, 223, 224
self-renewal, 230
September 11 (9/11), 7, 8, 13, 108
service learning: collaborative model, 108–10; outcomes, 110–11; planning for, 107–8

social: commitment, 77; consciousness, 152; democracy, 230
social justice, 37–39; and learning to teach, 22–24; theory into practice, 39–42
sociocultural patterns: creating space for critical conversation, 224–25; in pedagogical change, 224; rethinking role and structure, 224. *See also* pedagogies
special education cohort program, 187–88; evolution of, 188–89
standards and accountability, 14
standards-based teacher education, 204–6
standardization, 36, 47–48

TE Collaborative. *See* Teacher Education (TE) Collaborative
teacher dispositions, 120–24
teacher education, 235–38; a day in the life of, 206–10; as cultural agency, 14–17; as portraiture, 8–10; characteristics of reformed programs, x–xi; re-creating, 217–19. *See also* standards-based teacher education
Teacher Education (TE) Collaborative, 156–59, 160, 161, 165, 170, 171, 172, 173; Advisory Board, 163–64, 170; 20% partial intern program, 159–62
teacher preparation: as integrated whole, 43–47; as portraiture, 8–10; at UCLA, 34–35; challenges for, 6–8

UEN. *See* Urban Education Network
UNITE. *See* Urban Network to Improve Teacher Education
University of California, Los Angeles, xii, 33–34, 222
University of Nevada, Las Vegas, xi, 175, 222, 228
Urban Educator Network (UEN), 45–46, 49
Urban Network to Improve Teacher Education (UNITE), 56–57
Urban Immersion, 57–61
urban populations. *See* pedagogies, constructing alternative

About the Editors and Contributors

Patrick M. Jenlink, EdD, is professor of doctoral studies in the Department of Secondary Education and Educational Leadership and director of the Educational Research Center at Stephen F. Austin State University. He earned his Bachelor of Science degree with majors in sociology and biology, and his teaching certification in social sciences from Northwestern Oklahoma State University. Dr. Jenlink also earned his Master of Education with emphasis in counseling from Northwestern Oklahoma State University. His doctorate in educational administration was received from Oklahoma State University. Dr. Jenlink has served as a classroom teacher at the junior high and high school level, with assignments in social sciences and natural sciences, as well as serving as K–12 counselor. He has also served as building administrator and school district superintendent in Oklahoma. His university teaching experience includes Northwestern Oklahoma State University, Western Michigan University, and assignments in Europe with University of Oklahoma and NATO.

Currently, Dr. Jenlink's teaching emphasis in doctoral studies at Stephen F. Austin State University includes courses in ethics and philosophy of leadership, critical studies in politics and policy, and dynamics of change. Dr. Jenlink's research interests include politics of identity, social systems design and change, cultural-historical activity theory, democratic education and leadership, and postmodern inquiry methods. He has authored numerous articles, guest-edited journals, authored or coauthored numerous chapters in books, and edited or coedited several books. Currently he serves as editor of *Teacher*

Education and Practice and coeditor of *Scholar-Practitioner Quarterly*. His most recent book is *Dialogue as a Collective Means of Communication*, Kluwer Publishing. Dr. Jenlink's current book projects include the coedited *Scholar-Practitioner Leadership: A Post-formal Inquiry* (forthcoming from Peter Lang) and a coauthored book, *Developing Scholar-Practitioner Leaders: The Empowerment of Educators* (forthcoming from Falmer Press).

Karen Embry Jenlink, EdD, is a professor and serves as coordinator for MEd programs in secondary education in the Department of Secondary Education and Educational Leadership at Stephen F. Austin State University (SFASU) in Nacogdoches, Texas. She delivers instruction in both the doctoral and master's programs at SFASU, teaching courses related to human inquiry systems, teacher leadership, learning theory, and research methods. She also serves as an advisor for dissertation and thesis research with doctoral- and master's-level candidates. Following undergraduate and master's studies at East Texas Baptist University and the University of Texas at Tyler, respectively, Dr. Jenlink received her doctorate in education from the University of Texas A&M at Commerce.

A bilingual educator, Dr. Jenlink has a rich background in P–16 classroom teaching, including extensive experience in field-based teacher preparation. Her research interests include teacher leadership, cultural identity and recognition politics, democratic education, and social contexts of teacher preparation and educational leadership. Dr. Jenlink is the author of numerous articles in journals, book chapters, and technical reports in curriculum design related to occupational research. She recently coauthored *The Adams PRAXIS Test Preparation Guide* (Adams Media Press). A 10-year member of ATE, she is a past recipient of the LFTE Award, has served as president of Texas Teacher Educators, and has served as president of the Consortium of State Organizations for Texas Teacher Education. She is an associate editor of *Teacher Education and Practice*.

Beth Berghoff is associate professor of language education and chair of teacher education at Indiana University Purdue University Indianapolis (IUPUI). She teaches literacy classes for teachers and future teachers and researches multiple ways of knowing and arts-infused curriculum. She has served as president of the Indiana Council of Teachers of English and as

Language Arts Consultant for Indiana Department of Education. Beth's publications include *Beyond Reading and Writing* and *Arts Together: Steps Toward Transformative Teacher Education.* She has served on the editorial boards of *Language Arts* and the National Reading Conference and been on the NCTE Commission on Curriculum since 2000. Beth was also an elementary teacher for 12 years.

Jacqueline Blackwell is associate professor of early childhood and elementary education in the School of Education and a faculty associate for academic affairs (recruitment) in the Office of the Dean of Faculties at Indiana University Purdue University Indianapolis (IUPUI). She also is the 59th president of the Association for Childhood Education International (ACEI). Prior to coming to IUPUI, Jacqueline served as a classroom teacher in a model early childhood program and an administrator for a private child development and kindergarten center sponsored by the textile industry. She writes a regular quarterly column for *Childhood Education* and *Focus on Pre-k & K*. Her research interests include faculty recruitment and distance education.

Nona Burney is associate professor of secondary education in the College of Education, Roosevelt University. She teaches classes in methods of inquiry in the classroom for preservice teachers. Her research interests include public school reform, transformative leadership, and parental involvement in education.

Andy Carter is assistant professor of mathematics education with a joint appointment in the Mathematics Department and the College of Education. Over the past 30 years, his work as a public school teacher and as a staff developer in mathematics led to his interest in the social contexts that support learning. The primary focus of his research is the role of inquiry in the teaching and learning of mathematics. Specifically, Dr. Carter is interested in sociocultural theories of learning, the connections between inquiry and autonomy, and the use of mathematics lessons as learning experiments in the preparation of teachers.

Kelly Donnell is assistant professor of elementary and early childhood education in the School of Education and Allied Studies at Bridgewater

State College in Massachusetts. She formerly taught elementary school for over 10 years. Her research interests include learning to teach in urban schools, practitioner research, and teacher education for social justice.

James W. Fraser is professor of history and education at Northeastern University. For 2004–2005, he is visiting professor at the Steinhardt School of Education, New York University. He was the founding dean of Northeastern's School of Education, serving from 1999 to 2004. He has taught at Lesley University; University of Massachusetts, Boston; Boston University; and Public School 76 in Manhattan. His most recent books include *A History of Hope: When Americans Have Dared to Dream of a Better Future* (Palgrave-Macmillan, 2002), *The School in the United States: A Documentary History* (McGraw-Hill, 2000), and *Between Church and State: Religion and Public Education in a Multicultural America* (St. Martin's Press, 1999). Fraser holds a PhD from Columbia University. He is an ordained minister and pastor of Grace Church in East Boston and Union Congregational Church in Winthrop, Massachusetts.

Nicole Guttenberg earned her BS in biology and MEd from the University of Massachusetts, Amherst, and MS in medical biology from the Free University of Amsterdam, the Netherlands. Currently, Ms. Guttenberg is a doctoral candidate at the Boston College Lynch School of Education and is the associate director for Project QUEST, Quality Urban Education and Support for Teaching. It is sponsored by the Massachusetts Coalition for Teacher Quality and Student Achievement and funded by a Massachusetts Department of Education Teacher Retention Grant. Project QUEST is a university-sponsored mentoring program for beginning urban teachers designed to support the integration of social justice practices into the Massachusetts Professional Standards for Teaching. Her professional interests include education partnerships, principal/teacher leadership, and equitable instruction for all students.

Sheila Lane received a BEd from the University of Miami; an MA in the Teaching of English from Teachers College, Columbia University; and a PhD in education from UCLA Graduate School of Education and Information Studies. Her PhD was in educational psychology. Her dissertation was *Motivating Inactive Readers: The Effects of Video-Modeled Coping Training* *on the Metacognitive Acquisition of a Reading Strategy by Low-Achieving Readers*. She presented her doctoral research at an annual meeting of the American Psychological Association (1997). A recent publication is "Developing Novice Teachers as Change Agents: Student Teacher Placements 'Against the Grain'" in *Teacher Education Quarterly* with N. Lacefield-Parachini and J. Isken (Spring, 2003). She has had many presentations at annual meetings of the AERA and AACTE. Dr. Lane has experience teaching at both elementary and secondary levels (English) in urban schools.

Valerie Lava is an associate professor in the Department of Teaching and Learning at the Brooklyn campus of Long Island University. She prepares teachers in both the undergraduate, Inclusive Childhood Education Program and in the graduate program, Teaching Urban Children with Disabilities. Dr. Lava works with schools to promote the full inclusion of all students. Her research agenda includes examining issues in the areas of inclusive schooling, collaborative teaching methods, and personnel preparation.

Laurie Lehman is associate professor of special education at the Brooklyn campus of Long Island University where she has collaborated with colleagues to transform the teacher education programs to reflect the school's core principles of collaborative inquiry, valuing diversity, and social commitment. The focus of her scholarship has been student and teacher perspectives on inclusive education. Currently, she is collaboratively exploring the impact of autobiographies on student ideas about disability.

Nancy Lourié Markowitz is professor of education in the Department of Elementary Education at San José State University. She developed and has directed the Teacher Education Partial Internship Program since its inception in 1997. She was a Carnegie Scholar for the Advancement of Teaching where her research focused on the development of teacher educator inquiry within the TE Collaborative program. She currently teaches courses focused on creating effective learning environments in diverse, multicultural, urban K–8 classrooms. Her scholarly interests include the study of university/district collaboration, preservice teacher education, and inquiry into practices that promote effective learning environments.

Morva McDonald is an assistant professor in the Department of Curriculum and Instruction at the University of Maryland, College Park. She teaches doctoral-level courses and teacher education courses related to issues of multicultural education, social justice, diversity, and urban education. Her scholarly interests include the integration of social justice in teacher education, the relationship between teacher preparation for diversity and teachers' practices, students' opportunities to learn in and out of school, and sociocultural theories of learning.

Elizabeth Meadows is an assistant professor of elementary education in the College of Education at Roosevelt University. She enjoys supporting teachers' development by teaching undergraduate courses such as Teaching Science in the Elementary School and graduate courses such as Methods of Inquiry in the Classroom. Her current research interests include examining K–12 teachers' responses to faculty study groups on John Dewey's ideas about art, experience, and education, and exploring how the teacher-student relationship can help students learn optimally in school. Meadows is consulting editor for the new journal *Illinois Child Welfare*, whose mission is to improve child welfare services by publishing articles for practitioners, program managers, and policy makers that provide stimulating, relevant knowledge that honors the diversity of cultures and perspectives that constitute child welfare.

Eloise Lopez Metcalfe is director of the Teacher Education Program at Center X, University of California, Los Angeles. Her primary teaching interests include working with students as they develop teaching practices that are integrated with theoretical understandings and local community interests. Additional teaching interests are assisting students in their development of their social justice identity and their understanding of the influences of cultural and language backgrounds. The preparation of teachers for urban schools and the diversity of the teaching workforce are two of Dr. Metcalfe's research interests.

Lori A. Navarrete is an associate professor in the Department of Special Education at the University of Nevada, Las Vegas. Her teaching and research interests are in mild-moderate disabilities, multicultural and bilingual special education, diagnostic and prescriptive assessment, and teacher preparation. Her international interests have taken her to Mexico to examine special education teacher preparation programs and to Uganda and Hong Kong to explore gender issues in education and English as a second language (ESL) models, respectively. She has several years of experience working in professional development schools in the Midwest. Currently, Lori is coordinating a fast-track TESL endorsement program with the Clark County School District as well as developing a multicultural and bilingual special education program at UNLV.

Lori J. Olafson is an assistant professor in the Department of Educational Psychology at the University of Nevada, Las Vegas. Her research and teaching reconsider what constitutes "at-risk" learners, with a particular focus on adolescents. In addition, she conducts research that examines the relationship between teachers' beliefs and practices. For the past two years, Lori has been part of an IBM Reinventing Education 3 grant that has focused on developing and implementing a field-based teacher preparation program in partnership with two local elementary schools.

Brad Olsen is assistant professor of education at the University of California, Santa Cruz. His research focuses on teacher development (with emphases on teacher knowledge and identity), English education, and sociolinguistics. He can be reached at bolsen@ucsc.edu.

Tom Philion is chair of the Department of Teacher Education, and associate professor in the Language and Literacy Program at Roosevelt University. He teaches courses in young adult literature and reading and writing across the curriculum. His research interests and publications center on adolescent oppositionality, the use of technology in literacy instruction, and creative ways of overcoming adversity in urban schools and classrooms.

Jody Priselac is currently the executive director of UCLA's Center X and a member of the teacher education faculty in UCLA's Graduate School of Education and Information Studies. Her area of study is the teaching and learning of mathematics. She supervises, coordinates, and prepares secondary mathematics preservice students. She has been the writer, principal investigator, and director of successful grant proposals that focus on professional development of mathematics teachers. She has presented at local, state, and national conferences.

Rosalie M. Romano is an associate professor currently teaching undergraduate and graduate courses in cultural studies in the Department of Educational Studies at Ohio University. Her research interests include moral dilemmas of teaching, relationality in education, cultural criticism, and critical curriculum for social justice, as well as democracy in education. She is the author of *Forging an Educative Community: The Wisdom of Love, the Power of Understanding, and the Terror of It All* (2001) and *Hungry Minds in Hard Times* with C. Glascock (2003).

Jeffrey C. Shih is assistant professor of elementary mathematics education in the Department of Curriculum and Instruction at the University of Nevada, Las Vegas. Dr. Shih is also a senior scientist in the UNLV Center for Assessment and Evaluation. His current research interests revolve around the study of alternative forms of assessment, including developing measures to assess the extent of implementation of innovative classroom practice and evaluation and alignment issues in mathematics education. Dr. Shih has worked closely with the Clark County School District, serving as primary investigator on multiple grants examining the use of student work as a context to focus on the Nevada state standards.

Marguerite Sneed is former dean of education at Alverno College, Milwaukee, Wisconsin, and was instrumental in innovative changes to the college's teacher preparation programs. She coordinated fieldwork and elementary and middle school programs and also initiated development of a distinctive literacy education program. In large part because of that program, the U.S. Department of Education presented Alverno's elementary teacher preparation program its National Award for Effective Teacher Preparation. Often called upon to consult with schools and universities on issues of literacy learning, assessment, program development, and standards-based teaching and learning, she also contributes to development and implementation of the INTASC (Interstate New Teacher Assessment and Support Consortium) academies. Dr. Sneed is now reading and language arts consultant for the Kenosha Unified School District in Kenosha, Wisconsin.

Andrea J. Stairs is a doctoral candidate, a teaching fellow, and clinical faculty in the Department of Teacher Education, Special Education, and

Curriculum and Instruction at the Lynch School of Education, Boston College. Ms. Stairs is a former middle and high school English teacher. Her research interests include urban teacher education, school-university partnerships, and issues of social justice in education.

Gordon Suzuki is a teacher education faculty member in Center X, University of California Los Angeles. His interests include issues related to urban schooling, performance assessments of beginning teachers, mentoring and supporting the development of beginning teachers, and building partnerships with urban schools and communities.

Patricia Swanson is associate professor of education at San José State University where she teaches curriculum and instruction courses in mathematics and social studies. She has taught students in the TE Collaborative 20% Internship Program for seven years and continues to explore strategies for tightly linking coursework to field experiences. Her teaching and scholarship focus on preparing teachers to foster the development of thinking skills in academically and linguistically diverse classrooms.

Cecilia Traugh is director of the Center for Urban Educators (CUE) and associate dean for research and faculty development in the School of Education on the Brooklyn campus of Long Island University. Some of her areas of concentration are descriptive school-based inquiry, curriculum development and evaluation, including qualitative evaluation, and the preparation of teachers for urban schools. Among her scholarship interests are longitudinal studies of students learning to teach in urban settings, the role of classroom-based inquiry in teacher education, and descriptive inquiry methodologies.

Siri Voskuil is professor of education at Alverno College in Milwaukee, Wisconsin. In addition to teaching courses in the foundations of education, her time and efforts are devoted extensively to the ongoing development and improvement of the teacher education program, specifically to those components that involve fieldwork and student teaching. She has been instrumental in creating a document that takes the knowledge, performance, and disposition benchmarks of the Wisconsin Standards for Teacher Development and Licensure and restates them in specific language that defines an

Alverno teacher candidate at various points in the program. This document is now being used in all education course and field experiences at Alverno to guide the development of goals and objectives and to provide assessment criteria. Dr. Voskuil is an advocate for social justice in education and has recently made this the focus of her teaching and research.

Andrea Whittaker is an associate professor in the Department of Elementary Education at San José State University. She teaches teacher education courses in multicultural education, young adolescence, and classroom-based assessment. Her scholarly interests include equity-based pedagogy, case methodology, and the design of authentic assessments of student and teacher performance. Recent publications include *Using Assessment to Teach for Understanding: A Casebook for Educators*, coedited with J. Shulman and M. Lew (Teachers College Press, 2002); and *Learning Together What We Do Not Know: The Pedagogy of Multicultural Foundations* (in press), coauthored with M. McDonald and N. Markowitz (to appear in *Teacher Education Quarterly*, Summer 2005).

Rae Jeane Williams, a faculty advisor in the UCLA teacher education program, teaches curriculum and instructional decision making, knowledge and inquiry in the classroom, and secondary reading methods. She edits the *Center X Forum*, and codirects the UCLA National Board for Professional Teaching Standards Project. Her current research interests are integrating literacy into secondary content courses and the effectiveness of inquiry projects in assisting beginning teachers to reflect upon their practices.